BEYOND
REFORMATION?

BEYOND REFORMATION?

An Essay on William Langland's *Piers Plowman*

and the End of Constantinian Christianity

DAVID AERS

University of Notre Dame Press
Notre Dame, Indiana

University of Notre Dame Press
Notre Dame, Indiana 46556
www.undpress.nd.edu

Manufactured in the United States of America

Library of Congress Cataloging-in-Publication Data

Aers, David.
Beyond reformation? : an essay on William Langland's Piers Plowman
and the end of Constantinian Christianity / David Aers.
    pages   cm
Includes bibliographical references and index.
ISBN 978-0-268-02046-0 (pbk. : alk. paper) —
ISBN 0-268-02046-9 (pbk. : alk. paper)
1. Langland, William, 1330?–1400? Piers Plowman.
2. Christian poetry, English (Middle)—History and criticism.
3. Literature and society—England—History—To 1500.
4. Religious thought—Middle Ages, 600–1500.
5. Religion and culture.   I. Title.
PR2015.A38   2015
821'.1—dc23

2015032655

This book is dedicated to three teachers and friends:

Elizabeth Salter

Derek Pearsall

Stanley Hauerwas

Mirabile ergo mysterium Christi sedentis ad dexteram Dei:
occultum est ut crederetur, subtractum est ut speraretur.

(This is a wonderful thing about the mystery of
Christ's enthronement at God's right hand:
his presence is hidden that he may be believed in
and withdrawn that he may be hoped for.)

—St. Augustine, *Enarrationes in Psalmos*, 109.8

et certe videmus nunc per speculum in aenigmate,
nondum facie ad faciem. et ideo, quamdiu peregrinor abs te,
mihi sum praesentior quam tibi at tamen te novi nullo modo posse violari;
ego vero quibus temptationibus resistere valem quibusve non valeam, nescio.

(Without question, "we see now through a mirror in
an enigma," not yet "face to face" [1 Cor. 13:12].
For this cause, as long as I am a traveller absent from you
[2 Cor. 5:6], I am more present to myself than to you.
Yet I know that you cannot be in any way subjected to violence,
whereas I do not know which temptations I can resist and which I cannot.)

—St. Augustine, *Confessions*, X.5.7

CONTENTS

PREFACE

I would think that the whole Christian faith,
and all Christ's promises about the Catholic faith
lasting to the end of the age, and the whole Church of God,
could be preserved in a few, indeed in one.

—William of Ockham, *A Letter to the Friars Minor*

Because this is a somewhat idiosyncratic little book, the preface offers a brief account of some of the contexts that fostered its making and within which it ruminates. While this will not justify its existence, it suggests the kind of questions that inform the inquiry. I hope that even a very brief articulation of such questions may encourage at least some to read on who are not based in an English department and do not share (yet) my own love of Langland's work. To help readers new to the poem I have included, at the end of the preface, Derek Pearsall's excellent summary of the final version of *Piers Plowman*. This comes from his edition, *Piers Plowman: A New Annotated Edition of the C-Text*. Throughout *Beyond Reformation?* I have followed quotations of Langland's poetry with translations by George Economou. I am grateful to Derek Pearsall, George Economou, and their publishers for permission to quote from these works.[1] I hope the outline and the translations welcome new readers of the poem and nonmedievalists since this essay does raise in the margins, however tentatively, questions about cultural change and continuity from the Middle Ages to the English reformations of the sixteenth and seventeenth centuries.

But the most obvious and determinate focus of this book is the greatest English poem of the Middle Ages, *Piers Plowman*, which according
to its brilliant nineteenth-century editor, Walter Skeat, was a poem that
its author kept writing and revising throughout his life. The three versions that have reached us catch this process at different stages. The outcome of modern editing has confirmed both Skeat's picture of the process of writing and the view that it was made by one author, William
Langland.[2] The present book addresses the work in its latest version.[3] Its
reading concentrates on Langland's modes of writing, on his extraordinarily rich ecclesiastic politics, and on his account of the Christian virtues and the struggles of Conscience to discern how to go on in his often
baffling culture. Langland's complex allegory engaged with almost all the
institutions and forms of his culture. In doing so it necessarily explored
moral languages and principles in relation to current practices and tendencies. His vision included a strange sense that in his own historical moment some moral concepts were being transformed and some traditions
he cherished were becoming unintelligible. Here he grasped subtle shifts
which were hardly discernible in fourteenth-century England but would
have increasing and lasting force in the future. One of the questions emerging from Langland's explorations is hardly predictable, even hardly imaginable in terms of most versions of the Middle Ages in medieval and early
modern studies. Understandably so because it concerns signs and forces
of what Langland sees as de-Christianization. I will argue that, however
hegemonic the hold of what Eamon Duffy calls "traditional religion," the
issue of de-Christianization is indeed taken up by the late fourteenth-
century writer.[4] And in pursuing it I will sometimes bring Langland into
dialogue with Pope John Paul II writing in the 1990s—for the poet's responses to the pressures that led him to such a concern have striking implications for John Paul's ecclesiology. Langland's responses, however idiosyncratic they may be, might even engage those who give us big stories
about the relations between the Middle Ages, the Reformation, and modernity. Yet, as far as I am aware, Langland has been given no attention in
the plethora of grand narratives over the past twenty-five years.[5] If the
present book were to suggest to people with serious diachronic interests
that they should become careful readers of Langland it would have fulfilled a part of its purpose. It has, after all, been written in conversation
with people concerned, in very different ways, to explore and write grand

narratives of modernity involving the Middle Ages and what is currently widely known as the early modern period.[6] But such conversations, however important to my own reflections, provide a mostly implicit context for what is a close reading of a late medieval text and its analysis of its own culture in light of the journey of Christ into the far country and his homecoming.

For me, to attempt a close reading of this utterly gripping work is crucial even if this creates obstacles for even composing a grand narrative. Close reading: I have tried to remember Thomas Aquinas's admonition that "ex modo loquendi datur nobis doctrina," that the teaching we receive is inextricably bound up with the mode in which it is composed. He makes this remark in a commentary on the Pater Noster, but we find similar urgings in the *Summa Theologiae*. We must, he says, attend not only to what is signified but also to the "modus significandi." Failure to do this can lead to serious theological error, something St. Thomas finds illustrated in Joachim of Fiore's teaching on the Trinity.[7] This guideline is especially important in a study which finally argues that there is an intimacy between Langland's ecclesiology and the forms of writing he pursues. Commenting on the Book of Job, Aquinas takes great care to distinguish the work's different voices, since "truth may shine forth from debating back and forth."[8] I shall try to follow his admirable example as I read *Piers Plowman*. For in this essay I address a work that is dazzlingly polyvocal, multigeneric, and dialectical.[9]

I am also trying to understand Langland's own inventive, sometimes thoroughly idiosyncratic engagements with the Christian traditions he inherited, ones that included but were certainly not circumscribed by Eamon Duffy's "traditional religion in England." As Alasdair MacIntyre observes in *After Virtue*, "All reasoning takes place within the context of some traditional mode of thought, transcending through criticism and invention the limitations of what had hitherto been reasoned in that tradition: this is as true of modern physics as of medieval logic." It is true, moreover, that "when a tradition is in good order it is always partially constituted by an argument about the goods the pursuit of which gives to that tradition its particular point and purpose." If it is flourishing, a tradition will "embody continuities of conflict." Indeed, a living tradition "is a historically extended, socially embodied argument precisely in part about the goods which constitute that tradition."[10] Langland himself certainly found "deep-cutting disagreements, some of them seemingly irresolvable," in the contemporary form of his tradition.[11] Whether he considered this part of a tradition "in good order" and whether he himself thought some contemporary disagreements "irresolvable" are questions informing the inquiry of this book. Whatever the answer to these questions, such are the terms in which I approach the relations between late medieval Christianity and the Reformation, an approach that seems taught by *Piers Plowman*.

Perhaps two phrases in this book's title need some comment: "Beyond Reformation" and "Constantinian Christianity." First, a few points about reform in the Middle Ages.[12] In *A Secular Age* Charles Taylor noted that ideologies of reform, commitments to reform the church and individual Christians, were a constitutive part of medieval and early modern Christianity. He named this the "Reform Master Narrative."[13] Such commitment could take many forms and have very different sources. Reform could be initiated by ecclesiastic authorities. It could be initiated by agents outside the hierarchy and then embraced and ordered by the hierarchy. Sometimes it emerged among clergy and laity in ways that the authorities of the church would not tolerate, let alone assimilate. When this happened intransigent reformers were classified as heretics and persecuted by the church. Those classified as heretics were judged to have gone beyond legitimate reform, to be acting outside its paradigms and acting defiantly. In the *Summa Theologiae* St. Thomas maintains that such Christians should be separated from the church by excommunication and then killed ("per mortem a mundo excludi").[14] Of course, nobody judged as a heretic freely described themselves in this language. On the contrary, they tended, in the later Middle Ages, to see themselves as disciples of Christ seeking to reform the modern church to the practices of the early church.[15] They too came from dynamics of reform intrinsic to Christianity. This fact highlights one peculiar feature in Eamon Duffy's wonderful depiction of "traditional religion" in the later Middle Ages and its violent destruction in the sixteenth century. The dynamic I am discussing seems unknown to his Middle Ages. Of course nobody can write about very many aspects of a culture even in as massive a book as Duffy's, especially when offering the kind of detail and attention so impressively displayed in *The Stripping of the Altars*. But Duffy's "traditional religion" of the later Middle Ages seems timeless except in the sacred times of the liturgy and the time of the parishioners who performed it. Only with the attack on the people's church led by a coterie of evangelicals around Henry VIII and Edward VI do we suddenly encounter political agency and events in a restless, conflicted process of reformation, iconoclasm, and centralizing innovation.[16] In James Simpson's monumental study of English literary history and "the complex history of freedoms" from 1350 to 1547, the processes that comprise the "stripping" of Duffy's title are described as "cultural revolution" and sharply contrasted with the kind of "reform" intrinsic to medieval culture, including its literary forms. The latter is celebrated as both freedom and creativity, in contrast to the revolution of those who came to be called Protestants. For this fine literary historian, Langland is an admirable model of medieval reform as against (prophetically against, in Simpson's view) the sixteenth-century "revolution."[17] Neither Duffy nor Simpson, with their very different archives and disciplinary training, can find any spiritual, theological, and political vitality among any Wycliffites (also known as Lollards). None of us can, of course, approach all the writers and historical subjects we encounter with one love. But these Christians elicit nothing but condescension and scorn from Eamon Duffy.[18] Whether Langland shared the dispositions of Simpson or Duffy toward such Christians passing beyond reformation acceptable to traditional authorities remains a question that this book addresses. For one of its central questions is whether Langland himself goes "beyond reformation" in his ecclesiology and political theory. The answer that emerges is that he did indeed do so but in a somewhat enigmatic ecclesiology for "fools."

As to the phrase "Constantinian Christianity" in this book's title, Langland explicitly introduces reflections on this subject. He does so in the discourse of one of the poem's teachers, Liberum Arbitrium, "Cristes creature" and well known "in Cristes court" (XVI.167–68).[19] In Passus XVII he offers a grand narrative of the church as part of his criticisms of its modern practices. In this story the donation of Constantine to the church of the fourth century was a formative disaster:

> Whan Constantyn of his cortesye holy kirke dowede
> With londes and ledes, lordschipes and rentes,
> An angel men herde an hye at Rome crye,
> "*Dos ecclesie* this day hath ydronke venym
> And tho that haen Petres power aren apoysened alle."
>
> (XVII.220–24)

───────

[When Constantine out of his courtesy endowed Holy Church
With lands and peoples, lordships and incomes,
Men heard on high an angel cry at Rome:
"*Dos ecclesie* has this day drunk venom
And poisoned are all who have Peter's power."]

This alleged exchange between emperor and papacy initiates the endow-ment of the church with lands and political power. To Langland it repre-sents the immersion of the church in the political, coercive, and economic fabric of the social world. Trying to understand this process and its moder-nity is part of the task Langland set himself in writing *Piers Plowman*. The donation is "venym," poisoning those that claim "Petres power" because it turns Christians away from living as disciples of Christ. It directs their at-tention to all that is symbolized by Constantine. Christianity becomes the social cement, the political ideology of the current form of *saeculum*. This category, Constantinianism, became important in the work of the Men-nonite theologian John Yoder. But while I hope I have learned from his writings, my own usage of the phrase "Constantinian Christianity" remains Langlandian rather than Mennonite.[20] So does my account of its ending. Hardly surprising given the intense focus of this book on Langland's work.

One other feature of this book probably needs some explanation: the absence of chapters and chapter headings. The book is composed instead as seventeen steps or "passus." These belong in what I envisage as an "essay," as the work is identified in the subtitle. This seems to me the appropriate form for developing an argument around a close reading of Langland's poem that is, I hope, driven by his own dialectic. Chapter divisions, with conventional headings, would be alien to what I am trying to do and the kind of reading I am seeking to encourage. I hope this rather unusual fea-ture will gradually make as much sense to the reader as it does to me.

⌒

Beyond Reformation? has been written from both a Divinity School and an English department. It evolved in graduate courses predominantly located in the Divinity School of Duke University but including students from the English department concentrating on medieval and early modern studies.

I am extremely grateful to all those students who have participated in the range of courses relevant to the making of this book. I am very grateful to Stanley Hauerwas for agreeing to teach with me a course on grand narratives focusing on the place and version of the Middle Ages in such stories. His theological wisdom, profound learning, and generosity have been great gifts to me since I came to Duke University. I am also grateful to Thomas Pfau, friend and colleague both in the Divinity School and the English department. I hope I have learned from extensive discussions with him about the transformation of Western culture that made the modernity that makes and unmakes us. It was a great delight to read his own extraordinary grand narrative in manuscript, now published as *Minding the Modern* (2013). I continue to benefit massively from sustained conversations with my friend and colleague Sarah Beckwith. These conversations have continued over many years and over most of the subjects that engage this book. My debts to her are truly immeasurable. I thank Nicky Zeeman for many discussions about Langland and some of the questions shaping this book. Her encouragement was especially important when I was wondering whether some arguments unfolding in parts of the work were becoming too strange to pursue. James Simpson has been a prominent, critical conversation partner during the making of this book. Not only through his *Reform and Cultural Revolution* together with his later book, *Under the Hammer*, but also through copious discussions as coeditor, with Sarah Beckwith, of the current series of books published by University of Notre Dame Press under the title, ReFormations: Medieval and Early Modern. I thank Russ Leo for many conversations that proved relevant to this book. I have benefited from Anne Hudson's willingness to give me nuanced and learned responses to questions about Wycliffite writing and practice. I thank Jennifer Herdt for inviting me to write on Langland and the virtues in a special issue on the virtues she edited for the *Journal of Medieval and Early Modern Studies* (42, no. 1 [2012]): this provided essential encouragement to writing the present book to which it has been assimilated. I wish to thank Will Revere, who has been a superb research assistant during the making of this book, someone with an exceptional grasp of current grand narratives and working across the medieval/early modern divide. I am grateful that Jessica Hines and Cullen McKenney agreed to help Will Revere in the final stages of preparing this book. I have been greatly helped by Michael Cornett, managing editor of the *Journal of Medieval and Early*

Modern Studies, who with skill and care worked on the manuscript and edited text. Once more I thank Catherine Beaver for her central role in sustaining the English department at Duke over many years. Any writer is dependent on the editor of the press who takes on her or his book, and I am truly grateful for the advice and support of Stephen Little at University of Notre Dame Press, both for this book and for the press's series ReFormations: Medieval and Early Modern, mentioned above.

I cannot write about Langland's work without expressing boundless gratitude to my great teachers, Elizabeth Salter and Derek Pearsall. They directed my doctoral dissertation and continued to teach me after that in person, in friendship, and through their writings. Rereading all of Elizabeth's work on Langland while writing the present book brought home its massive influence on me, even when I go in directions she herself would, perhaps, have criticized. To her, to Derek Pearsall, and to Stanley Hauerwas I dedicate this little book. Finally, yet again, I thank Christine Derham who continues to be my closest friend and my wife, still agreeing to negotiate that great divide constituted by the Atlantic, separating Lollard Earsham from North Carolina: "For a further union, a deeper communion / Through the dark cold and empty desolation, / The wave cry, the wind cry, the vast waters / Of the petrel and the porpoise" (T. S. Eliot, "East Coker," in *Four Quartets*).

⌒

Outline of the Story Langland Tells in the Final Version of *Piers Plowman*, from Derek Pearsall, *Piers Plowman: A New Annotated Edition of the C-text* (Exeter University Press, 2008), 4–6

The C version of the poem begins with a Prologue, the dreamer's vision of the world in its corrupted state as a "field full of folk," dominated by self-seeking. A "Westminster interlude" shows the higher levels of church and state subjected to the same turbulent misrule. In Passus I, Holy Church explains the dreamer's vision to him, shows him how a right use of worldly goods would be in accord with God's Law, and answers his urgent entreaty, How may I save my soul? (I.80), which in a sense initiates the whole movement of the poem, with a preliminary outline of the doctrine of Charity. But the dreamer wishes to understand more of the ways of the world, and is presented in Passus II–IV with the vision of Meed the Maid, a brilliant allegorical portrayal of the corruption of every estate and activity of society through the influence of perverted ideas of reward and of money. The king (an ideal king) wins a measure of control over Meed with the help of Conscience and Reason, whom he takes as his chief advisers, and a golden age, it seems, is about to begin. But administrative reform alone cannot bring this about: men's hearts must be purged of sin so that they may be reformed inwardly. After offering his own "confession," therefore, the dreamer shows us Reason calling on the folk to repent and to seek Truth (V). The confessions of the Seven Deadly Sins follow (VI–VII), wound up by the prayer of Repentance for general forgiveness. The people rush forth in high enthusiasm to seek for Truth, but find no way until they meet Piers Plowman, who tells them where Truth may be found (in obedience to God's Law) and promises to lead them there when he has finished his ploughing (i.e. the well-organized Christian community must be based on a well-organized economy). All the folk, of all estates, are to help him. But not everyone works with a will: wasters and layabouts refuse to do their share and Piers has to call in Hunger to force them to work, an admission of defeat, since outward coercion is no substitute for inward and voluntary reformation. The passus (VIII) ends with Piers's programme of reform in some disarray, but he receives in the next (IX) a pardon from Truth granted to all those who help him: its terms as they apply to all estates of society are related in detail, but it is not in the end a satisfactory answer to the quest for Truth. It promises salvation for those who do well but does not explain what doing well consists of. Piers Plowman disappears at this point, and the dreamer, pondering on his dream and on dreams in general, takes up the search for Dowel.

At this point the poem makes a new beginning, as if to signal the movement from the outer to the inner, from the outward reform of society to the inward reform of the individual. The dreamer's search for Dowel is first within himself (X), for the answers provided by his own intellectual faculties (Thought, Wit). These answers are not fallacious, but they are partial, and as he goes on to meet a series of personifications of learning (Study, Clergy, Scripture) the dreamer, initially stubborn and complacent, becomes increasingly bewildered (XI). The answers he receives concerning Dowel and salvation are conflicting and confusing, and he falls into a stupor of worldliness, a fast subservience to Fortune, in which his life is dreamed away. The dreamer temporarily loses his identity, his place being taken by Rechelesnesse, who solaces the gnawing of doubt with his easy answers, crude simplifications and bold disparagement of what he does not understand. Witnesses of Truth, like Trajan and Leaute, are glimpsed briefly before being submerged in the prevailing murk, and hints of understanding on the part of Rechelesnesse, as of the virtue of poverty, are swallowed in presumption and vociferous anti-clericalism. This is without doubt the most difficult and in many ways the most profound part of the poem (XII). The dreamer resumes his identity only to make a grotesque misinterpretation of the vision of Middle-Earth (XIII) that he is granted, giving continued evidence of his unredeemed pride and presumption. At last he meets Imaginatyf, the sum of all the intellect can do. Imaginatyf provides interim answers to his questions about salvation and learning as they relate to the life of Dowel, but also, more importantly, embodies the first full and explicit recognition that Dowel consists precisely in not asking the kinds of question he has been asking, but in preparing the self, through humility and patience and voluntary submission of the will to the will of God, for the admission of Charity (XIV).

In the next passus, the dreamer is given an opportunity to exercise this active virtue of patience when he is invited to the feast with the learned and gluttonous friar (XV); for the first time speculation gives way to action, and talking about doing well gives way to doing well. After a momentary intervention by Piers Plowman, an epiphany of Truth and promise of grace for the dreamer, Patience takes on the role of guide and instructs the dreamer and Activa Vita (another *alter ego* for the dreamer, through whom something of the life of common humanity is brought into the search for truth) in the true nature of patient poverty and the voluntary acceptance of God's will (XV–XVI). The achievement of this understanding of God's will is for man true freedom, and the next guide is appropriately Liberum Arbitrium (Free Will), the highest faculty of man as he lives in concord with God. Liberum Arbitrium offers the fullest understanding of true Charity that is accessible to man in his human state, unaided by grace or revelation, and shows the relation of the clergy and the Church to this true Charity (XVI–XVII). He also shows, in the vision of the Tree of Charity (XVIII), how man's growth towards charity is thwarted by the devil's work. Man stands in need of an act of divine grace, and the dreamer glimpses what form this will take in a brief account of the life of Christ. But before this vision of grace can be fully granted, Langland must show how the ascent of the soul to the full life of Charity in the reception of Christ reenacts and embodies the processes of Christian history. So we return to Abraham (Faith) and Moses (Hope) and see how their partial understanding under the Old Law, of divine truth and specifically of the Trinity is to be crowned in the New Law of mercy and love as it is expounded (XIX) by the Good Samaritan (Charity), a figure who subsequently merges into Piers Plowman and into Christ.

The world and the dreamer's soul are now prepared for the great act of divine intervention, the fulfillment of the promise of redemption, and Passus XX is devoted to an account of the Crucifixion and Harrowing of Hell. From this high climax the poem returns to a vision of the establishment of Christ's Church on earth through the gift of grace; the dreamer, suffused with the glory of revelation, must still doggedly pursue the truth and be shown how the machinery of redemption is to operate, and how it has operated in the centuries of Christian history since the Redemption (XXI). The descent to the world of fourteenth-century England is swift, and the poem ends (XXII) with the Church of Unity besieged by the forces of Antichrist, the deadly sins, and infiltrated by the subtler temptations of the friars. The end of the poem is a resumption of the search for the true Christian life, as it is embodied in Piers Plowman.

BEYOND REFORMATION?

An Essay on William Langland's *Piers Plowman*
and the End of Constantinian Christianity

l

Having offered above Derek Pearsall's outline of the story Langland tells
in the final version of his work, I set out here with Passus XX. This passus
culminates in the powerful and complex oration of Jesus Christ as he lib-
erates enslaved human beings from the prison house of hell. We are given
a glimpse of immense divine power:

> "A spirit speketh to Helle and bit to vnspere the yates:
> *Attolite portas, &c.*"
> A vois loude in that liht to Lucifer saide,
> "*Principes* of this place, prest vndo this gates
> For here a cometh with croune, the kynge of all glorie!"
> .   .   .   .
> "Dukes of this demme place, anoen vndoth this yates
> That Crist may come in, the kynges sone of heuene!"
> And with that breth helle braek, with alle Belialles barres;
> For eny wey or warde, wyde open the yates.
> (XX.270–73, 362–65)[1]

> ——————

> ["A spirit speaks to hell and bids the gates be opened."
> *Lift up your gates.*
> A loud voice within that light said to Lucifer:
> "*Princepes* of this place, quickly undo these gates,
> For he comes here with crown, the king of all glory!"
> .   .   .   .
> "Dukes of this dim place, undo these gates now
> That Christ may come in, the son of heaven's king."
> And with that breath hell with all of Belial's bars broke;
> Despite all prevention, the gates were wide open.]

The creatures' technologies of war and fortifications disintegrate in the
"breth" of the word spoken in Jesus. But the words themselves concentrate
not on power but on the divine thirst to save humans, on the ties that bind
Jesus to his brethren, the mercy of his kingly power determined to be kind
to his kin (XX.403–44).[2] Unlike so many theologians of the later Middle
Ages and the Reformation, Langland constantly disciplined his writing

about divine power by the Christocentric narratives of the New Testament.[3] In his theological paradigms it is impossible to entertain many of the speculations about God's power encouraged by the fascination with God's *potentia absoluta* among the *moderni*. For example: that God could order Christians to kill innocent people; that because God creates creatures out of an untrammeled will he can do whatever he likes with them, so that if somebody always loves God and does all the works God demands, God can annihilate such a loving person or damn him eternally without any injustice; that God can deceive the faithful and could have deceived Christ, causing him to deceive his disciples concerning the future.[4] Langland gestures toward such theological discourses at least twice in *Piers Plowman*. At one point he is considering contemporary discussions of the Trinity at feasts of the wealthy:

> Nowe is the manere at the mete when munstrals ben stille
> The lewed ayen the lered the holy lore to dispute,
> And tellen of the trinite how two slowe the thridde
> And brynge forth ballede resones, taken Bernard to witnesse
> And putten forth presumpcioun to preue the sothe
> Thus they dreuele at the deyes the deite to know
> And gnawen god with gorge when here gottes fullen.
>
> (XI.33–39)

> [Now is the custom at meals, when the minstrels are silent,
> The ignorant take on the learned to debate holy doctrine,
> And talk about the Trinity how two killed the third
> And bring forth flimsy arguments, take Bernard to witness,
> And put forth a presumption to prove the truth.
> Thus they drivel on the dais, the deity to know,
> And chomp on God in their throats when their guts fill up.]

The laicization of theology here involves a parodic imitation of the church's theologians in their Latin academies. Parodic, yes; but also, distinctly, imitation. For what Langland has identified is the way philosophical theology in the modern university produced an immense discourse on the relations and processions of the Trinity which not only sidelined the narratives of scripture but was a committedly antinarrative genre.[5] True enough, this

genre comprised theologians whose apprenticeship involved both commenting on the *Sentences* and commenting on scripture as conventionally
read in the Catholic Church.[6] But such training legitimated the development of theology (around the *Sentences*) in which the doctrine of God was
abstracted from scriptural stories and elaborated in the categories of Aristotelian logic, physics, and metaphysics.[7] Langland evaluated the outcome
in the passage quoted above. Inattention to the disciplines of relevant narratives in scripture sponsored a freewheeling discussion of God's power
and nature. He returns to his critical evaluation of modern theology in the
critiques of the modern church which fostered this discourse, a critique
ascribed to Liberum Arbitrium:

> Freres fele tymes to the folk ther they prechen
> Mouen motyues, mony tymes insolibles and falaes,
> That both lewed and lered of here beleue douten.
>   (XVI.231–33)

> ———

> [Many times friars when they preach to the people
> Frequently raise fallacious and insoluble questions
> That put both the learned and ignorant in doubt of their belief.]

In shorthand, Langland points toward the institutionalization of theology
so richly illustrated by Hester Gelber in her remarkable doctoral thesis
and in her more recent studies.[8] The issues include Langland's suspicion
that the church now legitimizes a version of Christian theology in which
the narratives and histories through which God is revealed are subordi-
nated to modern forms of Aristotelian logic. Theologians (led by friars) are
lured to invent theological truth as suprahistorical or nonhistorical, quite
autonomous of the stories on which the church depends and acknowledges in the liturgy. While Langland includes disputations in an academic
mode in his own work, they are subjected to the overall dialectic in which
they exist, one finally shaped by Chistocentric and Pentecostal narratives.
For however fragmented and paratactic Langland's work may often feel,
Langland has a story to tell, one from which his theology and ecclesiology
emerges.

The Christ of *Piers Plowman* is the Christ whom the New Testament
describes as being sent to fulfill the promises of the divine covenant with

Abraham and Moses, to save sinners in the manifestation of God's love figured by the father, the shepherd, and the woman of Luke 15. Christ's oration in hell affirms his kindness and kinship with human beings despite their persistent rejection of God. What he says in the context is congruent with an exemplary exchange between Jesus and his disciples when they are rejected by a village of Samaritans: "And when his disciples James and John had seen this, they said: Lord wilt thou that we command fire to come down from heaven, and consume them?" (Luke 9:54–56).[9] The disciples' model of a prophet mediating divine power is Elijah summoning fire from heaven to kill more than a hundred Samaritans in proof that he is "a man of God" (4 Kings 1:1–12). Jesus's response reiterates a common declaration in the evangelical narrative: "the Son of man is come to save that which was lost" (Matt. 18:11; see too Luke 19:10). He is the one whom the Pharisees rebuke for keeping an open table: "This man receiveth sinners and eateth with them" (Luke 15:2). And he is the one who responds to this charge not by denial but by parable upon parable to show that this practice is itself a decisive revelation of the divine will (Luke 15:3–32). Langland himself cites one of these parables in his beautiful and moving depiction of Wille's first conversion in the poem (V.92–101).

How then does Langland return from the emancipating power of God revealed by Christ's acts and words in hell to the place in which he will complete his work for humanity: the present world and the church? The poet chooses to do so by way of the risen Christ's commission to Piers the Plowman, now figuring the apostle Peter, and a representation of Pentecost with an unusual commentary on this event.

Langland ascribes his account of the risen Christ to Conscience, the figure who replaces faith as Wille's guide at the opening of Passus XXI (XXI.9 ff.; cf. XX.6–34). The shift in guide indicates that this Conscience is one informed by faith and reflecting Wille's move toward "scientia" (knowledge) based on faith.[10] Wille begs Conscience "to kenne me the sothe" (XXI.9). What is puzzling him at this point is the relationship between the transformed figuration of "Peres the plouhman," just before the canon of the Mass, and Jesus, whom Wille has seen jousting on the cross against the powers that bind and terrorize humanity (XXI.1–14; cf. XX.6–34a). He is puzzled about the relations between the name of Jesus and the name of Christ (XXI.15–25). Conscience explains this relation to Wille by retelling the life of Jesus with his victory over death and devil: *Christus Resurgens*

(XXI.140–81a). Conscience's narration also completes Wille's long quest for Dowel, Dobet, and Dobest, those modes of virtue, by displaying them in Christological form, fulfilled in Christ. So, for example, Dowel becomes the evangelical law in which love of enemy is not a counsel of perfection but a precept of the new law initiated by Jesus Christ who makes law into gospel, a precept for all Christians to follow (XXI.108–23).[11]

This is the context in which Langland situates Christ's commission to the apostle Peter. Dobest completes the activity of the risen Christ among his disciples:

> And when this dede was doen, do best he thouhte
> And yaf Peres pardoun and power he graunted hym,
> Myhte men to assoyle of alle manere synnes,
> To alle manere men mercy and foryeuenesse
> In couenaunt that they come and knoleched to pay
> To Peres pardoun the plouhman *Redde quod debes.*
> Thus hath Peres power, be his pardoun payed,
> To bynde and to vnbynde bothe here and elles
> And assoile men of alle synnes, saue of dette one.
>
> (XXI.182–90)

———

> [And when this deed was done, he thought about Do-best
> And gave Piers the power and pardon he granted
> To all manner of men, mercy and forgiveness;
> Gave him might to absolve men of all manner of sins
> Provided they come and acknowledge they must pay
> To Piers the plowman's pardon *Redde quod debes.*
> Thus Piers has the power, if his pardon is paid for,
> To bind and unbind both here and elsewhere
> And absolve men of all sins, except for their debts.]

This is Langland's final account of what the papacy claimed as its origins. What Langland finally does with this claim is a major part of the story he will tell. At the moment, however, the apostle Peter is merged with Piers the poem's plowman as the risen Christ gives him the power to mediate Christ's mercy and forgiveness to "alle manere men" who fulfill the law of the gospel, the new covenant.[12] Christ's gift also resolves Wille's puzzles about indulgences and the purchase of masses so eloquently expressed much earlier in the poem, at the end of Passus IX. To appreciate the implications of this resolution we should recall the treatment of pardon and papacy in that passus.

There, Wille had woken from his vision of an encounter between "Peres the plouhman" and a priest who "impugnede" the pardon allegedly received from Treuthe as "no pardoun" (IX. 293–352a; 289; see IX.1–292 passim). Ruminating on the issues raised in this dramatic clash, Wille interprets the priest's judgment as congruent with his own suspicions about indulgences in the late medieval church together with the papal power they assume and papal authority.[13] He suspects that virtuous practice (Dowel) far surpasses any salvific role of indulgences, or of masses purchased for the souls of the dead to ease their path through purgatory, or of pilgrimages (IX.321–24).[14] But Wille wants to remain an orthodox member of the contemporary church and checks the direction of such thoughts by affirming papal power:

> Yut hath the pope power pardoun to graunte
> To peple withouten penaunce to passe into ioye.
> (IX.325–26)

———

> [Yet the pope has power to grant pardon
> To people to pass without penance into joy.]

This is a strikingly unqualified affirmation of papal authority and power in the economy of salvation. It smacks of just the kind of undifferentiated claims to plenitude of papal power so extensively criticized, in different ways and to different ends, by Marsilius of Padua and William of Ockham earlier in the century.[15] Langland emphasizes this scope by immediately glossing the statement about the pope's "power" to open the gate of heaven without any penitential reconciliation with God and neighbor: "Quodcumque ligaveris super terram erit ligatum in caelis" (Whatsoever thou shalt bind upon earth shall be bound also in heaven) (Matt. 16:19). This comes from Jesus's words to Peter after the apostle recognized him as "Christ, the Son of the living God" (16:16). Jesus blesses Peter and promises, "upon this rock (*petram*) I will build my church" (16:18). For Augustine, the rock on which the church stands came to mean Jesus Christ, the one whom Peter confessed to be "the Christ, the Son of the living God." In his *Retractions* he observes that Jesus says, "Thou art Peter," and not "Thou art the rock." There is no commitment to any exegesis that would make the "rock" represent the Roman papacy.[16] In a sermon apparently "some time between 410 and 412," Augustine observes that Christ bestowed the name Peter on the apostle Simon to represent the church: "Because Christ, you see, is the *petra* or rock; Peter, or Rocky is so called from rock, not the rock from Rocky; just as Christ is not so called from Christian, but Christian from Christ." So the rock on which Christ promises to build his church, Augustine states, is the Christological confession uttered by Peter when Christ says that he will build his church; Augustine glosses the promise: "that is, on myself, the Son of the living God . . . I will build you on me, not me on you."[17] Augustine's exegesis was well known in the Middle Ages and found a place in Aquinas's commentary on the Gospels.[18] But papal apologists appropriated the text, set aside Augustine's reading, and projected onto Matthew's Gospel their own ideology. To Ockham, such late medieval exegesis was quite unwarranted and led to "many heretical absurdities" in the papalist claims. True enough, Jesus said, "whatsoever thou shall bind upon earth, it shall be bound in heaven" (Matt. 16:19). But if these words are "understood without any exception Christ would have promised blessed Peter power equal to God's and Christ's." Another "heretical absurdity is that the pope could licitly and by right kill innocent people, and universally do all things contrary to divine and natural law."[19] Ockham goes on to expose the errant theory and practice of exegesis on which such papalist doxology rests.[20] Into such waters Langland steps with his quotation from Matthew 16:19, "whatsoever thou shalt bind upon earth, it shall be bound also in heaven" (IX.327a). But for the moment he does not explicate or unfold the sharp controversies in his church's reception of this evangelical text. Nevertheless, he will address the substance of such conflicts toward the end of the poem, and we should not imagine that the quoted text had a consensual interpretation.[21] Wille's own position here on papal authority and power is certainly not the poem's last word on this topic. In fact, even in Passus IX Wille's affirmation of papal power is followed by warnings about the contemporary norms presided over and encouraged by the modern papacy. Church and pope support the aspiration of wealthy people to "purchase" the pardons and papal bulls, notes Wille, but his support for the system is troubled.[22] As he considers Christ's final judgment, his language about papal dispensations becomes dismissive. He ponders how Christ's concern is with our daily practice and keeping of evangelical law. As for the church's economy of salvation mediated through papal indulgences and pardons:

> And how we dede day be day the doem wol reherce.
> A pouheful of pardon there, ne prouinciales lettres,
> Thow we be founden in the fraternite of alle fyue orders
> And haue indulgences doublefold, but Dowel vs helpe
> Y sette nat by pardon a pese ne nat a pye-hele!
>
> (IX.342–46)

———

> [How we led our lives here and kept his laws
> And how you acted day by day the doom will recount.
> A sackful of pardon there, nor provincials' letters,
> Though we be found in the fraternity of all five orders
> And have doublefold indulgences, unless Do-well help us
> I don't count pardon worth a peascod or piecrust!]

One might argue that Wille's vacillations merely reflect orthodox warnings about the abuse of indulgences. But such an argument overlooks the contested nature of the relevant network of practices, theological legitimizations, and Langland's own intense interest in this contest. Whatever pardon Piers may have received at the opening of Passus IX and however he may have understood or misunderstood it, Langland generated dramatic, irresolvable clashes between the massive gloss on the pardon (a gloss composed by numerous voices, including Piers's) and what turns out to be just two lines of judgment from the Athanasian Creed:

> And Peres at his preyre the pardon vnfoldeth
> And Y byhynde hem bothe byheld alle the bulle
> In two lynes as hit lay and nat a lettre more,
> And was ywryte ryhte thus in witnesse of Treuthe:
> *Et qui bona egerunt ibunt in vitam eternam;*
> *Qui vero mala in ignem eternum.*
> "Peter!" quod the prest tho, "Y kan no pardoun fynde
> Bote Dowel and haue wel and god shal haue thy soule

And do yuele and haue euele and hope thow non othere
Bote he that euele lyueth euele shal ende."

(IX.283–92)

———

[And Piers at his request unfolds the pardon
And I behind them both beheld the entire bull
In two lines as it lay and not a letter more,
And was written exactly thus in witness of Truth:
They that have done good shall go into everlasting life;
They that have done evil into everlasting fire.
"Peter," said the priest then, "I can find no pardon,
But only 'Do well and have well and God shall have your soul
And do evil and have evil and expect nothing other
But he that lives evilly shall have an evil end.'"]

Disturbed by this clash, this conflict of interpretation, Wille wanders without food and without money on Malvern hills, musing on this dream (IX.293–97).[23] Not until many passages later, and only after participation in the founding narratives of Christian teaching, are Wille's puzzles over papal power and the keys to the kingdom to be resolved. For now, we are left with Piers unable to answer the priest's charge that his alleged pardon is "no pardoun" and Wille's ambivalence over papal claims to the powers of the keys in the economy of salvation.

The resolution will emerge during the passage in which the risen Christ gives Piers power to mediate the forgiveness flowing from Christ's victorious battle over death and devil. This forgiveness had been manifested in his great oration during the liberation of prisoners held in hell (XXI.182–98; XX.370–475), the passage from which we set out. Conscience now tells Wille that such mediation is a gift given with a determinate condition, a divine gift that belongs to a new covenant in which law and gospel are inseparable. Wille is shown what he had forgotten and what Langland thinks the contemporary church has forgotten. Namely: Ockham was quite right to argue that Christ set clear limits to Petrine power even in its sublime origins, let alone in its modern Roman version. Furthermore, these limits mean that whatever a pope might claim, absolution will not be given by Christ unless the new covenant is fulfilled by the Christian paying back what he owes: "*Redde quod debes*" (Rom. 13:7; Matt.

18:28). That is to say, evangelical forgiveness is inseparable from evangelical justice. Just as Conscience had argued against Mede, it turns out that God "gyueth nothyng that *si* ne is the glose" (i.e., God's gifts are always glossed by an *if,* a certain condition, III.329). After invoking the condition, "*Redde quod debes,*" Conscience reiterates that only if the person seeking forgiveness renders what is owed, enacts just restitution, does Piers have the power to pardon, to "bynde and to vnbynde" (XXI.188–90). So emphatic is Conscience about this that he reiterates the conditionality of pardon in his account of Christ's ascension (XXI.191–98). The theological inflection here is unambiguous: Christ's minister can declare Christ's saving forgiveness only to those who fulfill Christ's conditions. So Ockham was, indeed, correct in discerning determinate limits to Petrine power even if his focus was in a different sphere of conflict.[24]

From Passus XVIII Langland's work had converged with the liturgy, and in Passus XXI he moves from the feast of the Ascension to Pentecost.[25] As in the celebration of Easter, we see Wille, quite unusually, participating in collective worship, singing *Veni creator spiritus* with "many hundret" (XXI.210–11). His encounters with Abraham (Faith) and with Christ as the Samaritan had included teaching about the Trinity, teaching replete with parable and narrative, a corrective to academic approaches mentioned earlier (XVIII.181–268a; XIX.26–278). He now receives a vision of the Holy Spirit. In this vision time present is joined with time past in a way that is characteristic of the liturgy. The contemporary church, in the feast of Pentecost, remembers and identifies with the apostolic church in which *Spiritus Paraclitus* first appeared "to Peres and to his felawes." Wille witnesses the presence of the Holy Spirit in the likeness of fire on all the disciples which brings them the knowledge of "alle kyne langages" (XXI.199–206; Acts 2:1–4). This vision terrifies Wille, but Conscience assures him that *Spiritus Paraclitus* is indeed the messenger of Christ who should be welcomed and worshipped (XXI.207–12). The hymn in which Wille joins is a prayer for the illumination of grace and bodily well-being from the "*Creator Spiritus*" who is called "*Paraclitus.*" It also includes a prayer for protection from enemies, for peace, and for knowledge of God the Father, recognition of God the Son, and belief in the Spirit of both.[26] After the celebration of Pentecost, Langland gives us his model of apostolic evangelization in the formation of Christ's church. In following this I shall focus on political and ecclesiastic implications.

II

From the first Pentecost the Holy Spirit, "Grace," accompanies "Peres plouhman," still figuring the apostle Peter, to make the church of Christ (XXI.213–335). Grace's first advice to Piers is also advice to Conscience who is close to Piers: "And conseilede hym [Piers] and Consience the commune to sompne [summon]" (XXI.214). All are to be gathered together so as to receive the gifts of grace. Langland glosses this episode by directing his readers to Paul's discussion in 1 Corinthians 12, teaching about the diversity of gifts from the one Spirit acting on the community of Christians. The Holy Spirit promises that the gifts he dispenses are sufficient treasures for a lifetime (XXI.215–18, 225–26). He thus returns to the language of Wille's first teacher:

> "When alle tresores ben tried, treuthe is the beste—
> I do hit vppon *Deus caritas* to deme the sothe.
> Hit is as derworthe a druerie as dere god hymseluen.
> For who is trewe of his tonge and of his two handes
> And doth the werkes therwith and wilneth no man ylle,
> He is a god by the gospel and graunte may hele
> And also lyk oure lord, by saynt Lukes wordes."
>
> (I.81–87)

> ["When all treasures have been tested, Truth is the best—
> I adduce *Deus caritas*, to deliver this fact.
> It is as precious a prize as dear God himself.
> For he who is true in his tongue and his two hands
> And works that way, wishing no man evil,
> Is a god, says the gospel, and grants health
> And resembles our Lord, in Saint Luke's words."]

Holy Church, for she is the teacher here, offers an extremely condensed introduction to a Christian language for evoking the commitment of divine love ("*Deus caritas*," or God is charity, 1 John 4:7–19) to draw humans into the divine life. Constant acts informed by truth create dispositions of the will which transform the human into "a god." The human creature becomes "lyke our Lord," becomes "a god" but not God. Holy Church goes on to associate this teaching with an exquisitely beautiful lyric on how "Treuthe" teaches that "love" is the "salue" (ointment, healing remedy) given to humankind. It is "the plonte of pees, most precious of vertues," brought into human lives through the incarnation of God (I.146–67). As St. Augustine preached to his congregation one Christmas day, "*Today Truth has sprung from the earth* (Ps. 85:11); Christ has been born from the flesh . . . in order to make gods of those who were merely human, one who was God made himself human; without forfeiting what he was, he wished to become what he himself had made. He himself made what he would become, because what he did was add man to God, not lose God in man."[27] Thus Langland's Holy Church and thus Augustine. But Holy Church's answers to Wille's question ("How Y may saue my soule," I.80), a question so dazzling in its excess of meanings, included a gesture toward "werkes," toward truthful action with one's "two handes." And this raised, but set aside, a question taken up time and again throughout *Piers Plowman* and now at Pentecost. Namely, what kind of community is constituted by the gifts of grace, the gifts that flow from the Incarnation?

In answering this question we should begin by noting how the grace given by the Holy Spirit is both communitarian and individual. It enables each person to be self-guided in a relative autonomy. Grace "yaf vch man a grace to gye with hymsuluen" (gave each man a grace to guide himself with) (XXI.227). This unequivocal affirmation of gifts that sustain individual choice and responsibility is combined with a focus on the range of gifts needed to sustain the Pentecostal polity. Langland's interpretation of St. Paul's "*divisiones gratiarum*" (diversities of graces) is striking. For he introduces a range of human labor that is both outside Paul's attention and belongs specifically to Langland's own world. His aim is to show how the gifts of grace can sustain a social formation in which practices that have been displayed in the poem as inclining their agents to habitual sin can be ordered to virtue. Let us consider some of his examples.

From the Prologue through to the confessions of capital sins (Passus VII) Langland represents contemporary England as a culture in which relations between humans as well as between humans and God are being deformed by commodification, by selling and buying. Law, marriage, the exegesis of scripture, and the sacrament of penance are all assimilated to the kind of production and exchange encouraged by market relations where traditional virtues and their language become unintelligible (Prol.; II–IV;

VI–VII). But in the Pentecostal polity Grace teaches members of the polity trade ("craft") with the requisite skill in buying and selling to gain their livelihood (XXI.234–35). Earlier in *Piers Plowman* lawyers represented the total subjection of God's gifts of language, the word, into words spoken only for material profit in a culture where Mede organizes all aspects of the law (Prol. 160–66; III.450–51; III–IV passim). At that stage Conscience's frustration drew him into a fantasia composed in an apocalyptic mode where he envisaged the revolutionary transformation of law into manual labor (III.452). Revolution, distinctly, rather than an ameliorative process of reforms. But in the Pentecostal community Grace bestows "wyt with words" and enables lawyers to earn their livelihood "with Trouthe" (XXI.229–31). Perhaps Langland is imagining the fusion of gospel and law within contemporary divisions of labor. Lawyers formed in Christian virtues earn their livelihood by using their special gifts to facilitate among their neighbors the union of justice and mercy, truth and peace, fulfilling the promise of the new covenant (see XX.459–75). Certainly Grace's Pentecostal gifts produce a realm of manual labor free from the conflicts around the Statute of Laborers, work disciplines, and the price of labor in the communal pleasures of the pub (XXI.236–39; cf. Passus VIII).[28] As Langland composes his vision of Pentecostal, liturgical time, he has moved from Acts 2:1–4 to late fourteenth-century England. His development of Paul's instruction on "spiritual things" (*de spiritualibus*) addresses modes of production and subsistence set aside in 1 Corinthians 12.

One of the most startling gifts of the Holy Spirit is the gift of grace-formed violence directed to remedy the unjust actions of "false men." Grace enables and guides some people to ride out and recover what had been unjustly seized:

And somme to ryde and rekeuere that vnrihtfulliche was wonne:
He wissede men wynne hit ayeyn thorw wihtnesse of handes
And fechen hit fro false men with Foleuiles lawes.

(XXI.245–47)

[And some to ride and recover what was unrightfully gained;
He showed men strong-armed ways to win it back
And take it from false men with vigilante law.]

Grace must envisage a more effective version of the courteous knight who had promised Piers to help his agrarian labor by enforcing labor discipline, including the Statute of Laborers (VIII.19–34, 324–38). Called upon by Piers to subject the laborers who insist on working as they will rather than at Piers's commands, the knight had threatened to "bete" them according to "the lawe" and put them "in stokkes" (VIII.149–63). This law is the Statute, with its coercive enforcement, passed by parliament to hold down wages to pre-plague levels and passed especially for the benefit of employers against the interests of laborers, in particular landless laborers utterly dependent on selling their labor. The "werkemen" curse the king who assented to the legislation and "alle the kynges justices" who tried to enforce it and impose penalties on those who persisted (VIII.337–38). But in Passus VIII the knight's threats and the labor laws are treated with contempt. Both prove totally ineffectual.[29] Grace thus seems to offer a more forceful agency of just coercions in the Pentecostal community but also one that is directed to obtaining restitution from "false men" who had wrongfully taken materials from their neighbors and refused to render what they owed according to Christ's own law (XXI.186–87, 191–98). This remedial coercion is a fascinating perspective on Langland's Pentecostal politics, one perhaps made more tricky by the citation of the Folvilles.

For this name conjured up the role of violence that could be practiced by local groups of gentry in late medieval England.[30] We encountered something that looked a little like the historical Folvilles in Passus IV. There a member of the armed elites carries out a series of violent acts against local people to strengthen his own dominion and wealth. Langland names him "Wrong" and his victim is called "Pees" (IV.45–65). Wrong is supported by Mede who seeks to compensate Peace so richly that he will withdraw his complaint and prevent the subjection of Wrong to royal justice administered from Westminster (IV.66–98). Without any ambiguity, Langland is exemplifying such violence and Mede's corruption of restitution as acts against Reason, Conscience, and Justice (IV.99–161). So despite some possible cultural memories of the historical "Foleuiles" that might associate them with Wrong and Mede, when the Holy Spirit advocates "Foleuiles Lawes" for the Pentecostal polity, he intends them to organize action against figures represented by Wrong. However tricky the allusion, Grace is asserting the sanctification of some forms of violence committed to the restitution of unjustly appropriated goods. It is committed only to that remedial activity and holds no legitimation for self-serving deployments of force ("Wrong").

Christians often appealed to Paul's letter to the Romans when thinking about the justification for force in the polity. There Paul accepted the sword as a power given to the higher powers ("potestatibus sublimioribus") by God (Rom. 13:1–8). Obedience was thus a matter not merely of necessity, but for conscience ("propter conscientiam").[31] Langland does not invoke this text in his own sanctification of coercive restitution against "false men." But he does quote from this chapter (Rom. 13). He reiterates the demand he ascribes to the risen Christ, the demand that conditions the forgiveness Christ mediates through Piers: "*Reddite omnibus debita*" (Render to all their due) (Rom. 13:7). Folville's laws and the Pauline citation give an extremely unusual edge to the feast of Pentecost. But it is an eloquent reflection of Langland's conviction that even the Pentecostal community will include armed people to recover what has been taken "vnrihtfulliche" (XXI.245–47). Pentecost does not restore all Christians to the state of innocence, despite the pouring forth of the gifts of the Holy Spirit. But Grace's limitation of coercion to such restitution of just relationship will come to seem a paradise in comparison to post-Pentecostal lay elites and their versions of justice and legitimate use of force.

The Pentecostal community is also granted a version of artisanal work which would, in Langland's culture, have entailed a revolution in social relations. Instead of competition, hierarchy, and hostility between different groups of artisans competing in the market, the Holy Spirit generates relations of Christian fraternity and humility (XXI.252–55).[32] Langland's assimilation of Paul's Corinthian letter to his own Pentecostal contexts is subtle. Perhaps most important to his vision is that Paul taught the church in Corinth to have a thoroughly egalitarian way of perceiving the diversities of the Spirit's gifts. This helps Langland compose a distinctively antihierarchical version of the church, therefore one at odds with the late medieval church. Using the body analogically, Paul writes that those who seem "more feeble members of the body are more necessary" and that those conventionally considered "less honourable members of the body, about these we put more abundant honours." Even so, God's gifts and our celebration of them are ordered so that "there might be no schism [*scisma*] in the body; but the members might be mutually one for another [*pro invicem sollicita sint mem-*

bra]" (1 Cor. 12:22–27). In the previous chapter Paul had rebuked this church for their "schisms" (*scissuras*) as for the way rampant individualism and division of status are displayed, even when all meet to celebrate the Lord's Supper (11:18–22). Such assumptions, however habitual, are evidence that the Corinthian Christians forgot what Jesus said to his disciples at supper on the night he was betrayed: "as often as you shall eat this bread and drink the chalice, you shall shew the death of the Lord, until he come. Therefore, whosoever shall eat this bread, or drink the chalice of the Lord unworthily, shall be guilty of the body and of the blood of the Lord[,] . . . not discerning the body of the Lord" (11:26–29). *Discerning* the body of Christ must include *discerning* how all gathered together are "members of the body, whereas they are many, yet are one body: so also is Christ. For in one Spirit we are all baptized into one body" (12:12–13). This is what Langland recapitulates and applies to contemporary social relations. To discern the body in this way is to free perception from the norms of hierarchy and status. From freed perception Grace will enable egalitarian relations suited to a Pentecostal polity. To oppose this will be a mark of communities in which the body is not discerned: "he that eateth and drinketh unworthily eateth and drinketh judgment to himself, not discerning the body of the Lord" (11:29). In Langland's church the body of Christ habitually worked to sacralize the very sharp sense of hierarchy naturalized in its society.[33]

As one ponders the theology and politics of Langland's passage one comes to its version of priesthood. In the medieval church the characteristic definition of what constitutes a priest was his consecration of the wafer and the wine on the altar of the Mass into the body and blood of Christ, the Galilean body. Through the priest's actions, in Thomas Aquinas's memorable terms, Christ would be present: "not only the flesh, but the whole body of Christ, that is, the bones and nerves and all the rest" (non solum caro, sed totum corpus Christi, idest ossa et nervi et alia huiusmodi) (*ST* III.76.1, resp. and ad 2). This teaching had become so central in the late medieval church that those who rejected it were judged to be heretics and from 1401, in England, risked being burned to death.[34] Yet, in this context, the Holy Spirit's declaration about priesthood is striking. It is far from the customary exaltation of priesthood over laity, an elevation that was theological, liturgical, judicial, cultural, and plainly embodied in the spaces of the church building. The Holy Spirit presents the grace of priesthood in this way:

Som wyes he yaf wyt with wordes to shewe,
To wynne with treuthe that the world asketh,

As prechours and prestes and prentises of lawe:
They leely to lyue bi labour of tonge
And bi wit to wissen othere as grace hem wolde teche.

(XXI.229–33)

———

[Some men he gave intelligence as a way with words,
To earn with truth what the world asks us,

And preachers and priests and apprentices at law:
They to live loyally by labor of tongue
And by intelligence to train others as Grace would teach them.]

Here Langland's *modus loquendi* concerning the priesthood seems quite remarkable in the context of the normative discourses of his church. As Aquinas taught, theology is inextricably bound up with its forms of language, the *modi loquendi*.[35] And Langland sets priests on even ground with apprentices of law and with all whose livelihood comes from truthful uses of intellect and language. Rather than being identified as consecrators of the Eucharist and placed in an exalted segregated station, appropriate to those who handle Christ's body, they are linked by alliteration with preachers as well as with "prentises of lawe." Of course, those who spoke for the medieval church, before as well as after Wyclif, had insisted that only priests in their parishes and those licensed by the local bishop could preach licitly.[36] But the Holy Spirit knows nothing about such hierarchies and boundaries. Indeed, he chooses not to give any warrant for any kind of sacerdotal supremicism in the Pentecostal community. On the contrary, the creation in which the gifts of intellect and language are bestowed on the priesthood seems more congruent with the missionary church of martyrs held up as a model by Liberum Arbitrium earlier in the poem. And he had advocated this model as a far more faithful witness to Christ than the one offered by the contemporary church and its leadership (XVI.242–XVII.320, esp. XVII.214–91a). As for the identity of that speaker: he is "Cristes creature" and "in Cristes court yknowe wel and of his kynne a party" ("I am Christ's creature . . . and a member of his family, / And well known in Christ's court and to Christians in many a place") (XVI.165–78).

Furthermore, Holy Spirit's donations include some conspicuous absences. Conspicuous, that is, in the contexts of the late medieval church so relentlessly criticized by Langland. Holy Spirit apparently knows nothing about Franciscan claims to have discovered and chosen the status of perfection, the life of absolute poverty initiated by the sixth angel of the Apocalypse.[37] He simply ignores these conventional and grandiloquent claims together with the intense, protracted battles they had caused in the thirteenth- and fourteenth-century church. Holy Spirit actually seems to know nothing about friars who, according to Chaucer's Wife of Bath, have displaced the world of elves and fairies:

> As thikke as motes in the sonne-beem,
> Blessynge halles, chambres, kichenes, boures,
> Citees, burghes, castels, hye toures,
> Thropes, bernes, shipnes, dayeryes—
> This maketh that ther ben no fayeryes.
> For ther as wont to walken was an elf
> Ther walketh now the lymytour hymself.
>   (*Wife of Bath's Tale*, *CT* III.868–74; trans. 299–300)[38]

> [As thick as motes that speckle a sun-beam,
> Blessing the halls, the chambers, kitchens, bowers,
> Cities and boroughs, castles, courts and towers,
> Thorpes, barns and stables, outhouses and dairies,
> And that's the reason why there are no fairies.
> Wherever there was wont to walk an elf
> To-day there walks the holy friar himself.]

Like Chaucer, Langland's Conscience remarks on the immense number of friars in the modern church, complaining that they have multiplied "out of nombre," becoming a figure of hell which also is "withoute nombre" (XXII.253–72). Despite this strong post-Pentecostal presence, Holy Spirit does not include *any* mendicant way of life as an object of his grace or part of the Pentecostal community. Given the poem's focus on mendicant orders and the role played by friars in the final passus, this judgment is hardly surprising: but it is, nevertheless, replete with significance.[39] Nor does Holy Spirit mention his founding of monasteries, that religious order so severely attacked earlier in Reason's sermon (V.146–79). But, in contrast, he *does* say that he has inspired some Christians to live in poverty, patience, praying "for alle cristene" and longing to leave this world (XXI.248–49). These people are certainly not mobile, mendicant, preaching friars involved in administering the sacrament of penance. Perhaps Carthusian monks devoted to contemplation, devotional writing, and prayer might be included in this group, but the latter sounds very like the institutionally detached contemplatives so warmly praised by Langland in his Prologue. These were described as "ankeres and eremites that holdeth hem in here selles, / Coueyten noght in contreys to cayren aboute" (Prol. 30–31).[40] Liberum Arbitrium also held up such Christians and their detachment from the church's most prominent institutions as models of sanctity:

> Holy writ witnesseth ther were suche eremytes,
> Solitarie by hemsulue in here selles lyuede
> Withoute borwynge or beggynge bote of god one,
> Excepte that Egide a hynde other-while
> To his selle selde cam and soffred be mylked.
>
> . . . .
>
> Y can nat rykene hem riht now ne reherse here names
> That lyueden thus for oure lordes loue monye longe yeres
> Withoute borwynge or beggynge, or the boek lyeth,
> And woneden in wildernesses amonges wilde bestes.
> (XVII.6–10, 25–28)

[Holy writ testifies there were such hermits,
Solitaries, living by themselves in their cells
Without borrowing or begging but from God only,
Except that to Giles' cell from time to time a doe
Came, though not often, and let herself be milked.

. . . .

I cannot count them right now or rehearse their names
Who lived thus many long years for our Lord's love

Without borrowing or begging, or the book lies,
And dwelled in the wilderness among wild beasts.]

This perspective, no encouragement to contemporary friars or landholding monasteries, is now shown to be Pentecostal. While observing this, we
should also note that in Passus XXI Holy Spirit does not create a new hierarchy in which "such eremytes" constitute the status of supreme perfection claimed by friars and carefully explained by Thomas Aquinas.[41]

III

Perhaps even more important is the absence of any mention of a pope
in the Pentecostal community. Holy Spirit seems to pour his sanctifying
gifts to priests, preachers, apprentices of law, contemplatives, astronomers,
philosophers, manual laborers, traders, and armed groups responsible for
the enforcement of justice against those who steal. But in this rich and
idiosyncratic reading of Paul's instructions to the church in Corinth (1
Cor. 12) the Holy Spirit does not mention any unique vicar of Christ, any
head of the church under Christ, any ecclesiastic leader bearing a plenitude of power and coercive jurisdiction in alleged succession to the apostle
Peter. One can bring out the force of Langland's choices by thinking of
two places in which Aquinas, the common doctor of the Catholic Church,
addresses the Pauline text cited by Langland. Discussing the diversity of
offices in the church (in the *Summa Theologiae*), he emphasizes that they
must be ordered and all confusion avoided in diverse offices, status, and
ranks. Yes, as Paul said, the members should be mutually careful for each
other. And this needs hierarchy. In the commentary on Paul's letter to the
Corinthians ascribed to Aquinas, he discusses 1 Corinthians 12 at length.
Its approach is very different from Langland's. Characteristic of this is
Aquinas's reading of Paul's images of head and feet as prelates and their
subordinates. When Aquinas glosses Paul's statement about the necessity
of members who seem more feeble (1 Cor. 12:22) he thinks of agricultural
workers: they are lowly but necessary to enable social life. This is, of
course, a commonplace of medieval discourse about estates and hierarchy
but neither exactly Paul's preoccupation nor the focus of Holy Spirit in
Langland's account. But perhaps most illuminating in the present context

is Aquinas's response to Paul's wish to avoid "schism in the body" (*schisma in corpore*) by encouraging mutual solidarity among Christians (12:25–27). Aquinas takes this as a discussion of the church's peace and introduces comment on the governance of the church (prelates, archdeacons, parish priests). When there is no governor ("gubernator") the people fall (quoting Prov. 11:14). If we turn back to the treatment of schism in the *Summa Theologiae*, we find Aquinas maintaining that it involves not holding fast to the head from which the body is nourished (citing Col. 2:19). This head is Christ whose surrogate in the church is the pope ("cuius vicem in Ecclesia gerit summus Pontifex"). So schism is the rejection of papal supremacy ("schismatici dicuntur, qui subesse renuunt summo Pontifici").[42] It is worth recalling here that when he addressed heresy in the *Summa Theologiae* he had similarly placed the authenticity of the universal church in the pope (*ST* II-II.11.2, ad 3). Langland is choosing to set aside such approaches as he figures the founding of the church.

They are, however, a central strand of orthodox ecclesiology in the Middle Ages and the increasing centralization of papal power and its monarchic form. The ideology of this form achieves particularly clear articulation in Boniface VIII's bull *Unam Sanctam* (1302). Having stipulated that outside the church there is no remission of sins nor salvation, it affirms that this church has one body and one head, namely Christ *and* Christ's vicar Peter, together with Peter's successors. The pope declared that the church has two swords in her power, one "spiritual," the other "temporal." Boniface VIII insists that "he who denies that the temporal sword is in the power of Peter, misunderstands the words of the Lord, 'Put up thy sword into thy sheath' [John 28:11]. Both are in the power of the Church, the spiritual sword and the material." The latter is to be wielded by lay powers at the church's command. Whoever resists papal power resists the ordinance of God while "it is altogether necessary to salvation for every human creature to be subject to the Roman pontiff."[43] This political theology was bound up with Neoplatonic metaphysics and the ecclesial model of Pseudo-Dionysius. Such a combination had been common in orthodox formulations of hierarchy, authority, and obedience in the church. Perhaps it remains so in the theologians of so-called Radical Orthodoxy. But lay sovereigns like Edward I of England and Philip IV of France did not subject their own power to its scheme. And Langland's Pentecostal politics, with its own version of Peter, goes sharply against its grain. In fact, Langland's vision of the Holy Spirit's formation of Christian community and church rejects a papal and hierocratic model. The commentary I offer below on Langland's history of the church in Passus XXI–XXII will unfold this view of his political theology. He was not without company, and I will also consider some of his affinities with Ockham and Wyclif.

But the reading offered above with the comments from Aquinas and from *Unam Sanctam* demand a return to Langland's Piers. What exactly is his role in the Pentecostal community, and what are the implications of this role for the papacy in the late medieval church?

In his vision of Pentecost Langland continues to identify the apostle Peter with Piers, his poem's plowman and increasingly mysterious figure (cf. VIII; XV.127–49; XX.6–34; XXI.6–14; XXI.182–90). Present at the gathering of the disciples in Jerusalem "when the days of the Pentecost were accomplished" (Acts 2:1), Wille discerns *Spiritus paraclitus* coming "to Piers and to his felawes" (XXI.199–212). After the gift of languages to the disciples and prayer to the Holy Spirit, the latter counsels "Peres plouhman" and Conscience to gather "the commune" for the reception of gifts I have been exploring (XXI.213–18). As we have seen, the Holy Spirit dispenses his grace without any mediatorial, ministerial role being given to Piers. Before he does so, he issues a prophetic warning about the forces that have the power to crush even Conscience, informed as he is by Christian teaching. Only if Christ himself helps Conscience will this be prevented (XXI.219–20). Once again, Holy Spirit does not mention any vicar of Christ, any human being required to mediate the mediator Jesus Christ. On the contrary, those who put themselves forward as mediators formed in the modern church will turn out to be deluded:

And false profetes fele, flateres and glosares,
Shal come and be curatours ouer kynges and erles.
And thenne shal pryde be pope and prince of holy chirche,
Coueytise and vnkyndenesse cardynales hym to lede.
(XXI.221–24)

———

[And many false prophets, flatterers, and con men,
Shall come and over the souls of kings and earls have the cure.
And then pride will be pope and prince of Holy Church,
Covetousness and Unkindness cardinals to lead him.]

Coming from the Holy Spirit this is an extremely disturbing prophecy about the church and its hierarchy. The leaders of the church will be driven by the lust for dominion as the papacy becomes the embodiment of the capital sin associated with Lucifer and the transformation of heavenly angels into demons (see too I.107–14). Those responsible for electing the pope, and leading the church with him, will become subjects of covetousness and "unkyndenesse." Covetousness was one of the capital sins which most preoccupied Langland as he traced its normalization in his culture (VI.196–397; Prol.), while unkindness was singled out by Christ the Samaritan. That figure of divine charity revealed unkindness as the one unforgivable sin, the mysterious sin against the Holy Spirit:

> So is the holy gost god and grace withouten mercy
> To alle vnkynde creatures, as Crist hymsulue witnesseth:
> *Amen dico vobis, nescio vos.*
> Be vnkynde to thyn emcristene and al that thow canst bidde,
> Dele and do penaunce day and nyht euere
> And purchase al the pardoun of Pampilon and of Rome
> And indulgences ynowe, and be ingrate to thy kynde,
> The holy goest hereth the nat ne helpeth the, be thow certeyne.
> For vnkyndenesse quencheth hym that he can nat shine
> Ne brenne ne blase clere for blowynge of vnkyndenesse.
>
> (XIX.218–26)

———

> [So is the Holy Ghost God and grace without mercy
> To all unkind creatures, as Christ himself witnesses:
> *Amen I say to you, I know you not.*
> Be unkind to your fellow Christians and all that you can pray for,
> Deal alms and do penance day and night forever
> And buy all the pardon out of Pamplona and Rome
> And indulgences enough, and be *ingratis* to your kind,
> The Holy Ghost won't hear you or help you, you can be sure.
> For unkindness quenches him so that he can't shine
> Or burn or blaze clear because of unkindness' blowing.]

Now the Holy Spirit is prophesying that the church, called into existence as the community of sanctification by the Holy Spirit, is to be led by those who systematically enact the sin against the Holy Spirit: *unkyndenesse*. It is hard to imagine any description of the church more forceful in its authority. The confidence of this judgment is indicated by Langland ascribing it to the Holy Spirit who is, in his doctrine of God, the third person of the Trinity (e.g., XIX.96–200). Nor does Langland allow readers to blunt the implication of the Holy Spirit's prophecy of the church's history by sliding into the pleasures of metaphysical speculation so central in the training of medieval theologians.[44] Furthermore, he is about to pour immense intellectual and poetic work into showing the fulfillment of the prophecy in the final two passus of *Piers Plowman*, a fulfillment that forces us to read the treatment of the church from the prologue onward in its light. But before the prophecy is unfolded, Langland has more to say about Piers/Peter and his relations to the contemporary papacy.

After forming the Pentecostal polity, the Holy Spirit makes Piers his "procuratour" (agent), his "reve" and his "registere to reseyuen *Redde quod debes*" (XXI.258–59). This is the role given him by the risen Christ (XXI.182–90). The Holy Spirit develops this task into an extended and traditional allegorization of plowing, harrowing, and sowing seed (XXI.261–316).[45] Piers is thus returned to the earlier scene in which he attempted to plow and sow the land (his "half-aker" or "croft") to provide subsistence for the whole community (VIII.1–18). Piers had been a Christian layman of the third estate serving "Treuthe" in "alle kyne craftis" related to plowing (VII.182–99). In his representation of this service in agrarian production, Langland chose to figure forth an extraordinarily rich fable addressing agrarian conflicts and political ideology in late fourteenth-century England. As I have shown elsewhere, at the heart of the conflicts explored by Langland in Passus VIII is the Statute of Laborers, legislation passed by landholding gentry, merchants, and lawyers in parliament to hold down wages and to control the mobility of laborers seeking to benefit from the demographic collapse caused by the plague of 1348–49, which killed almost half the population. In these political struggles working people who resisted the prejudicial legislation were habitually represented by those aligned with the legislating classes as *wasters*, as greedy dissidents.[46] It is worth noting that local justices of the peace (gentry, lawyers, sometimes judges) set wage rates for various occupations and conditions for labor discipline. Servants (laborers) had to be sworn in twice a year before village constables, and those who refused to take oaths or refused to take work at the set rates when ordered by constables to do so were prosecuted. Research by Richard Smith has shown that "there is substantial evidence to indicate that petty constables bore the bulk of the labourers resentments" against "unpopular legislation." It was the village constables who were often the ones trying to enforce the "statuyt" opposed by the laborers in Passus VIII who curse the king and all "the kynges justices" responsible for assenting to the labor legislation (VIII.337–40).[47]

This is the ideological and social context in a brilliantly engaging, dialogic, and dramatic passus (VIII). Piers takes on the role of local constable trying to guarantee subsistence production on the "half-aker" (VIII.2–4) within the terms of the "statuyt" (VIII.337–40). Langland depicts Piers meeting strenuous resistance from those who had been working but consider themselves to have done enough. Piers calls on the knight, representing the dominant lay estate, to enforce labor discipline with the available means of violence—for after working the laborers withdraw to the ale house to spend their wages singing "hey trollilolly." As the Protestant editor of Piers Plowman (1550) glossed: "Jolye workmen."[48] The knight courteously threatens to beat them "by the lawe" and set them in the stocks (VIII.122–63). The law stipulated that those who resist should be put in the stocks by lords, stewards, bailiffs, and constables or sent to the nearest jail until they submit.[49] As they did in reality so in Langland's fable the laborers resist the knight (VIII.163–66). One might well wonder what role the church plays in this conflict among its members? All it does is threaten the laborers with excommunication, which, so Piers says, they treat with contempt (VIII.159).

At this point Piers invokes the personification of Hunger to impose labor discipline and give him control over the agrarian workers, "*pur charite*" (for charity's sake). Invoking the theological virtue which would be central in Passus XVII–XXII, Piers unselfconsciously calls for revenge on the disobedient. Hunger duly obliges. He batters the disobedient people into fawning obedience to Piers, their constable. This seems a more effective subjugation than any achievable by the armed ruling class. Not "Jolye workmen" now.

But Piers is not only a constable and plowman imposing one group's version of social order (the common good) on another. He is also a devoted servant of Treuthe. A wise Christian layman, he had earlier been able to offer lost penitents a map to "the hye gate of heuene" and a vision of Grace. In this teaching we find how Treuthe guides Charity to build a church within each Christian (VII.205–69). We also find, as Elizabeth Salter has shown in an illuminating and characteristically understated essay, that this layman's modes of talking and teaching converge with contemporary contemplatives, especially Walter Hilton and Julian of Norwich.[50] So the apparent resolution of social conflicts through force and in a spirit of revenge (VIII.158, 170) cannot satisfy him. His discipleship of Christ takes him beyond the knight's force, beyond "Foleviles laws," and beyond his own wrath. The exercise of dominion and power, even in what the Christian takes to be a good and necessary political cause, is not tolerable. Why not? Piers gives a lucid, decisive answer:

> "Meschef hit maketh they ben so meke nouthe
> And for defaute this folk folweth myn hestes.
> Hit is nat for loue, leue hit, thei labore thus faste
> But for fere of famyen, in fayth," sayde Peres.
> "Ther is no filial loue with this folk, for al here fayre speche,
> And hit are my blody bretherne, for god bouhte vs alle.
> Treuthe tauhte me ones to louye hem vchone
> And to helpe hem of alle thyng ay as hem nedeth."
>
> (VIII.211–18)

––––––

> ["Misfortune makes them so meek now
> And for want only these guys follow my orders.
> It's not for love, believe it, they labor this hard
> But for fear of famine, in faith," said Piers.
> "There is no filial love in these people, for all their fair speech;
> And they're my blood brothers, for God bought us all.
> Truth taught me once to love each one of them
> And to help them in all things always as needed."]

Certainly "fayre speche" toward Piers has replaced the working people's threats and abuse ("bad hym go pisse with his plogh," VIII.149–51; see too VIII.164–66). But as the quotation from Piers just above makes clear, their new obedience is the product of fear rather than love. This is the problem with coercive jurisdiction, one Piers had not anticipated. Most important, it goes against the grain of Christian discipleship, as Piers now recognizes. He has acted in anger, calling down punitive hunger in revenge on those who opposed his version of order and unity: "Awreke [revenge] me of this wasters, for the knyhte wil not" (VIII.170). Let us recall an evangelical text cited in the first part of this essay and compare the story of the Samaritan villagers who refuse to receive Jesus because he is going to Jerusalem. The disciples are outraged at this rejection and ask Jesus if he would like them to "command fire to come down from heaven and consume them," in accord with what might seem good precedent from the history of Israel (4 Kings 1:10, 12; see too 2:23–24). But Jesus rebukes his disciples: "You know not of what spirit you are. The Son of man came not to destroy souls, but to save" (Luke 9:51–56). Piers now remembers the hard model he seeks to follow. To those who have rejected him he is bound in fraternal solidarity formed by Christ's acts, not Cain's. He confesses: They are "my blody bretherne, for god bouhte vs alle" (VIII.216). Such a moving affirmation of kinship and its sublime kindness constituted the core of the narratives of salvation as Langland so dramatically represents them (XX.403–40). As he overcomes both his wrath and his pleasure at restoring dominion with order, Piers shows the virtues of Christian discipleship, the greatest of which is charity (1 Cor. 13).

So in Passus VIII we have encountered the limits of what we will come to see as Piers's "olde" plow, the carnal plow with which he tried to organize production in contemporary England. We have also encountered an apparently irresolvable contradiction between coercive jurisdiction and the imitation of Christ's own *kyndenesse*, one which included a sacrificial kinship with humankind resulting in Christ's affirmation, "we both brethren of o bloed" (XX.418). We must remember the details of Passus VIII and its historical allusiveness when we explore its allegorization in Passus XXI. For as medieval theologians taught, distinctly Christian allegory interprets and builds on the historical narratives while Christ alone is the hermeneutic key to scripture.[51]

In Passus XXI Piers at no point makes a claim to coercive jurisdiction, nor does he make the slightest move in such a direction. Coercion is left entirely in the "wihtnesse of hands" (strength of hands) of those led by Grace to recover what has been stolen, to fetch this "fro false men with Folevilles laws" (XXI.247, discussed above). We are given no indication that Piers himself has any concerns with controlling or deploying even such remedial temporal power. In no way does he give the remotest encouragement to the theory of two swords regurgitated in *Unam Sanctum*. On the contrary, his Christ-given "power," confirmed by the Holy Spirit, is directed to declaring the forgiveness of sins in the covenant made by Christ and to cultivating "treuthe" in the Pentecostal polity (XXI.182–90, 258–61). Some medieval theologians construed Peter as head of the apostles and projected their own hierarchical church onto him and the apostles. And some commentators on Langland do the same, assimilating his work to such papal ideology.[52] But this goes against the grain of Langland's writing. For he could easily have supplied us with such images of Pope Piers as the head of the church deploying the kinds of dominion, temporal powers, and coercive jurisdiction *intrinsic* to the late medieval papacy. However, he does no such thing. In fact, if we set him in relation to the papacy of his own church, we emerge with a thoroughly critical image which aligns Langland's views with earlier fourteenth-century works by William of Ockham, or even some moments in Marsilius of Padua, rather than with Giles of Rome, or Augustine of Ancona, or *Unam Sanctam*, or even Thomas Aquinas.

I am not proposing any direct influence on Langland from the brilliant and very different analysis of the contemporary papacy and Christian tradition in William of Ockham. Rather I am thinking about the scope of political theology and its stories available in the fourteenth century as Langland composed the figure of Piers and considered his relation with the modern papacy. I see no good reason to assume that his ecclesiology must be congruent with the putative norms of the late medieval church and its hierarchy. Such assumptions may have been encouraged, paradoxically and ironically, by the considerable attention given to Wycliffism over the past fifty years. As Langland differs in some decisive ways from Wyclif, as shown by Pamela Gradon and Anne Hudson, then he must be an orthodox ecclesiologist.[53] But even if one, bizarrely enough, prohibited the possibility of his theological inventiveness, Langland had more options than those offered by Wyclif or by those determining orthodoxy by attacking Wyclif. It seems worth recalling at least one of the strands in pre-Wycliffite heterodoxy with which Langland had some affinities in the area now under discussion: the later work of Ockham, written after his withdrawal from obedience to the papacy and from the new leadership of his own religious order.

Ockham wrote at great length against the forms of power and juris-diction he confronted in the fourteenth-century church. He rejected papal claims to plenitude of power that included wide temporal, secular power. He argues that Christ did not give Peter coercive jurisdiction over emper-ors since he himself, as incarnate, was inferior to lay judges and rulers. He liked to quote St. Bernard's *De consideratione ad Eugenium Papam*, stress-ing that Peter lacked gold and silver (Acts 3:6), while in his temporal power the modern pope is "the successor not of Peter but of Constantine." Ockham concurs: "From these words we gather that in abundance of riches the pope has succeeded, not blessed Peter, but Constantine. This implies that the pope is not Christ's vicar in any temporal matters what-ever."[54] Peter's primacy among the disciples led Ockham to elaborate a vi-sion of spiritual leadership as nondominative. In the *Breviloquium* (Short Discourse) of the early 1340s, he laments papal usurpation of power in "both divine and human matters" such that the claims by modern popes to "fullness of power" in "both temporal and spiritual" matters is "dangerous to the whole community of the faithful" and actually "heretical."[55] Like Langland's Piers, "the pope is only a steward," he is one of "the stewards [*dispensatores*] of God's mysteries" (*Breviloquium* II.6; 1 Cor. 4:1). As Ar-thur McGrade shows, Christ taught "the limits of papal power accord-ing to Ockham, when He rejected a lordly (*dominativum*) mode of ruling consisting principally of severe physical punishment, even when it was offered Him by others. In order to show perfectly that the judgement of blood was not to be exercised either by Himself or a mortal man, or by His vicar, He was unwilling either to give sentence on the woman [taken in adultery, John 8:3–5] Himself or to commit her to another for the full measure of justice or even to say what punishment should be inflicted on this sort of woman by an appropriate judge." In this example, Peter and all popes "were instructed not to exercise such judgement regularly, either personally or through another."[56] In the same chapter of the *Breviloquium* (II.19), Ockham recalls a text he often mentioned: Jesus rebuking James and John for their offer to punish those who rejected Jesus (Luke 9:55). He also quotes another he frequently invoked, one that can illuminate my reflection on Piers and his transformations between Passus VIII (where, as plowman, he deploys temporal jurisdiction) and Passus XXI (where, as plowman, merged with the apostle Peter, he does not):

"You know that the rulers of the nations lord it over them [*princeps gentium dominantur eorum*], and those who are greater exercise power [*potestatem exercent*] over them; but it will not be so among you. Whoever wishes to become greater among you, let him be your servant; and who wishes to be first among you will be your slave; as the Son of Man did not come to be served but to serve" (Matt. 20:25–28). By these words Christ prohibited to all his apostles the power of world rulers. He taught explicitly, therefore, that some power is to be excepted from the words he had previously spoken to Peter, "Whatever you bind" etc. [Matt. 16:19]. (*Breviloquium* II.19)

This eloquent evangelical narrative is applied to limit the hierarchy's claims to binding and loosing. In McGrade's words, what Ockham offers "as a compelling model for the normal operation of papal government is a mild pastoral care, a *ministerium* which explicitly allows for acts of power but only when these are urgently necessary for the good of the church. This view stands in marked contrast with the traditional hierocratic contention that judicial power is the essence, and its exercise the glory of the papal office."[57] Indeed, in *On the Power of Emperors and Popes*, Ockham emphasizes how Christ has set Christians under "the law of perfect liberty, viz., the evangelical law."[58] This is a form of life which shapes all relations with authority, including the interpretation of scripture. The Christian's freedom must not be coerced to assent to ecclesial articles of faith whose substance and warrant she or he does not see. As McGrade shows, "Ockham's treatment of evangelical liberty clashes sharply with the hierocratic ideal of comprehensive direction of man's spiritual life from above."[59] It is, after all, not just within the scope of *all* Christians to weigh and judge the determinations of the papacy; it is also their *duty* to oppose whatever she or he takes to be heresy. Whatever, that is, the person thinks is opposed to scripture, reason, and the tradition of the universal church, understood as all the individual faithful who have ever lived (not some corporate personage allegedly spoken for by the papacy in modern Avignon).[60] In accordance with this vision of Christian life is Ockham's unwillingness to assume the adequacy of "implicit faith" for most laypeople. On the contrary, "all believers are equal in that each Christian bears the duty of knowing explicit faith, commensurate with his status." It is less surprising, in light of such views, that Ockham maintained women should be represented at a general council.[61] Finally, in these brief remarks on an Ockhamizing option in the fourteenth century, we should note that Ockham's critical ecclesiology is completely untouched by the kind of "dualism" intrinsic to Wyclif's insistence that the true church is only the congregation of the predestined (whom nobody knows anyway).[62] We should also note that despite his Franciscan commitments and his late identification of the current papacy with Antichrist (in *On the Power of Emperors and Popes*, chap. 27), there are, as Brian Tierney writes, "no traces of Joachimite fantasy" in his theology.[63]

IV

It seems to me that remembering some of Ockham's contrasts between a true, Petrine pope and the contemporary papacy with its hierocratic ecclesiology helps one grasp some of the choices Langland himself was making in his Pentecostal vision and its aftermath. The earlier narrative of agrarian production and the formation of a Christian community showed how impossible it was for Piers to join coercive jurisdiction enforcing the Statute of Laborers with Christ's love for his "blody bretherne" (VIII.216). In the Pentecostal polity Grace commissions Piers to practice an evangelical agriculture. This involves allegorizing the earlier episode.[64] Gone is the Statute of Laborers as Grace gives Piers a "newe plouh" with a team of four great oxen, the four evangelists, with John the "most gentill," indeed the "pris neet of Peres plouh" (the prize ox of Piers's plow) (XXI.262–73a, 426). Together with this he gives two harrows pulled by four horses. Allegorically: grace gave Augustine, Ambrose, Gregory, and Jerome to teach the faith and harrow all Holy Scripture with the Old and New Testament of the covenant. By prioritizing these gifts Langland emphasizes that scripture with patristic exegesis and patristic theology are the chief resources of the church's mission. This may seem a traditional, uncontroversial model. After all, Aquinas had opened his *Summa Theologiae* by taking "sacra Scriptura" and "doctrina" as synonymous (*ST* I.1.2, ad 2).[65] But Langland was writing in a different context, one in which the church authorities were confronting people who used this perception to drive a wedge between scripture and the authority of the contemporary church, including its authority as interpreter of scripture and judge of what constituted orthodox tradition.[66] In such a context, the Holy Spirit's decisions may have important implications for authority and hierarchy in the modern church. But any such implications will be unfolded later.

For the moment, Christians once plowed and harrowed by scripture and patristic exegesis are ready to receive the grain seed from the Holy Spirit. Allegorically, these graces are the infused cardinal virtues.[67] Infused cardinal virtues are not different from the acquired cardinal or political virtues that could be cultivated outside the church. But they are directed to a different end. The acquired cardinal virtues enable someone to flourish as a human being and achieve an end proportionate to created nature. Infused cardinal virtues, the gift of the Holy Spirit, have an end which exceeds all proportion to our created nature and our unaided, natural abilities. Their end is the vision of God, eternal life. This end is above the nature of every creature and beyond the grasp of natural reason.[68] So these infused virtues are part of the answer to the crucial question Wille had put to Holy Church so long ago: how may I save my soul? (I.79–80). Langland's vision of Pentecostal polity thus shows how Christ's victory over sin, death, and hell is mediated through his spirit to bring humanity to a harvest beyond the happiness of natural man in the earthly city (XXI.274–334). Characteristic of Langland's theology of grace, humans are passive receivers of divine gifts beyond comprehension or merit *and also* active agents. They are figured as the earth that is plowed, harrowed, and sown with divine grain: they are also figured as eating the grain (XXI.274–316).[69] Eating implies a decision to eat, and this implies the possibility of not eating: so, allegorically, grace may be resistible even when intimately offered, sown in the soul.

Such are the mysterious legacies of the Fall. Besides singing "Veni Creator Spiritus," with its prayer for love to be poured into their hearts ("Infunde amorem cordibus"), those in Langland's church would also know another Pentecostal hymn, "Veni Sanctus Spiritus." In this they would confess that in the absence of the Holy Spirit humans are empty and far from harmless ("Sine tuo numine, nihil est in homine, nihil est innoxium"). So after sowing the deeds he has been given, Piers must continually cultivate love and the virtues with the harrow of old and new law as patristic teachers did. Justified by Christ, sanctified by the Holy Spirit, Pentecostal Christians remain sinners, and Langland figures this through the tough weeds that include "cammokes," those W. W. Skeat glossed as "the rest-harrow" (short for arrest-harrow).[70] These weeds spoil "the fruyt in the feld" (XXI.312–16), alluding to the fruit of the tree of Charity (XVIII.1–180). So we see how the laborers who resisted Piers and the Statute of Laborers in Passus VIII have been assimilated to the weeds which resist Piers's evangelical work. But now the tropological dimensions of Langland's allegory acknowledge the presence of the forces that resist divine grace in the soul. This allegory does not allow the blaming of one social group with the exonerating of others, the representation of those who resist the Statute of Laborers as sinners while not so naming those who legislate and enforce such partisan, self-serving laws in the polity. Weeds pervade the field: what makes it a Pentecostal one is the presence of the Holy Spirit with the obedient evangelist, Piers. Under their protection the grains will ripen into a bounteous crop that will need storing in a house which the Holy Spirit tells Piers to build (XXI.309–18).

Piers, the model for any prelate, *disclaims* the ability to construct or sustain such a house: "'By god! Grace,' quod Peres, 'ye moet gyue tymber / And ordeyne that hous ar ye hennes wende'" ("'By God! Grace,' said Piers, 'you must give timber / And ordain that house before you go away'") (XXI.319–20). The figuration shows us how this evangelical leader, *this* Peter has absolutely no sense that he himself is the rock on whom the church is built or the rock on whom it stands. We are given no encouragement to impose a conventional papalist exegesis of "Tu est Petrus et super hanc petram aedificabo ecclesiam meam" (Thou art Peter; and upon this rock I will build my church) (Matt. 16:18). On the contrary, Langland's figuration invites one to recollect the Augustinian tradition recapitulated by John Calvin in his *Institutes of the Christian Religion* (1559). In this tradition we find an exegesis which is totally Christocentric. Jesus Christ is the *rock* on which the church is built, the chief cornerstone. Peter has just confessed that Christ is the Son of God (Matt. 16:16), and on *this* rock Christ builds his church. As St. Paul wrote, "other foundation no man can lay, but that which is laid; which is Christ Jesus" (1 Cor. 3:11).[71] In his *Retractions*, we recall, Augustine mentioned Matthew 16:16, "Thou art Peter, and upon this rock I will build my church." He remembers earlier exegesis in which he read the rock as Peter. But since then, he observes, he has frequently taught that the rock is Peter's Christological confession: "the rock was Christ," writes Augustine, quoting Paul (1 Cor. 10:4).[72] This is far removed from the papalist claims and metaphysics, illustrated earlier from

Unam Sanctam, as it is from those displayed by Michael Wilks, such as, "The pope then is God in human form, a reincarnation of Christ."[73] Such papalism is made quite unintelligible in Langland's work, by design.

Piers confesses in humility that far from being the rock of the church's foundation he depends entirely on the Holy Spirit's agency. Invited by Grace to build "that hous," we noted how Piers demurs, "'By god! Grace,' quod Peres, 'ye moet gyue tymber / And ordeyne that hous'" (XXI.317–20). The Holy Spirit does not disagree but immediately provides the church's foundation: the signs and merciful effects of Christ's passion (XXI.317–24). With that he gives a roof composed of Holy Scripture and names the house "Vnite, Holy Chirche an [in] Englisch" (XXI.325–28). This is the fulfillment of Love's song after Christ's harrowing of hell: "*Ecce quam bonum et quam iocundum, &c.*" (Behold how good and how pleasant it is for brethren to dwell together in unity) (XX.466–66a; Ps. 132:1). A song, as Augustine observed celebrating a "love and fraternal unity" (*dilectio et unitas fratrum*) which points to the Pentecostal community (Acts 4:32–35).[74] Having built the house called "Holy Chirche," Grace provides further mediations for bringing home the harvest: two parts of the sacrament of penance (contrition and confession), with priesthood figured as "hayward" (XXI.329–32). Appropriately enough, a "hayward" was "a manor official appointed to prevent trespass on the cultivated land by animals or persons."[75] This is an emphatically limited and humble version of priesthood but exemplifies ministry in the Pentecostal church. The figure also recalls Reason's attempt to establish Wille's vocation in Passus V. There his questions include one concerning Wille's ability to act as *hayward:* "And kepe my corn in my croft fro pykares and theues?" (And guard my grain in the field against pilferers and thieves?) (V.12–17). Of course, at that stage of his journey, Wille could not fulfill the role of literal or figurative hayward, servant of Reason or of the Holy Spirit.

As soon as Grace has shaped the gifts of Christ's redemptive acts into a house, the church, he sets out on an evangelical mission *taking Piers with him* (XXI.332–34). This gives us the divine warrant for Liberum Arbitrium's insistence that the church should be committed to a universal, evangelical, and nonviolent mission. It should, that is, follow the church of the martyrs. This makes an eloquent contrast with the hierocratic late medieval church of immense temporal possessions and political power so fiercely criticized by Liberum Arbitrium (XVI.231–85; XVII.6–320a). Piers has primacy in the Pentecostal church, but this is a primacy without temporal jurisdiction and without worldly power. And here I need to say more about the significance of the Holy Spirit and Piers setting out from "that house Vnite, Holy Chirche an Englisch." *Leaving that house.* For this is a moment replete with theological and ecclesial meaning, one closely re-lated to the poem's final lines when Conscience follows them. What is Langland saying through the act of the Holy Spirit drawing Piers with him? I will return to this moment on more than one occasion. But it ex-plores what Christians might have to do, and be, if they want to continue as disciples. They can only build a Christological, spiritual house under-stood through allegorical imagery. So, for example, they would *not* build anything like the friars' church, with its extremely costly windows where the names of wealthy donors are engraved, an imposing carnal architec-ture whose funding inevitably draws the church into commodification of its ministry even when that ministry claims to embody absolute poverty (III.45–76). They would *not* seek, with the friars, to institutionalize pov-erty, thus unleashing a host of ironies by which Langland, like many before him, was much engaged.[76] They would *not* do anything that opens the path to Constantinianizing the church (XVII.208–38), to merging prelates, priests, and religious with the sources and customs of dominion: "ye leten [consider] yow alle as lordes, youre lond lyth so brode," complains Rea-son (V.140–68; see too Prol. 56–94). Once the walls, *not* of stone, but of Christ's passion, have been built and roofed with sacred scripture, then Christians would go. Where? Into the world, evangelizing, plowing with these "foure grete oxen" (the Gospels), four horses (the fathers), and the exegetical harrow (XXI.262–73a). They would thus become as nomadic as Piers. Or Wille! This departure of the Holy Spirit and Piers presents us with a model for detachment from formal structures. No carnal hierarchy; no political powers; no need for the so-called defense of the church by armed lay powers, whether the knight in Passus VIII or the expropriating Crown and lords in Passus XVII; no Constantinianism, whether Liberum Arbitrium's threat or Wyclif's anticipation of Henry VIII.[77] So despite his moments of despair, despite his fall into "the Londe of longynyng" (XI.164–98), the nomadic Wille may figure forth a model for the church of Christ: a church which should travel light, as befits "pilgrims and strangers on earth" (Heb. 11:13), traveling, as Wille tells Reason he himself does, "Withoute bagge or botel" (V.52). Such a church might recall in its modes of being how "god, as the gospel saith, goth ay as the pore" (XII.101), how "oure Ioye and oure Iuel, Iesu crist of heven, / In a pouere mannes apparaille pursueth vs euere" (B XI.185–86).[78] This eschews, of course, the wealth and power of institutionalized poverty. So the Holy Spirit and Piers leave before the church can develop material and formal organizations making it indistinguishable from the *world*, with its concentrations of power, dominion, wealth, and coercive jurisdictions. Such a setting out, a leaving, figures a revolutionary model of the church in relation to contemporary realities and conventional reformism.

V

Having established the Pentecostal church and corrected modern misprisions of papal power, Langland decides to initiate an exploration which addresses fundamental concerns in his great work. How did we get from Grace's Pentecostal polity to the contemporary polity and its church? It is not, we recall, that Langland had represented the Pentecostal community as a return to the state of innocence, to Eden. It was a community for sinners redeemed by Christ and being sanctified by the Holy Spirit. It included the need for coercive restitution against "false men" who had stolen goods. Not surprisingly, it also included the need for spiritual disciplines to cultivate souls always likely to produce weeds. So Langland gives us not a narrative of fall from a sinless Eden into sinful history. Rather we witness a condensation of all the forces resisting Grace and the labors of his plowman, Piers. This happens as the Holy Spirit and Piers are pursuing the universal, evangelical mission of Christ's church: "teach ye all nations [*docete omnes gentes*]. . . . Teaching them to observe whatsoever I have commanded you" (Matt. 18:19–20). This commitment takes Piers "As wyde as the world is" (XXI.332–33). It emphasizes the absence of any authoritarian plans for the church concerning dominion, control, order, and unity. Merged with St. Peter, Piers has disappeared from the church without offering *any* word concerning a putative successor. We are thus given no hints of any links between Piers and modern cardinals who propagate an ideology of Petrine succession and claim that they are the ones chosen to determine it. Indeed, the figure of the poet had offered this perception in the Prologue:

I parsceyued of the power that Peter hadde to kepe,
To bynde and to vnbynde, as the boke telleth,
Hou he it lefte with loue as oure lord wolde
Amonge foure virtues, most vertuous of vertues,
That cardinales ben cald and closyng-yates
Thare Crist is in kynedom to close with heuene.
Ac of the cardinales at court that caught han such a name
And power presumen in hemself a pope to make,
To haue the power that Peter hadde inpugne hem Y nelle . . .

(Prol. 128–36)

———

[Some of the power given Peter I perceived,
To bind and unbind, as the book tells us,
How he left it with love as our lord wished
Among four virtues, most virtuous of virtues,
That are called cardinal and on which the gate hinges
By which Christ in his kingdom closes off heaven.
But the cardinals at court that the name also claim
And its power presume in their choosing a pope,
That power from Peter I would never impugn . . .]

These lines anticipate the careful description of Peter's power from the risen Christ together with its careful restriction to the reception of restitution in the mediation of divine forgiveness (XXI.182–92). Already the passage in the Prologue binds the apostolic power of binding and unbinding to love in the practice of the four cardinal virtues. As Aquinas explained, a human being is a political creature ("animal politicum") who needs to cultivate the political or cardinal virtues to develop a flourishing life which can draw him or her toward the divine vision.[79] In the Prologue there is not yet an attempt to distinguish acquired from infused virtues because the understanding of such a distinction's force depends on the narratives of the Incarnation, Crucifixion, and Resurrection in Passus XVIII–XXI. The infused virtues given by the Holy Spirit draw people to their supernatural end disclosed by Christ the mediator, "God our goal, man our way" (*quo itur Deus, qua itur homo*), in Augustine's words.[80] The political or cardinal virtues teach us to do well in a manner proportionate to our human nature. And in this context the writer's attention is on the present political moment, generating the ironic play on both the words *cardinals* and *court/caught*.[81] The contemporary church had produced a papal "court," the curia, modeled on the courts of lay elites, a court displaying powers far beyond the carefully limited specificities of Piers's power to mediate God's reconciliation with humanity (XXI.182–90). At the court of Rome the cardinals of the church have become parodies of the cardinal virtues. They are characterized as those who have appropriated the power of making popes, an appropriation extended at the Third Lateran Council in 1179.[82] Langland's gorgeous puns mark the way cardinals at the papal "court" have "caught" the name of cardinal and "power presumen in hemself a pope to make." The language of "caught" evokes what the speaker sees as usurpation, taking, as Bennett noted, "the name without the virtues that go with it."[83] Similarly, in describing the cardinals as those who "power presumen," Langland indicates both their pride (presumption) and the lack of good warrant for their claims and so for a foundational practice in the church.

In his commentary on the B version of the Prologue, J. A. W. Bennett observed that this passage "probably alludes, if cryptically, to the election of an antipope in Sept[ember] 1378."[84] In both the B and C versions of the Prologue, Langland has the speaker promise not to challenge the immediate cause of this catastrophic event, the cardinals' appropriation of electoral powers, even as he does so. In the C version, Conscience is named as the speaker and concludes this critical passage on the cardinals, papal power, and the Great Schism of 1378 by issuing a command against opposing the election of the pope: "'Contreplede hit noght,' quod Consience, 'for holi kirke sake'" ("Don't contradict it for Holy Church's sake," said Conscience) (Prol. 138). On many occasions in *Piers Plowman* Langland supports theologians' arguments that Conscience can err, sometimes, as we shall see, in extremely serious matters. In the Prologue, however, the reader is presented with advice not only contradicted by Conscience's own preceding criticism of the cardinal and the papal curia but also overwhelmed by current events in the church. *Which* election should we not oppose ("contreplede")? After all, contested elections have now provided two popes. And soon Wille receives a vision of "Holy Churche" descending from Truth's kingdom in which she assures him that her wealthy, amoral adversary Mede is as familiar in "the popes palays" as herself (II.5–24). This is a devastating confession from one of the poem's most authoritative teachers, straight from "the castel," from the tower where "Treuthe is ther-ynne" (I.3–13, 72). It casts light on the contexts of papal election alluded to a few lines earlier and on "the power that Peter hadde to kepe" (Prol. 128). In Passus XXI Langland returns to the consequences of the schism, and sustained attention is devoted to the contemporary church in the final passus. But for now I will return to the account of events after the Holy Spirit leads Piers on the mission of universal evangelization.

These events begin with a recapitulation of attacks designed to pre-vent and destroy the fruit of charity in Passus XVIII (28–49). Pride leads "a grete oeste" (army) to blow down, break, and bite in two the roots of the virtues cultivated by Grace and Piers in the fields of faith and in human souls (XXI.335–38). Langland is putting questions about the formation of Christian habits across time and across generations, in communities, and in individual lives. The initial attack involves pride and the malicious distortion of the gifts of language aimed at the destruction of love in the community (XXI.339–43). The adversaries of the Pentecostal polity offer a confident prophecy designed to evoke despondency and mistrust. They predict that the seeds sown by Piers, the cardinal virtues, will be lost. Far from the seeds having established the roots of good habits, the prediction is that they will prove more like those falling on the wayside where the fowls of the air devour them, or on rock where they sprang up but soon withered away for lack of moisture, or among thorns which choked them (Luke 8:4–15). We remember the "cammokes [rest-harrow/arrast-harrow] and wedes" identified by Piers as the sowed and harrowed (XXI.312–13). Through Pride's followers, Langland offers a brilliant insight into the un-making of the Pentecostal polity. He focuses on the ways in which prac-tice, practical reasoning, and language are inseparably intertwined. A shift in one shifts the whole cultural configuration.

In the polity inspired by the gifts of Grace, social and political identi-ties gave people the practices which in themselves constituted doing well. There was no need for a nomadic, deracinated figure to wander around asking what might count as "do well" and where he could find "do well." Wille's obsessive questioning about these virtues had finally been an-swered in the life of Christ (XXI.26–190) and his legacy to the Pente-costal community through the Holy Spirit. We are shown how the infused cardinal virtues kindle the acquired virtues which are, as we have seen Aquinas observing, "the political virtues." These show us how to do well ("bene operari") toward the whole community and to all its parts, toward each household and every single person ("aliquam singularem personam" [*ST* I-II.61.5, ad 4]). The Pentecostal community gives people the roles whose fulfillment would constitute doing well, a life congruent with the outpouring of the Holy Spirit's gifts in daily practice.

But what the adversaries of this polity promise is an unmaking that will render Wille's form of life with its continual dislocations and confusion normal rather than eccentric and aberrant. Think of merchants. Early theologians harbored suspicion and hostility toward this occupation as tending to encourage covetousness, instability, and a range of vices. By the later Middle Ages, the church, inhabiting societies replete with markets and trade, had revised its teachings so that it could acknowledge the possibility of virtuous merchants distinct from bad ones. We have seen traces of this cultural and theological story in *Piers Plowman*. In Passus IX it is said (by someone hard to identify) that merchants pose special problems in relation to the pardon from Truth:

Marchauntes in the margine hadde many yeres,
Ac no *a pena et a culpa* no Treuthe wolde hem graunte
For they holde nat here haliday as holi chirch hem hoteth
And for they swere by here soule and so god mote hem helpe
Ayen clene consience for couetyse of wynnynge.

(IX.22–26)

———

[Merchants in the margin had many years' remission
But no *pena et a culpa* would Truth grant them
For they don't hold their holidays as Holy Church commands,
And they swear by their souls and say may God help them
Against clear conscience for coveting gains.]

This traditional view that the practices internal to being a merchant inevitably generate mortal sins has been unfolded in the confession of Covetyse (VI.196–314). But immediately there is a qualifying response:

Ac vnder his secrete seal Treuthe sente hem a lettre
That bad hem bugge boldly what hem best likede
And sethe sullen hit ayeyn and saue the wynnynges,

Amende meson-dewes therwith and myseyse men fynde
And wykkede wayes with here goed amende
And brugges tobrokene by the heye wayes
Amende in som manere wyse and maydones helpe,
Pore peple bedredene and prisones in stokes
Fynde hem for godes loue and fauntkynes to scole,
Releue religion and renten hem bettere.
"And Y shal sende yow mysulue seynt Mihel myn angel
That no deuel shal yow dere ne despeyre in youre deynge
And sethe sende youre soules ther Y mysulue dwelle
And abyde ther in my blisse, body and soule for euere."
Tho were marchauntes mury; many wopen for ioye
And preyde for Peres the plouhman that purchased hem this bulle.

(IX.27–42)

———

[But under his secret seal Truth sent them a letter
That bade them buy boldly what they liked best
And after to sell it again and save the profits
To repair hospitals and to provide for troubled men
And improve bad roads with their goods
And broken bridges on the highways
Repair in some way and to help maidens,
Poor bedridden people and prisoners in stocks
To support them for God's love, and send children to school,
Relieve religious orders and endow them better:
"And I shall send you myself my angel Saint Michael
So that dying no devil shall hurt you or bring you to despair
And after to send your souls where I myself dwell
And abide there in my bliss, body and soul forever."
Then the merchants were merry; many wept for joy
And prayed for Piers the plowman who obtained them this bull.]

Here is a figure of redeemed mercantilism. The practices of the occupation and its motivations—the desire to make material profit—are affirmed. Merchants can continue to buy and sell boldly. They can concentrate on making profits ("wynnynges"). But while the practices and their energetic performances are just what the church had rejected as "couetyse of wynnynge," there is now the possibility of changed intention, of changed will informing what appear to be the very same practices. Without changing their institutional form of life merchants can now manifest the love of neighbor and love of God.

How can this be? Aquinas had answered clearly enough in the *Summa Theologiae*. The treatise on justice addressed contemporary forms of trade and the quest for profit. The danger of this work is that it encourages insatiable desires to accumulate material goods so that accumulation without end becomes the perverse end. However, Aquinas determines that practices aimed at profit need not generate such sinful habits. It can be directed toward benevolent activity in the community, such as helping the poor, or public benefit of providing their county's needs, or sustaining their own households (II-II.77.4).[85] This passage is reflected in the marginalia of the pardon Piers is said to receive and in a letter allegedly sent from Treuthe "vnder his secrete seal" (IX.22, 27). This tells merchants to buy "boldly" whatever they most like and then sell at a profit to be deployed in a wide range of good works in their communities (IX.27–36). This passage anticipates the Pentecostal community in Passus XXI, for there the Holy Spirit teaches some people to learn "craft and konnynge of syhte, / With sullyng and buggynge here bileue to wynne" (skill and keen sight / With buying and selling to earn thier livelihoods) (XXI.234–35).[86]

But soon there will be a separation between social identity and the ethical practices embodied in this identity. The adversaries predict that choices will have to be made in changed circumstances where even people with good intentions will encounter unprecedented difficulties in moral discernment. The very criteria for ethical judgment will become disputable. Let us stay with merchants. Instead of the Holy Spirit's merchants in a community shaped by the virtues, we are promised that merchants will inhabit a social formation in which practices have become so complex that traditional discernment seems impossible:

Ne no manere marchaunt that with moneye deleth
Where he wynne with riht, with wrong or with vsure!
                              (XXI.349–50)

———

[Nor any manner of merchant who deals with money
Whether he earns rightly, or wrongly, or with usury.]

No longer will the occupation in which one has been apprenticed give clear guidance as to what constitutes *do well*. In the Pentecostal community, "sullyng and buggynge" (selling and buying) could be practiced with assurance that they belonged to a web of practices informed by Grace (XXI.234–35). No longer will this be so. The very act of dealing with money could compel one, however unwillingly, into usurious relations which could no longer be reorganized as such. In these reflections Langland was responding critically to important shifts in late medieval culture, gradual and slow but decisive changes in the history of Western culture. The relevant practices and adjustments in moral theology have been explored in some fine historical works.[87] One could summarize the relevant changes to which Langland's vision responds in some such ways as the following, crude as this is. Once upon a time, Christian theologians determined that any repayment of a loan exceeding the sum lent was a usurious transaction. Urban III had introduced to the discourse on usury another strand, Christ's words in Luke 6:35: "lend, hoping for nothing thereby" (*mutuum date nihil inde sperantes*). This encouraged an analysis of usury with a focus on intention, a central concept in the medieval exploration of sin and the making of a good confession. But the revolutionary transformations of markets, exchange, and long-distance trade from the twelfth century reconfigured the contexts of borrowing and lending. It no longer made sense simply to imagine the borrower as a needy laborer or small-scale agricultural producer whose desperate needs in the face of delayed or failed produce was being exploited by cruel usurers defying obvious Christian teaching about charity. Among borrowers were powerful and wealthy merchants or landowning aristocracy seeking loans to enhance wealth, seeking credit in their own pursuit of power. These increasingly complex relations put new pressure on the church's lawyers and theologians. Did no *lenders* need protection too? Should borrowers, perhaps merchants, rich knights, and kings, be free to break the terms of *contracts* without compensating the lender? Should the lender not be able to include in his loan compensation for profits he could himself have made by deploying the sum he lent to a wealthy client? Traditionally, of course, any such compensation had identified the transaction as usurious, as against nature, *unkynde* in Langland's vocabulary, a mortal sin disqualifying the lender from Christian burial. But could one keep the traditional language concerning the wickedness of usury (think of Dante's location of usurers,

Inferno XVII) while classifying a range of practices that would once have been judged usurious (hence against nature) as licit (hence congruent with nature)?

The answer seems to have been yes. The church's analysts would gradually designate a new range of compensations on loans as exceptions, as extrinsic titles exempt from being judged as usury. The two cases mentioned above (compensation for breach of contract and compensation for profit the lender could have made with the money he lent) were justified as *damnum emergens* and *lucrum cessans*. While one theologian might accept both as licit, another (such as Aquinas) might accept the former and reject the latter.[88] So here was a classic source for the development of an increasing casuistry for the church's experts, canon lawyers and theologians. Such casuistry would accommodate traditional moral rhetoric to enable a range of contemporary practices from which precapitalist markets and mercantilism developed, at least with hindsight, forms of credit and interest.[89] Writing about a hundred years before Langland, Giles of Lessines had composed an intriguing study, *De Usuris*, in which he tried to clarify the emerging casuistry in this domain. A former student of Aquinas, Giles made the *intention* of the lender a paramount consideration. Did the person lend with the hope of profit (*spes lucre*)? Yet he is clear about the difficulty of judgment concerning inner states. He begins by acknowledging that in our times we hear many controversies between doctors of theology on moral issues where there is great danger to souls and especially concerning usury.[90] He rehearses traditional definitions and condemnations of usury as a mortal sin against nature ("contra naturam," chap. 4, 416). He worries, however, that nowadays certain statements by experts seem to excuse usury in some loans and contracts, opening out extremely dangerous paths for Christians, paths that seem legitimizations of covetousness. He attempts to maintain traditional accounts of usury, including those concerning the evils of selling time (which is God's) and a focus on intentions of the lender (chaps. 5–8). Nevertheless, as Lester Little shows, in *De Usuris* there is a "wide range of specific credit situations that Giles proposed and treated sympathetically. In all such cases interest would be tolerable as compensation for loss but not as sought-after profit."[91] Little also discusses an early fourteenth-century tract on usury by the Franciscan theologian Alexander of Lombard. In this the Franciscan discussed "twelve major types of cases in which to accept something in return over the original amount paid out was legitimate. Then he went on to a series of cases where there was no doubt." Where there is doubt Alexander displays conflicting opinions among experts.[92]

Lester Little understood such later thirteenth- and fourteenth-century developments in casuistry surrounding the ethics of usury as an attempt to accommodate tradition to "new social realities" with the aim of "giving guidance" to those trying to make their living and their profits in such realities.[93] Unlike the modern historian, Langland does not seem to envisage Christian teaching, "guidance," appropriately accommodating itself to "new social realities." But he does seem to have seen something close to Little's account of the late medieval changes in practice and theology. Nevertheless, from Langland's perspectives, "the new social realities" undermine ethical understanding necessary to the cultivation of the virtues even as they dissolve the Pentecostal community of virtues. True enough, the earlier parts of his poem had shown how the virtues and vices of trade were central to modern life for Christians (Prol.; II–IV; VI). But he had tried to clarify the definition of vices in the exchange of goods and the uses of money by deploying traditional forms of satire to do so, for example, Mede and Covetousness.[94] In Passus XXI, however, Langland is suggesting that what tradition had identified and satirized as aberrant had become hegemonic. If this was indeed characteristic of emerging circumstances, then the critical norms on which such satire depends would themselves become eccentric. He showed Conscience struggling against Mede's practices and her self-legitimizing ideology (III.216–85) even as he also showed this ideology being accepted in all social groups, including "the popes palays" (II.23; see II–IV). He also showed the figure of Covetousness finding the language of restitution unintelligible (VI.233–38) even though restitution was an essential prerequisite for the sacrament of penance. But however ominous this situation, Repentance and Conscience in Passus II–VII have the necessary resources of discernment. They are not puzzled or confused over the constitution of usury, the sins of the market, and the criteria of moral judgment. Passus XXI, however, foresees a new and worse situation.

Then nobody will be able to differentiate licit forms of trade from usury. Good intentions will not be adequate. If so, what unfolds in the post-Pentecostal Christian world is something much closer to an insight offered by Aquinas in his treatise on law in the *Summa Theologiae*. He addressed the question of whether the natural law can be deleted from the human heart (I-II.94.6). While he answers that in one sense its fundamental principles are indelible, in another sense its precepts *can* be blotted out from the human heart. This can come about through vices, through bad reasoning, through depraved customs and corrupt habits. So among some people even theft and other vices "against nature" (*contra naturam*) are not judged to be sins. He is reminded of the situation Paul outlines in his letter to the Romans (1:24 [*ST* I-II.94.6, resp.]). In an earlier article he had observed that natural law may fail and be perverted through the collective habits inculcated by bad traditions. He exemplified this by the normalization of theft among the Germans even though theft is explicitly against the law of nature ("cum tamen sit expresse contra legem naturae" [I-II.94.4, resp.]). Aquinas is thinking of the pagan Germans whose customs he found in Julius Caesar's *De Bello Gallico*, book 6. But could such *unnatural* practices become normalized in a Christian community? Could a Christian community, with a church in its midst, generate *de-Christianization*?

Langland's answer is a resonant *yes*, introduced by the observation on usury in Passus XXI (348–50). That which had been clearly present as against nature, as *unkynde* (VI.294), can no longer be discerned as such by many Christians. Natural and unnatural kind and "unkynde" begin to merge. In Langland's theology this is a catastrophic development. For sin against *kynde*, against *kindness*, in his view, involves the special sin against the Holy Spirit. So convinced is he about this that he represents Christ himself, in the figure of the Samaritan, teaching that "unkyndenesse" is the one sin that quenches the light and fire of the Holy Spirit, the one sin that divine love will not forgive (XIX.111–232, 255–300). Whoever chooses the sin against the Holy Spirit extinguishes the torch of mercy and is left in darkness and freezing winter:

> Be vnkynde to thyn emcristene and al that thow canst bidde,
> Dele and do penaunce day and nyht euere
> And purchase al the pardoun of Pampilon and of Rome
> And indulgences ynowe, and be ingrate to thy kynde,
> The holy goest hereth the nat ne helpeth the, be thow certeyne.
> For vnkyndenesse quencheth hym that he can nat shine
> Ne brenne ne blase clere for blowynge of vnkyndenesse.
>
> (XIX.220–26)

[Be unkind to your fellow Christians and all that you can pray for,
Deal alms and do penance day and night forever
And buy all the pardon out of Pamplona and Rome
And indulgences enough, and be *ingratis* to your kind,
The Holy Ghost won't hear you or help you, you can be sure.
For unkindness quenches him so that he can't shine
Or burn or blaze clear because of unkindness' blowing.]

Unkindness encompasses a range of acts. It includes lack of gratitude, lack of compassion (illustrated by Dives in the parable from Luke 16:19–31 related by Langland in XIX.230–54), theft, and murder (XIX.255, 261). Usury too was named as *unkind* in Passus VI, so we now learn that the Christian community, in its inability to recognize usury, will be unable to recognize the unkindness which is the sin against the Holy Spirit.

Emerging in this prediction is the medieval writer's glimpse of a strange new situation. From within the Christian community itself comes the kind of de-Christianization of culture associated by Pope John Paul II with the later twentieth century in his encyclical *Veritatis Splendor* (The Splendor of Truth). He thought he had found a distinctively modern tendency. This is not "limited and occasional dissent" from Christian doctrine but "an overall and systematic calling into question of traditional moral doctrine."[95] It might seem that any link between the pope's identification of what he calls "a new situation" (4/14) and Langland's vision is, at best, wildly anachronistic. After all, does not Langland write from within the world of "traditional religion," long before the "stripping of the altars" and the revolution of early modernity?[96] In the familiar terms of conventional grand narratives, does he not write within the medieval world that preceded the "unintended" consequences that are said to include secularism, capitalism, the modern state, and anarchic hermeneutics?[97] He did indeed. But the fact that Langland's vision of his world may not fit the Middle Ages of Eamon Duffy, Brad Gregory, Charles Taylor, or many other tellers of grand narratives should not mean that he is compelled to sing their songs, nor that he should be ignored by the composers of grand narratives whose point of departure, that which precedes modernity, is the Middle Ages. While I shall return to such issues at the close of this book, for now I follow Langland's vision of new challenges to the church and his highly critical account of the church's responses.

VI

The post-Pentecostal church is led by Conscience. This seems not to have much interested, let alone surprised, most commentators.[98] But I think Langland's choices here and their implications deserve careful scrutiny. This scrutiny will contribute greatly to our understanding of his ecclesiology and its relations to the contemporary church. Let us begin this inquiry by returning to the Pentecostal church and shifting our focus to Conscience's presence there.

After the distribution of graces, considered earlier in this study, the Holy Spirit orders the community to crown Conscience "kyng" (XXI.252–57). What kind of figuration is this, and what kind of king? The context is one in which the poet is about to allegorize the earlier plowing episode of Passus VIII. Piers is now cultivating truth with evangelical oxen, patristic horses, and infused cardinal virtues as seeds (XXI.258–318). He watches Holy Spirit build "that hous Vnite, Holy Chirche an [in] Englich" (XXI.328), a house made from Christ's acts of love. No sooner is this done than the Holy Spirit turns its outcome into a universal mission of evangelism: "As wyde as the world is with Peres to tulye [till] treuthe / And the londe of bileue, the lawe of holi churche" (XXI.329–34).[99] In this allegory we see the making of the church that Liberum Arbitrium had held up as a model, namely, the evangelical and nonviolent church that embodied "Charite" (XVII.125), the church of the martyrs (XVII.262–320a). He had explicitly contrasted this with the modern, *Constantinian* church (XVII.125–38; XVI.231–85). Liberum Arbitrium's model is akin to one we find in texts of the New Testament and early church in which Christians are envisaged as "resident aliens" or "settled migrants" in the empire who are "answerable finally to the law of another city."[100] Their task is not to provide the social cement for the empire and Roman civilization, not to become a new civic religion like that so powerfully described and analyzed in Augustine's *City of God*.[101] That is why Liberum Arbitrium was among those who say the donation of Constantine and all it symbolized was a disaster for the church:

Whan Constantyn of his cortesye holy kirke dowede
With londes and ledes, lordschipes and rentes,
An angel men herde an hye at Rome crye,
"*Dos ecclesie* this day hath ydronke venym
And tho that haen Petres power aren apoysened alle."

(XVII.220–24)[102]

———

[When Constantine out of his courtesy endowed Holy Church
With lands and peoples, lordships and incomes,
Men heard on high an angel cry at Rome:
"*Dos ecclesie* has this day drunk venom
And poisoned are all who have Peter's power."]

The endowment of the church with material power ("*Dos ecclesie*") is poison because it weaves the church into the very fibers and nerves of the corporal world, dissolving the critical tensions between God and mammon ("No man can serve two masters. . . .You cannot serve God and mammon" [Matt. 6:24]). Liberum Arbitrium declares that the remedy for this disaster is in the hands of the armed lay elites, the lords, and the king. Like Wyclif, he thinks a coercive act of ecclesial disendowment would be an act of charity (XVII.225–32). As all commentators note, here Liberum Arbitrium is a fellow traveler of Wyclif and his sympathizers.[103] This is a moment in a complex dialectical process and, as we shall see, very far from being Langland's last word on ecclesial reform. But it is a very forceful expression of what had become a distinctively Wycliffite proposal. What I want to emphasize here is that such a model of reformation involved an exorbitant increase in the Crown's power and wealth. This is clearly articulated in Wyclif's *De officio regis*, where the king is made supreme over the church and over the priesthood.[104] It is hardly surprising that Wyclif was seen as the morning star ("stella matutina") of the English Reformation, a reformation in which the king disendowed the church and became supreme head of a monarchic church: a form of caesaro-papism.[105] Such are the range of literary, theological, and historical contexts in which I return to the question put above: when Conscience is made "kyng" what kind of figuration is this, and what kind of king is it who becomes leader of the church in Passus XXI and XXII?[106] One recent glossator of the poem maintains that Conscience "is likely to suggest the secular authority in its capacity of 'joint' religious leader with the clergy."[107] But in Langland's historical moment it is not at all clear what might be meant by "secular authority" which is "'joint' religious leader with the clergy." Perhaps putting "joint" in scare quotes hints at some recognition that this formulation would "suggest" contentious equivocation to those puzzling over relations between lay elites and ecclesiastics in later fourteenth-century England. It may be helpful to reconsider Conscience's role in relation to Liberum Arbitrium before addressing his form of kingship in the church of the final two passus.

According to Langland, Conscience is enfolded in Liberum Arbitrium. The poet has the latter explain the relationship to Wille: "when Y chalenge or chalenge nat, chepe [choose; buy] or refuse, / Thenne am Y Concience ycald, goddes clerk and his notarie" (XVI.191–92). So Conscience is an act of Liberum Arbitrium. The term is often translated "free will," but this is so misleading in the culture of modern English that it is best avoided. For it risks importing a split between will and understanding in discussions of freedom, a split of immense historical significance for our understanding of humans but one that is really only identifiable in later writers.[108] We need to English Liberum Arbitrium along lines that yoke freedom and decision or judgment. It is a power constitutive of our humanity, the power through which we move ourselves to act. As befits such a divine gift, "Cristes creature" (XVI.167), Liberum Arbitrium also describes himself as love, as "Amor" or "Lele Loue" (XVI.195–96). Langland's Conscience is intimately related to him.[109] We should also remember his grasp of Christology and his recognition of the Holy Spirit. This emerges after Wille invokes him to explain the contemplative vision of Christ with "Peres armes" which he has received during Mass on Easter Sunday (XXI.4–210). The allegorical modes in this part of the poem together with Langland's insistence on drawing Conscience into such closeness with Piers, Christ, and the Holy Spirit, showing us how he is indeed "goddes clerk" (XVI.192), prevents us from fixing him as "the secular authority."

Instead of this, let us note that the Holy Spirit has just exhorted the Pentecostal community to fraternal love and humility before he tells the people to crown Conscience king and make "Craft" (Skill) the steward who will guide the way they clothe and feed themselves (XXI.254–57). Such a command, in such a fluid figurative context, directs those who have just received the "diversities of graces" (XXI.228a) from the Holy Spirit to be ruled collectively and individually by "goddes clerk," the intimate of Liberum Arbitrium ("in Cristes court yknowe [known] wel and of his kynne a party" [XVI.168]). He is also the explicator of Christ's relation to Piers and of Christ's life, the teacher of Wille and one who can recognize the Holy Spirit, "Cristes messager" come from God (XXI.207–10). Living out such acknowledgment in the Pentecostal community would be to obey the Holy Spirit and live under the rule of a Conscience formed by Christ. Such a life, in such a community, is gifted with all the resources flowing from Christ's life mediated by the Holy Spirit and poured into "that hous Vnite, Holy Chirche an Englisch," an allegorical process I have already discussed (XXI.258–332).

But, as I also observed, Langland makes the completion of this edification also the moment in which the Holy Spirit and Piers set out from the church in an evangelical mission as "wyde as the world is" (XXI.332–34). They pursue Liberum Arbitrium's model of the early church. And so we reach the point with which this section began. The Holy Spirit and Piers disappear, leaving Conscience in what is now the post-Pentecostal community. We did not find out exactly how the folk responded to Grace's command to crown Conscience king and make Craft (Skill) steward. Did they obey? If they did, could they sustain such obedience in the apparent absence of Piers and the Holy Spirit? In his study *Fundamental Authority in Late Medieval English Law*, Norman Doe discusses "the late medieval view of law in general as having a moral basis." Here conscience was crucial:

> Whereas reason may have been something of a technical idea of right understood largely by the common lawyers, conscience was a distinct moral force known directly, principally through the pulpit and confessional, by the ordinary citizen. Indeed, for the citizen, the psychological incentive to obey legislation was enhanced through promulgation in the counties when the authority of a statute was seen publicly to be built on conscience. Everyone knew that to offend one's conscience would imperil the soul.[110]

True enough, it was assumed that "everyone" knew this. After all, we are naturally disposed by God to grasp the basic principles for leading the kind of ethical life which will enable us to flourish as humans. And we are given conscience, such a prominent figure in *Piers Plowman* and one so intimately related, as we have seen, to Liberum Arbitrium and Reason.[111] But Langland wonders what happens to conventional teaching in contemporary Christian culture, how the people relate to the figure they have been told to crown and how Conscience will fare as "constable" of the church (XXII.214). He now explores these questions with his characteristic inventiveness in a brilliant dramatic narrative.

VII

As soon as the Holy Spirit and Piers set out on their evangelical mission as "wyde as the world is" Conscience, Christians, and the cardinal virtues come under attack from the capital sin Pride with a "grete oeste [army]" of vices many of whom were penitents in Passus VI and VII. The aim is to destroy the Pentecostal community and the church of Christ (XXI.335–54). Conscience responds by advising Christians to go immediately into the church ("Vnite"), stay within it, and pray for peace in Piers's "berne" (barn). He seems to experience the lack of the Holy Spirit for he is certain that without Grace's presence Christians are not strong enough to go against Pride (XXI.355–59). So he envisages the situation of the Christian community as a siege. It is as though, in the perceived absence of the Holy Spirit, Christians should retreat into the church imagined as an edifice. It is striking that Piers has disappeared without any word of a successor. Certainly neither he nor anyone else in the Pentecostal church gave any hint of links between himself and modern cardinals who appropriate the name of the cardinal virtues he had sown and arrogate to themselves the power to make a pope (Prol. 128–36, discussed above in section V). But we remember that in the "hous" composed by the Holy Spirit Grace "made presthoed" (XXI.332). Even if there is no successor to Piers/Peter there is "presthoed." Here, one might think, would be a source of appropriate guidance and a mediator of the sacraments flowing from Christ.

And yet instead of turning to one of the "presthoed" made by the Holy Spirit for life in the church, Conscience turns to Kynde Wit and accepts him as his teacher (XXI.360–61). In the circumstances now confronting Conscience, this is a strange and significant choice. For Kynde Wit is carefully placed in *Piers Plowman*. It is a natural power of the soul associated with human rationality. Holy Church, descending from the

Tower of Treuthe, considers Kynde Wit an appropriate guardian and dispenser of worldly wealth (I.3–4, 51–53). But Conscience is now confronted by "principalities and power" in a struggle against "the rulers of the world of this darkness, against the spirits of wickedness in high places" (Eph. 6:12). His needs will be for more help than Kynde Wit can give. And even Ymagenatyf had perceived the limitations of Kynde Wit with relevant clarity. He had warned Wille that a "kynde-witted" person cannot reach the beginning of the way to salvation through "kynde wit." In spiritual battles, concerning our supernatural end, a "kynde-witted" person is like a blind man in worldly battles: his weapons are useless. Ymagenatyf maintains that "kynde wit" is a "chaunce," in the sense that it depends entirely on the contingencies of the material world for its knowledge (XIV.33). It is confined to the realm of created nature. So dependence on it would lock such subjects into its realm taken as autonomous from God. As Aquinas so often argued, the end to which creatures are drawn is twofold, *duplex*. At the very beginning of the *Summa Theologiae* he tells us that God has ordained us to himself as our end, a goal which far exceeds the grasp of human reason. He quotes from Isaiah: "the eye hath not seen, O God, besides thee, what things thou hast prepared for those who love you" (64:4; see too 1 Cor. 2:9). We need to know this end so that we can order our lives to it. So it was necessary for our salvation that we should know through divine revelation what so exceeds human reason (*ST* I.1.1, resp.). Later, in the question on predestination, he emphasizes that we are drawn to an end which exceeds the proportion and power of created nature: eternal life which consists in the divine vision. But the end is "duplex." And the other end is proportionate to created nature. Such an end created nature can reach by the power of its own nature (I.23.1, resp.). Later still, in the treatise on divine grace, he considers an objection to his Augustinian position. The objector maintains we can know God by *kynde wit* ("per cognitionem naturalem"), not turned to God as the object of beatitude and the cause of our reconciliation with God, our justification (I-II.113.4, obj. 2 and ad 2). This "duplex" pervades Aquinas's thinking, and its reflections on the limits of *kynde wit* in our quest for the divine vision and salvation are congruent with Ymagenatyf's and with Langland's own.[112]

But Langland has not left our understanding of *kynde wit* dependent on Ymagenatyf and Aquinas. Christ, manifested in the figure of the Samaritan (Passus XIX), addresses this topic. Appropriately enough, the context of this discussion concerns human knowledge of God. Faith, embodied in Abraham, had told Wille that he follows one God in three persons. Wille is impatient with such trinitarian talk and dismisses it:

"This is myrke thyng for me," quod Y, "and for many another,
How o lord myhte lyue o thre; Y leue hit nat," Y sayde.
(XVIII.196–97; see 184–97)

———

["This is a dark thing for me and for many another,
How one Lord might live in three, I don't believe it," I said.]

Confronted with this unequivocal rejection of Nicene Christian teaching about God ("Y leue hit nat"), faith tries to draw Wille away from this unbelief toward orthodox Christianity and its affirmation of trinitarian relations in the divine life. Faith does so by offering analogies that he believes will disclose such orthodoxy in a persuasive way (XVIII.198–238).[113] In this sequence, Langland gives us a beautiful mode of faith seeking understanding:

"Muse nat to moche theron," quod Faith, "til thow more knowe
Ac leue hit lelly al thy lyf-tyme,
That thre bilongeth to a lord that leiaunce claymeth."
(XVIII.198–200)

———

["Don't muse too much on it," said Faith, "until you know more,
But believe it loyally all of your lifetime.
Three belongs to a Lord who claims allegiance."]

But there is no indication that Wille is persuaded by this or by the speaker's long elaboration (see XVIII.198–238).

For his doubts about trinitarian teaching return in the ensuing conversation he has with Hope, or Moses. The latter seems to assume a monotheism that "of no trinite ne telleth ne taketh mo persones / To godhead but o god and on god almyhty" (makes no mention of Trinity and gives no more persons / To Godhead but one God and one God almighty) (XIX.29–39). Wille thinks that this version of monotheism, unlike the trinitarian one, is easy for both unlearned and learned people (XIX.42–43).[114] But he cannot accept Hope's claims that God wants us to love everyone, liars as well as honest people (XIX.44–47). Wit had long ago proclaimed the virtue of loving and helping one's enemies, following Christ's explicit precepts (Matt. 5:43–48; Luke 6:27–35 [X.188–89]). But Wille finds Hope's version of this evangelical teaching unacceptable and disputes it. Indeed, he is as disputatious as he has ever been, and there is no warrant for those readings of *Piers Plowman* that assert a movement in the poem setting aside ratiocination and argument. The conversation between Wille, Faith, and Hope is "in the way" (XIX.48), and disputation "is the way" *intrinsic* to the life of Wille, the rational appetite, and to the Christian search for God: "Come then and confute me, saith the Lord" (*Et venite, et arguite me, dicit Dominus*). Or, "Thus saith the Lord . . . let us plead together: tell if thou has anything to justify thyself" (*iudicemur simul: Narra si quid habes vt iustificeris*).[115] Thus, "in the way," albeit in a "wide wildernesse" traveling with Faith and Hope, however contentiously, Wille now encounters Jesus Christ in the person of the Samaritan (XIX.48–54). So for Langland disputations, even disputation against orthodox trinitarian discourse, is *not* incompatible with Faith or Hope or encountering Christ.[116]

The new scene is a dramatization of Jesus's parable of the good Samaritan and the half-dead man wounded and stripped by robbers (Luke 10:29–37).[117] In the face of Semyvief ("semivivo relicto," Luke 10:30), both Faith and Hope (as the priest and Levite of the parable) are terrified. Wille complains about his companions' failure (XIX.53–82). The Samaritan defends them, explaining their limitations in the face of fallen humanity, and instructs Wille on the unique saving powers of Christ bestowed in the sacraments. Once again Wille expresses his troubles with Faith's doctrine of a triune God and Hope's ethics of universal love (XIX.96–107). The response of Christ in the figure of the Samaritan is as kind as it is clear. He determines that the teaching Wille has received from Faith (Abraham) and Hope (Moses) is indeed true:

"A saide soeth," quod the Samaritaen, "and so Y rede the also.
And as Abraham the olde of o god the tauhte
Loke thow louye and bileue al thy lyf-tyme."

(XIX.108–10)

["He told the truth," said the Samaritan, "and I advise you so, too.
And as old Abraham taught you about one God,
See you love and believe that all your life."]

At just this point he names the objector whom Wille has been following
in his rejection of Faith's trinitarian teaching, the teaching of orthodox
Nicene Christianity. The name given links this episode explicitly with Conscience's attempt to defend the church in Passus XXI and his acceptance
of a teacher named Kynde Wit:

And yf Kynde Wit carpe here-ayen or eny kyne thouhtes
Or eretikes with argumentis, thien hoend thow hem shewe.
(XIX.111–12)

[And if Common Sense or any kind of thoughts speak to the contrary
Or heretics with arguments, you just show them your hand.]

So the authoritative Samaritan, figuring Christ himself, teaches that Kynde
Wit is the source of serious resistance to what Langland considers a truthful understanding of the triune God. Acting beyond its limits, it will generate heresy. In the earlier version of this episode (Passus XVI of the B
version of *Piers Plowman*), the Samaritan warned Wille not only about
the limits of Kynde Wit but also about Conscience:

And if Conscience carpe þerayein, or kynde wit eyþer,
Or Eretikes wiþ argumentȝ, þyn hond þow hem shewe.
(B XVII.138–39)

[And if Conscience complains about this, or Kynde Wit either,
Or heretics with arguments, show your hand to them.]

In this warning Conscience is associated with the limits of natural reason
uninformed by the supernatural gift of faith. According to the B version
of *Piers Plowman*, Conscience is as likely to lead one to antitrinitarian
heresy as is Kynde Wit. This is particularly fascinating in relation to the
defense of the church I am considering from Passus XXI: "And thenne

cam Kynde Wit Consience to teche" (XXI.360; B XIX.360). It is impera-
tive, in my view, that commentators never conflate the B version of the
poem with the C version, and so one must note that the later version separates Kynde Wit from Conscience as the Samaritan warns Wille about potential sources for heresy. Nevertheless, the C version does keep the Samaritan's luminous warning that Kynde Wit is a power who can make trouble
for trinitarian Christians and so a power whose limits must be carefully re-
spected. So in both the B and the C versions Langland has given us good
warrant to recognize the risks if the church of Christ (founded by the Holy
Spirit) is being led by Kynde Wit and the risks in Conscience accepting
Kynde Wit as his teacher without any reservations (XXI.360). It is not, of
course, that Ymagenatyf and, more authoritatively, Christ the Samaritan
attack Kynde Wit as a part of the human soul, God's own gift. The issue is
the identification of its licit activities and the identification of the boundaries of its competence.

Yet Conscience quite fails even to raise such questions as he embraces
Kynde Wit as his teacher. From a perspective uninformed by Langland's
dialectical work, this embrace might seem both obvious and untroubling.
Conscience, like Kynde Wit, is as natural an act as synderesis is a natural
disposition: gifts from God that are part of our "kynde," what makes us
distinctively human beings. As Wit had earlier said to Wille in his lecture
on Christian anthropology, "lyf lyueth by inwit and leryng of Kynde,"
with Kynde glossed as "Creatour," as "fader and formour of al" (X.173,
151–55).[118] So one certainly finds conscience active in non-Christians
like Trajan (Passus XII) or like Judas Iscariot or Pontius Pilate. And, as
Aquinas teaches, natural reason and conscience may present believing in
Christ, something Christians understand as a good act necessary for salvation, as a bad action. If this happens, we are bound to obey such judgment
of reason and act of conscience, according to St. Thomas (*ST* I–II.19.5,
resp.).[119] I recall such conventional puzzles in this area of theological ethics because I think Langland becomes extremely interested in one of its
central topics: the sources and authority of an erring conscience. This will
not be the last time he shows Conscience making an error with dismaying
consequences for the church and its members. Such errors, in the contexts
Langland established earlier in Passus XXI, must be characterized as
Christian *amnesia*. For his Conscience, we will remember, recognized the

relation between Christ and Piers, instructed Wille on the life and names of Christ, recognized the Holy Spirit, and was called by the Holy Spirit with Piers. Now, apparently, under the massive pressures of Pride's assault and, perhaps crucially, split off from the absent Piers, *he forgets*. Langland is addressing a question Augustine put when preaching on the disciples' ship being tossed with waves in the midst of the sea (Matt. 14:24–33). As usual, the ship figures the church, and Augustine asks his congregation, "When you are firmly settled in the Church can you experience the absence of the Lord? When can you find the Lord absent?"[120] Same question; not, I think, quite the same answer.

Kynde Wit, accepted as teacher, shows Conscience how to defend the church. In his newly bestowed authority he "comaundede alle cristene peple / To deluen [dig] a dich depe aboute Vnite" so that the church will be "as hit were a pile [fortress]" (XXI.360–63). Conscience acts as Kynde Wit's echo as he reiterates this command (XXI.365–66). Christians must dig a ditch, make a great moat, and build fortifications. This may seem a rational way of life for the church in response to the vicious forces that threaten it. Some readers may recall the very different model offered by Piers so long ago, in Passus VII. There Christians were led to "a court as cleer as the sonne," where "The mote is of Mercy," and where Grace will disclose "Treuthe sitte in thy sulue herte" (Truth sitting in your own heart), where Charity will make a church to nurture "alle manere folke" (VII.232–60). This recollection might arouse unease at the contrasting model generated by Kynde Wit. But perhaps, as yet, such unease will remain rather vague in the face of the people's energetic obedience to their leaders' command. The "house" that the Holy Spirit and Piers had left as a vulnerable barn for storing ripe corn is now, allegedly, turned into a moated fortress (cf. XXI.317–31 and 367–80). The bad are kept out while those laboring to fortify "Vnite" are kept in and sanctified by penitential discipline. Conscience is delighted at the successful enactment of Kynde Wit's order. Triumphantly (proudly?) he declares that with such fine defenses he doesn't care about the assaults of Pride all this Lent (XXI.381–82; cf. Piers's satisfaction with those working in his "half-aker" at VIII.197–200). Kynde Wit's model of a fortress church has encouraged a conviction that the major threat to Christian discipleship is from *outside* the church. This will prove to be a profoundly mistaken conviction, but for the moment it seems that holiness has been achieved within the fortress. Yet this apparent success encourages everyone, including Conscience, to overlook both the contrast with the missionary church of the martyrs celebrated by Liberum Arbitrium (XVII.262–320a) and with the evangelical church led by the Holy Spirit and Piers cultivating truth as "wyde as the world is," teaching the evangelical law without boundaries, moats, or fences (XXI.332–34).[121]

There is a late fourteenth-century sermon by John Mirk which illuminates the contrasting ecclesial models I have been discussing. When Liberum Arbitrium wanted to illustrate a modern exemplar of the church of the martyrs, he chose St. Thomas of Canterbury, Thomas Becket (XVII.270–76). And to St. Thomas of Canterbury Mirk devotes a fascinating sermon, preached on his festival. Mirk ponders the murder of the archbishop by the Crown and lay elites. When the king's knights come to kill St. Thomas for crossing the king's power, the monks of Canterbury bolt the doors of the cathedral to protect the archbishop. But Thomas goes to the door, unbars it, and takes a knight by the hand, saying, "Hyt bysemeth not to maken Holy Chyrche a castel—cometh in, my chydren." They do so, and they murder him.[122] This powerful narrative not only gives a moving example of just what is entailed in Jesus's precepts concerning love of enemy (Matt. 5:43–48). It also discloses exactly what is at issue in the error made by Kynde Wit and Conscience in displacing the evangelical model of the church of the martyrs. "Hyt bysemeth not to maken Holy Chyrche a castel—cometh in, my chydren." Mirk and Langland's Liberum Arbitrium both celebrate a martyr who in the midst of "vnkynde cristene in holy kirke was slawe [slain]" (XVII.275). He is, for both writers, "a forbisene," an exemplary figure for Christians, individually and collectively. He also reminds Christians, most forcefully, that the killers are "vnkynde cristene," classic agents of Constantinian Christianity. How appropriate, how revealing that the English sovereign who declared himself head of the English church should publicly proclaim (1538) St. Thomas of Canterbury a rebel and a traitor. Henry VIII ordered that nobody must call Thomas Becket a saint (itself now made a treasonous act) and that his name was "to be erased from all liturgical books, and his Office, antiphons, and collects to be said no more." All images and pictures of Becket were to be disappeared.[123]

VIII

Although Langland never represents Conscience as a priest (in any version of the poem), Conscience offers the Eucharist to those who have built the holy fortress with their penitential labors. This act does not seem to have interested scholars, but it is as replete with significance as it is puzzling and, in the late fourteenth-century church in England, provocative:

> "Cometh," quod Consience, "ye cristene, and dyneth
> That haen labored lelly al this lenten tyme.
> Here is bred yblessed and godes body therunder."
>   (XXI.383–85)

———

> ["Come," Conscience said, "you Christians, and eat,
> Who have labored loyally all this Lenten time.
> Here is a blessed bread and God's body there-under."]

Conscience goes on to declare that Grace gave Piers power to consecrate ("to make hit") and people the ability "to eten hit aftur" (XXI.386–89). But Piers is absent from this eucharistic event. In fact he had been absent since his departure with the Holy Spirit on the mission of universal evangelization, absent from the project of turning the church into a fortress. So what exactly is Langland saying about the administration of the Eucharist here? What are the theological and ecclesial implications of the scene he imagines?

We have some truly outstanding studies on the practice and theology of the sacrament of the altar in the later Middle Ages.[124] Given this and given my own recent contribution to this literature, it is only necessary here to recollect a few features that seem especially relevant to the present rumination on Langland's intention in writing this passage.[125] The Mass was central to Christian life in the Middle Ages. Here Jesus Christ became present on the altar in the form of bread and wine. He did so at the prayer of consecration in the canon of the Mass, and he did so in his Galilean body, "not only the flesh, but the whole body of Christ, that is, the bones and nerves and all the rest" (*non solum caro, sed totum corpus Christi, id est ossa et nervi et alia hujusmodi*).[126] Eamon Duffy describes this event, at the heart of medieval Christianity, with eloquence and precision:

In the Mass the redemption of the world, wrought on Good Friday once and for all, was renewed and made fruitful for all who believed. Christ himself, immolated on the altar of the cross, became present on the altar of the parish church, body, soul and divinity, and his blood flowed once again, to nourish and renew Church and world. As kneeling congregations raised their eyes to see the Host held high above the priest's head at the sacring, they were transported to Calvary itself, and gathered not only into the passion and resurrection of Christ, but into the full sweep of salvation history as a whole.[127]

This brings out the fact that "for most people, most of the time the Host was something to be seen, not to be consumed" (95). Eating the consecrated wafer, the body of Christ, would be reserved, for most Christians, to the Easter Eucharist (95–107). As for consecration, Aquinas makes it clear that only a duly ordained priest has the power to consecrate in Christ's person ("in persona Christi," *ST* III.82.1, resp.). Indeed, by the later Middle Ages, Duffy observes, "no layman or woman might even touch the sacred vessels with their bare hands" (110).[128] However communitarian, inclusive, and committed to "corporate Christianity" with an immensely active laity, the late medieval church produced a version of the Eucharist which involved an immense affirmation and making of a quite distinctive and exclusive sacerdotal power.[129] No Christian accepted as orthodox in Langland's church would claim that the Eucharist could be, say, taken from the pyx (hung over the high altar of the church, containing the sacrament) and distributed by a layperson. But this is what Conscience does (XXI.383–85): perhaps the absent Piers had indeed left the consecrated bread in a pyx. By what warrant, under whose authority?

There certainly were Christians in Langland's society who held views on such matters which went against the grain of current orthodoxy. Take, for example, Walter Brut, an often-brilliant theologian who was a Latinate layman first accused of heresy in the 1380s and later compelled to set down his understanding of Christian doctrine in Latin.[130] During his profound and wide-ranging account, he wonders whether women can confect the body of Christ and administer the sacrament to the people ("an mulieres possint conficere corpus Christi et populo ministrare" [341]). What actually distinguishes priests from laypeople (341)? Working his way through history, theology, and ecclesiology, he concludes that he cannot think the church can licitly preclude laymen or laywomen from consecrating and administering this sacrament. He simply cannot see how the church could assume that it could compel Christ to conform his arrangements for the consecration of his body to the ordination of the Roman pope. And, after all, the church had long allowed women to administer the one sacrament it claims to be necessary for salvation, namely, baptism (346, 345).[131] Or take John Wyclif: in his admirably lucid *De Eucharistia (Tractatus Maior)*, he argues that no faithful Christian doubts that God can give a layman ("layco") the power to consecrate the sacrament.[132] Or, a little later (1428–31), Hawisia Mone of Loddon, in Norfolk: "Every man and every woman being in good lyf oute of synne is as good prest and hath as muche poar [power] of God in al thynes [things] as ony preset ordred be the pope or bishop."[133] But are we meant to see Conscience, distributing the sacrament in the absence of any priest, as a fellow traveler with Walter Brut or John Wyclif or Hawisia Mone? Is Conscience's laicization of the Eucharist's distribution affirmed by Langland? Is this event presented as a model for the church or only a model in the absence of Piers and any priests? In my view the passage invites such reflective questions while making sure they cannot be resolved with the resources Langland has chosen to offer at this point. However, by the time we conclude reading the final passus, a cluster of answers will be emerging. They may perhaps bring his work closer to aspects of Walter Brut's than is generally acknowledged.

But having raised this important issue, Langland continues with the Easter Communion offered by Conscience. It is offered without the customary elevation of the Host, and we should note that it is also offered as often as "ones in a monthe / Or as ofte as they hadden nede" (XXI.388–89), very much against the norm of Langland's church.[134] Displacing the habitual elevation and adoration of the Host, Conscience proclaims a condition to his distribution of the sacrament: people must pay to the pardon from Christ mediated by Piers, "*Redde quod debes*" (Pay back what you owe) (XXI.385–90). In doing so, he faithfully follows his earlier account of the condition attached to the new covenant by the risen Christ (XXI.182–87). Christ's pardon is contingent on its recipients making *restitution*. They must do so because this act restores the broken bonds of charity and justice in the community. Those who want to be disciples of Christ are thus obligated to attempt the imitation of Christ's reconciliation of law and gospel, of justice and peace in his work of divine love (XX.430–75). The response from the community of the holy fortress, in the Mass, is truly astonishing: outraged incredulity. Conscience reiterates his teaching. He aligns it with the cardinal virtues and reminds the people of the Pater Noster: "Et dimitte nobis debita nostra, sicut et nos dimittimus debitoribus nostris" (And forgive us our debts, as we also forgive our debtors) (XXI.391–94a; Matt. 6:9, 12). So Conscience has placed Christ's condition for his pardon as a condition for receiving "godes body" (XXI.385). After all, this sacrament represents and creates the unity of Christians in the church, so Conscience's counsel acknowledges that without the justice and charity of mutual restitution there is an impediment to participation in the body of Christ.[135] Given that the cardinal virtues had been internalized in the Pentecostal community (eaten and sown in souls), Conscience's expectation that his own judgment about restitution would be shared by all is hardly surprising. But the community's rejection of his counsel is unequivocal. So once more Langland chooses to display the incompletion of a central sacrament in his church. Once again penance has not been consummated in the Eucharist, although the Eucharist was the end of all the sacraments, the spiritual food which changes humans into itself, into the divine life (*ST* III.73.3, resp. and ad 2, quoting Augustine, *Confessions* VII.10). So the immediately preceding claim to have achieved "holinesse" in this church is contradicted and treated with irony. But Langland does not leave us with this disturbing enough irony. He has one of the church's members articulate the collective rebellion against Conscience, the cardinal virtues, and the sacrament.

The speaker is a brewer, one of the small-scale commodity producers on whose activity Langland bestowed considerable attention earlier in his work.[136] The brewer proclaims his priorities and teleology: maximizing profits in his trade while vehemently rejecting the virtue of justice. He tells Conscience to be silent and ridicules talk about *Spiritus iusticie*, that infused cardinal virtue given by Grace and sown by Piers (XXI.274–75, 297–308). The will to silence Conscience ("hold thy tonge, Consience") figures a will moving toward a fixed aversion from love of God and neighbor. This movement is encapsulated in the brewer's claim that his nature ("my kynde") is to pursue profits quite independently of the virtues and the quest for holiness (XXI.396–402). Langland is showing how practices normalized in the occupations of his culture can create a second nature that transforms one's "kynde," transforms a nature created in the image of

God (XVIII.1–7). In such a transformation the demand for restitution becomes unintelligible. Just as it has been for Covetyse (VI.234–38). This is a collective version of what Augustine describes so powerfully in his *Confessions*. Our choices and acts come to bind our will in chains of habit ("consuetudo") since habits which we do not resist become necessity, a second nature.[137] Earlier I observed Aquinas's interest in the way in which malevolent cultural habits can occlude the natural law. He maintained that a particular culture could normalize vicious acts into habits that were deemed virtuous. His example, we recall, was Germanic tribes in which theft (contrary to both natural and divine law) was normalized (*ST* I-II.94.4, resp.; see too I-II.94.6, resp.). Langland's brewer apparently has no memory of Grace making a community in which forms of exchange are integrated with Christian ethics in relations of friendship rather than predatory exploitation. Nor is there any memory of the specific conditions under which merchants will receive pardon, conditions that join the pursuit of profit with its charitable distribution (IX.22–42; see similarly *ST* II-II.77.4). Nor is there any recollection of Jesus's warning that covetousness and unkindness quench God's mercy (XIX.328, 184–85, 218–19, 255–57). Yet Langland emphasizes that this process of de-Christianization is happening within the Christian community currently gathered around "bred yblessed and godes body therunder," a process *within* the fortress church.

Conscience is not easily silenced, as Christian tradition always taught. He insists that the cardinal virtue of justice, dismissed by the brewer, is actually the "cheef seed that Peres sewe." Salvation, he maintains, is impossible without a life committed to *Spiritus iusticie*. Furthermore, he affirms that unless people continue to eat the seeds that are the cardinal virtues, and to feed on conscience, they will be eternally lost (XXI.403–8). Having erred in his subjection to Kynde Wit's model of the church, with its delusions concerning relations between what is within (holiness) and what is without (threat to holiness), Conscience now reaffirms the Pentecostal community. In doing so he is certainly acting as "goddes clerk and his notarie" (XVI.191–92). As for the brewer, we are not given his response to the Conscience he sought to silence. But we are being given some very disturbing answers to the question I noted at the end of section VI, namely, how the people obey the Holy Spirit's command to crown Conscience (XXI.256). There are more disturbing answers to come.

After Conscience's angry reply to the brewer, Langland introduces a new interlocutor (XXI.408–81). He is called a "lewed vicory," that is, as Derek Pearsall notes, "an uneducated parish priest (i.e. lacking in Latin)," while D.W. Robertson and Bernard F. Huppé observe that he is "unlearned in the sophistry of the friars."[138] Unlike much commentary on this extraordinarily resonant figure, this observation appreciates the irony in "lewed" and its direction.[139] He is "lewed," unlearned in a range of practices in the contemporary church witheringly criticized throughout *Piers Plowman*: he lacks such learning just as St. Paul lacked "wisdom" in his "foolishness" (1 Cor. 1:18, 21).

His experience as a "curator of holi kirke" confirms much that Langland has just shown in the community's rebellion against Conscience and against Christ's refusal to split off pardon from the demands of conversion in practice. The "lewed vicory" is familiar with Christians who are ignorant of cardinal virtues and disdainfully reject Conscience (XXI.404–12). Owing to Langland's own vision, we too are familiar with them. The priest couches his experience in a locution akin to Wille's earlier observations on his many years in London without encountering charity among "clerk nother lewed" free from covetousness (XVI.286–97; cf. XXI.410–12). Both the "lewed" priest and Wille identify a pervasive strand in *Piers Plowman*: the disclosure of decisive absences of virtues that constitute distinctively Christian communities.

Having confirmed the ignorance of cardinal virtues in the parish, the priest takes up the ironic punning on "cardinal" displayed in the poem's Prologue.[140] Instead of the cardinal virtues sown in the Pentecostal church, the modern church has cardinals sent from the pope. Instead of the infused cardinal virtues given by the Holy Spirit to Piers and the community as spiritual food, contemporary cardinals are takers and consumers, not bringers of gifts. The vicar thus develops a major critical strand of Langland's vision of the contemporary church, one designed to lay bare its material foundation and the consequence of such a foundation. We are moved from allegory and the spirit in Pentecostal agriculture to the letter and voracious carnal consumption in the hierarchy governing the church. Today's cardinals are funded and fed by "we clerkes" who pay for the elite's furs, for their horses' food, and for the predators in their retinues. The laypeople provide for the clerks who are compelled to fund the hierarchy, and the "lewed" priest recounts their responses: "The contreye is the corsedore [the more cursed] that cardinals cometh ynne" (XXI.417–18). These cardinals belong to the Constantinian church so fiercely and extensively attacked by Liberum Arbitrium ("Cristes creature . . . in Cristes court yknowe wel"), to which I shall return when discussing the poem's ending (XVI.167; XVII.200–235a). The vicar proposes a reformation of the church that would eject those exploitationary cardinals from England. As part of this reformation, they would have to remain with their financiers at the papal court in Avignon or Rome among the relics in the church to which they were affiliated: ironically, the relics of the early martyrs (XXI.419–23).

These remarks on relics, in the context of the hierarchy's finances, relate to one of the latest passages Langland wrote. In the Prologue to the poem's C version, he added an attack by Conscience on the sponsorship of idolatry as a component of fund-raising in contemporary churches (Prol. 95–124). The vicar's ecclesial reformation would also involve the return of Conscience to the royal courts where he had been trying to persuade the king to expel the forces of Mede from governance of the polity at all levels (II–IV). The "lewed vicory" calls for Grace and Piers to continue the work of universal evangelization so that "all men were cristene" (XXI.424–27). He imagines Piers in the role of emperor but envisages as peculiar a form of emperor as Langland's Christ is a peculiar kind of chivalric knight: riding an ass, bootless, without spurs or spear, and jousting on a cross while armed only with the vulnerable garment of *humana natura* (XX.8–25; XIX.48–52; XXI.12–14). As emperor, Piers, according to the vicar, will lead not armies but the plow of human subsistence production *and* of evangelical teaching. His reformist vision is modeled on the evangelical church of the martyrs celebrated by Liberum Arbitrium (XVII.262–94). No more a church fortress.[141] Like his author, the priest gives attention not only to the future, but to the present church, with Piers providing the critical comparison. Here we should remember the Holy Spirit's prophecy while founding the Pentecostal church. The pope, he warned, will become an embodiment of pride while the cardinals will lead the church with covetousness and "vnkyndenesse" (XXI.223–24). The latter is the sin against the Holy Spirit, the one sin that quenches the grace of God (XIX.153–278). The modern "lewed" priest discerns that the Holy Spirit's prophecy concerning the cardinals has been fulfilled. He rightly contrasts the pope with Piers. For he sees that both with his literal and his allegorical plow Piers aimed to imitate the God who patiently teaches and patiently loves his enemies. Most appropriately he explicitly invokes the following evangelical text:

> But I say to you, Love your enemies: do good to them that hate you: and pray for them that persecute and calumniate you: That you may be the children of your Father who is in heaven, who maketh his sun to rise upon the good and bad, and raineth upon the just and the unjust. (Matt. 5:44–45)

Such is the divine model of unconditional generosity and loving kindness. Never unlearned about what should matter to Christians, the "lewed vicory" comments accordingly:

> Ac wel worth Peres the plouhman that pursueth god in doynge,
> *Qui pluit super iustos et iniustos* at ones
> And sente the sonne to saue a corsed mannes tulthe
> As brihte as to the beste man or to the beste wommam.
> Rihte so Peres the plouhman payneth hym to tulie
> As wel for a wastour or for a wenche of the stuyves
> As for hymsulue and his seruauntes, saue he is furste yserued.
> (XXI.430–36; see 430–41)

––––––

> [But well may it go for Piers the plowman who in his deeds follows God,
> *Who raineth upon the just and the unjust* at once,
> And sends the sun to save a cursed man's crops
> As brightly as to the best of men or women.
> Just so Piers the plowman takes pains to raise crops
> Just as much for a waster or a woman of the streets
> As for himself and his servants, except he is served first.]

The "lewed" priest can recognize Christian discipleship when he encounters it. And plainly enough, this celebration of Piers includes a memory of his struggles in the field of agrarian production (see section III above). Despite his attempt to use coercive jurisdiction to enforce the Statute of Laborers, Piers had been overwhelmed by his recognition that those perceived as "wastour" or "wenche of the stuyves" are also his "blody bretherne, for god bougte vs alle" (VIII.213–28; XXI.434–36). Although the agricultural laborers threaten him violently, he acknowledges them as those whom "Treuthe tauhte me ones to louye hem vchone " (Truth taught me once to love each one of them) (VIII.211–18). However unpalatable and hard, as Wille objected on another occasion about Hope's teaching on love (XIX.40–47), such are the demands of Christian discipleship as the vicar, like Langland, maintains.

Against these apostolic virtues the priest sets contemporary popes. These are popes devoted to deploying coercive jurisdiction. The vicar objects to the material exploitation of the church by the papacy as well as the lust for dominion informing popes (XXI.442–43). Far from being literally unlearned ("lewed"), the priest's compressed commentary on the papacy converges with Ockham's own identification of the papal ambitions to imperial power. The pope, he objects, "claymeth bifore the kynge to be kepare ouer cristene" (XXI.443). We recollect how Ockham had denied that Christ had given Peter, let alone modern popes, plenitude of power over temporal goods and the political order.[142] The vicar considers the ways in which modern popes, antithetical to Piers, have often hired soldiers to kill fellow Christians in pursuit of their political ambitions. The papacy is immersed in habitual violence. The pope, he says, "soudeth [hires] hem that sleeth suche as he sholde saue. / . . . And counteth nat thow cristene be culde and yrobbed / And fyndeth folke to fihte and cristene bloed to spille" (And takes no account though Christians are killed and robbed / And pays people to fight and spill Christian blood) (XXI.428–29, 443–46a). The vicar is elaborating the earlier complaints of Liberum Arbitrium that the pope "with moneye maynteynneth men to werre [wage war] vppon cristene" (XVII.234). Liberum Arbitrium had combined this complaint with a forceful analysis of the determining and disastrous role of material "possession" in the governance of the modern church (XVII.220–38; XXI.428–29).[143] He had proposed the disendowment of the church by lay elites as the necessary reformation, but the "lewed vicory" does not suggest this. And with very good reason gives the vision of lay elites to which the poem is moving.

Although the vicar sets aside Liberum Arbitrium's idea of reformation by lay elites, he does allude explicitly to the Great Schism in the church from 1378. Its immediate cause was the action of the cardinals electing two popes, first Urban VI, then Clement VII.[144] Once again there is nothing debilitatingly unlearned about the priest's approach to the practices of the church in schism. He lucidly identifies the papal and ecclesial ideology legitimizing crusades against Christians aligned with the papal adversary (XXI.428–29). The ideology and practice is well exemplified by an English crusade against Christians across the channel whose allegiance was to a different pope. The "lewed" priest could be refering to the papal sponsorship of crusades against Christians that began in 1379, the year after the Great Schism. And he could be alluding to Bishop Despenser's crusade on behalf of Urban VI in 1383.[145] Whether Langland intended him to be doing the former or the latter or both has no consequences for the comments I am about to offer. For I take the English crusade led by the bishop of Norwich, Despenser, to be symptomatic of the church analyzed and attacked by both Liberum Arbitrium and the "lewed vicory." And, for that matter, by their author, Langland.

Let us begin considering some of the theological and ecclesial dimensions of this English crusade.[146] It displayed conventional doctrines of soteriology and the soteriological role of the church. Bishop Despenser had seen the possibilities of the schism to reindulge "his military tastes" manifested earlier in Italy and more recently in slaughtering agrarian workers involved in the great rising of 1381.[147] In November 1378, Urban VI had already issued *Nuper cum vinea*, which promised indulgences to people who fought against those aligned with his rival, Clement VII. Despenser sought and was granted papal bulls (1381), "which gave him powers both to grant indulgences to those who took part in or contributed towards a crusade against the anti-pope, and to dispense clerics to take the cross," a phrase used in that ecclesial culture without irony.[148] After receiving the third bull (*Dignum censemus*, May 1382) empowering him to preach the crusade and act against the pope's adversaries, he published all the bulls he had received, sent out fund-raisers, and "solemnly took the cross in St. Paul's cathedral."[149]

So the bishop now had papal authority to promise those who enlisted in the crusade plenary indulgences, a full remission of their sins. He was also licensed to promise such remission to those who paid for a particular soldier to fight in the forthcoming war and who contributed funds for hiring soldiers in general.[150] Christ, we remember, "yaf Peres pardoun and power he graunted hym, / Myhte men to assoyle of alle manere synnes" (XXI.183–84). Are Bishop Henry and Pope Urban deploying the gift Christ bestowed on Piers? Within their own ideology, of course. To Langland, however, this evangelical gift was inseparable from the law of the new covenant (XXI.182–96). Neither a figure of Piers nor a priest who followed the model of the nonviolent church of the martyrs espoused by Liberum Arbitrium, the bishop of Norwich nevertheless acted with full papal support and within the conventional theology and soteriology of the late medieval church, unequivocally supported by his archbishop, William Courtenay.[151]

It is illuminating to observe the terms chosen by Henry Knighton, himself a religious, in his contemporary chronicle to describe the theology and politics of this English crusade.[152] Knighton reports that the bishop had raised "an incalculable and unbelievably large sum of money," while "it was believed that very many gave more than they could afford, in order to secure the benefit of absolution for themselves and their devoted friends" (*ut beneficium absolucionis consequerentur pro se et suis benivolis amicis*) (324/325). Knighton emphasized that this pardon was efficacious not only for the donors and their living friends but also "for their friends who had died." Indeed, he states that the people "could not be absolved unless they contributed according to their ability and means" (*aliter non absolvebantur, nisi tribuerunt secundum posse suum et facultatem suam*) (324/325). This is an important observation on a line customarily taken by medieval and modern apologists, namely, that indulgences were issued only to those truly following the sacrament of penance. Knighton makes the reality of such exchanges perfectly clear: however penitent one might be for one's sins, such indulgences were issued only to penitents who supplied funds or who were prepared to fight their fellow Christians (also known as schismatics and heretics).

Who were the priests working as confessors and financial agents for Bishop Despenser? Prominent among them were friars appointed by the bishop. Whatever the views of a parish priest, even if he were a "lewed vicory" with critical views on such crusades and their theology, he was obliged to allow Despenser's mendicant agents to preach and to confess their parishioners. As for the friars, they were entitled to keep six pence of each pound they collected.[153] Such was the complex treasury of merits allegedly entrusted by Christ to the ecclesial hierarchy for distribution to the faithful in response to their participation in the sacrament of penance and holy war.[154]

Knighton's language in describing the conventional theology in these transactions is very helpful to anyone exploring Langland's work. Knighton claims that many people paid for soldiers and archers while others joined the holy war at their own expense, and he explains why:

> For the bishop had wonderful indulgences, with absolutions from punishment and from guilt [*indulgencias mirabiles, cum absolucione a pena et a culpa*] granted to him for the said crusade by Pope Urban VI, by whose authority both he and his agents absolved from punishment and from guilt both the living and the dead on whose behalf a sufficient contribution was made [*cuius auctoritate tam mortuos quam vivos, ex quorum parte contribucio sufficiens fiebat, per se et suos commissarios a pena et culpa absolvebat*].[155]

Indulgences assuring the recipient of pardon *a pena et a culpa*, remission of both punishment and guilt, now and beyond the grave, were extremely desirable, a plenary pardon indeed. Langland's Passus IX, woven around "a pardoun *a pena et a culpa*" sent from Treuthe to Piers, works around the theology and practice of such claims in his church (IX.1–8). But whereas Knighton offers no critique of the "wonderful indulgences" dispensed by pope, bishop, and friar confessors, Langland's exploration of the sacrament of penance, pardon, and indulgence unfolds across his whole work. He can certainly imagine Treuthe sending a pardon *a pena et a culpa* to his servant Piers struggling to discover the due relations between coercive jurisdiction and discipleship of Jesus Christ who had proclaimed a gospel of nonviolent love of enemies. But while he can imagine such a gift, he unveils this imagining in a passus which glosses the pardon with numerous voices. It also explores many topics and complex social issues before dissolving the pardon into two lines from the Athanasian Creed: "Et qui bona egerunt ibunt in vitam eternam; / Qui vero mala in ignem eternum" (And they that have done good shall go into life everlasting; and they that have done evil into everlasting fire) (IX.287–88). A priest notes that in these two lines, abstracted from their trinitarian and Christological contexts, "Y can no pardoun fynde / Bote Dowel and haue wel and god shal haue thy soule / And do yuele and haue euele and hope thow non othere / Bote he that euele lyueth euele shal ende" (I can find no pardon, / But only "Do well and have well and God shall have your soul / And do evil and have evil and expect nothing other / But he that lives evilly shall have an evil end) (IX.289–92).[156]

Returning from Langland's pardon to Bishop Despenser's, I wish to emphasize the incorporation of the crusading pardons in the sacraments (of order, of penance, and of the altar) in a complex network of political powers. So far I have discussed theological and ecclesial strands. But economic and political forces were interwoven. And this particular interweaving confronted all of Langland's explorations of the church and Constantinian Christianity.

The processes of state formation and centralization occurred earlier in England than in continental Europe, while its forms of feudalism were "of such a kind as to enhance the prestige of the crown" and to favor "the maintenance and then the extension of royal justice and administrative authority."[157] Thus Marc Bloch wrote in his last book before being killed by the Nazis. Another peculiarity of the English, as Philip Corrigan and Derek Sayer observe, was the way state formation involved the fusion of centralizing powers with "a high degree of involvement of local ruling elites in the exercise of governance," including Parliament, the apparatus of justice, and county government.[158] In this context it is not surprising that the crusade led by an English bishop could never have taken place without the consent of Crown and Parliament, both Lords and commons voting taxation to support this war-making. Contrary to Wyclif's model of lay elites virtuously disendowing the church of temporalities in an act of armed charity, a model adapted by Liberum Arbitrium in Passus XVII, this historical event discloses the fusion of all elite and ecclesiastic hierarchies. We must ask why lay elites would consent to this crusade and contribute to its funding.

Norman Housley's answer to this question centers on the influence of merchants, "London capitalists who dominated the commons." For these people, he argues, the wool trade with Flanders was extremely important. They could already see their profits being undermined by political conflicts in Flanders and were confident that an imminent French presence, in support of Clement VII, would be disastrous for their own economic interests.[159] Margaret Aston notes the drop in wool exports "from about 18,000 sacks in 1381–2 to about 11,000 in 1382–3" and the commercial difficulties this posed to English merchants. Their fears about the French were confirmed when in 1382 "Charles VI entered Bruges and confiscated the goods of English merchants. The wool traffic at Calais ground almost to a halt." As significant as the obvious economic interests involved in the readiness of the English to crusade in Flanders was the fact that the Commons included in their reasons for using taxes to support this enterprise a wondrously holy intention: "the salvation of Holy Church."[160] This declaration is an important witness to conventional relations between religion and politics in late medieval England. These fundamental relations are often obscured in the powerful and hugely influential work by Eamon Duffy on "traditional religion" before the Reformation stripped the altars and attacked the people's church.[161]

As for the Crown, royal finances were intermeshed with those of London merchants who were funding the long dynastic conflict over French sovereignty. But with Richard II only reaching his fifteenth birthday in 1382, John of Gaunt wielded substantial influence on government and himself had a distinctive agenda. This entailed his long-term attempt to occupy the throne of Castile and León (whose title he had acquired by marriage in 1372). In early 1382 he too had gained papal bulls from Urban VI to wage a crusade against the king of Castile, who was aligned with Pope Clement VII. As Aston has observed, "Dynastic ambitions of the house of Lancaster could now plausibly be represented in new disguise—a crusade of the orthodox papacy against the schismatic ally of schismatic France."[162] So Crown and Parliament had to choose one of the two English crusades on offer, or, of course, imagine a theology in which "the salvation of Holy Church" would demand the rejection of both crusades together with their Constantinian political theology. Such a rejection, however, in that culture of discourse, would have been outside the bounds of orthodoxy led by pope, archbishop, bishops, mendicant friars/fundraisers, Crown, and Parliament. So the balance of material and ideological forces led to a final decision in favor of the bishop's crusade made in the spring Parliament.[163] The crusade would be financed by taxation as well as by resources from the indulgences authorized by papal bulls, bishop's ministers, and the church's soteriology. We see an event weaving together king, lords, merchants, Commons, secular clergy, friars (as confessors, preachers, and fund-raisers), and lay Christians supporting the crusade with ideology, money, and, in some cases, their own bodies. This is just the religious and political fabric that Langland is exploring and on which the "lewed vicory" comments. Langland himself shows us how he would certainly concur with William of Ockham's eloquent remark on the papacy: "Christ, setting Saint Peter in authority over his sheep did not say, 'Shear my sheep and make yourselves clothes from their wool,' or 'Milk my sheep, and drink or eat their milk,' nor did he say 'Slaughter my sheep, and eat their meat,' but: 'Feed my sheep [John 21:17]', that is, 'Keep, rule, guard, and serve them, to my honour and their utility.'"[164]

After praying for the conversion of the church's cardinals, the "lewed" priest concludes his powerful oration by returning to "the commune." It was their rejection of Christ's covenant, the Eucharist, and Conscience's counsel on restitution as intrinsic to the new covenant which brought him into Langland's vision. His closing observations are perfectly in accord with what Langland has shown us and with what he will show us next. In this community, says the priest, only practices that tend to "wynnynge," to material gain, will be reckoned as cardinal virtues. So, for example, Guile is now celebrated as *Spiritus prudencie* (XXI.451–58). Langland is, quite brilliantly, imagining a history in which the meaning of moral concepts is transformed. This is also what he was exploring in Pride's prophecy envisaging a culture in which nobody could discern a difference between usury and just exchange (XXI.348–50). The Christian people turn *Spiritus prudencie*, a cardinal virtue intrinsic to practical reasoning and given by the Holy Spirit, into worldly wisdom, guile. To them, all the beautiful cardinal virtues seem vices: "And al tho fayre vertues as vises thei semeth" (XXI.456). As the brewer's contempt for *Spiritus iusticie* has so well illustrated (XXI.396–402). Langland is exploring how neither the meaning of vices and virtues nor the central concepts of Christian theology will be independent of specific social formations and the practices they elicit and normalize. Indeed, in the long run such independence would lead to the unintelligibility of inherited moral discourse. This dialectic, between ethical concepts and social practices, is one which preoccupies Langland throughout *Piers Plowman*. It is foregrounded with special sharpness in the last two passus of the work.

IX

The next two speakers are laymen who further exemplify and elaborate the critique of contemporary Christian culture offered by the "lewed vicory." They claim to speak for the infused cardinal virtues of justice and fortitude sown by Piers as the gifts of the Holy Spirit (XXI.274–75,

289–308). James Simpson comments that we are being shown "the slipperiness in the very meaning of words denoting the cardinal virtues."[165] While this is true, we are also being shown how words and versions of the virtues slip, slide, and perish because they belong to particular cultural practices and habits which themselves change, decay, and perish. Langland's work consistently resists idealist assumptions about language and its autonomy of determinate social formations. So he now introduces a lord who maintains that the ruthlessly exploitative and violent management of his manors is conducted with "riht and resoun," the gifts of the Holy Spirit ("*Spiritus intellectus*") and the infused cardinal virtue of courage or fortitude, "*Spiritus fortitudinis*." Thus:

> Thenne lowh ther a lord and "Bi this lihte!" saide,
> "Y halde hit riht and resoun of my reue to take
> Al that myn auditour or elles my styward
> Conseileth me bi here acounte and my clerkes writyng.
> With *Spiritus intellectus* they toke the reues rolles
> And with *Spiritus fortitudinis* fecche hit, wolle he, null he."
>
> (XXI.459–64)

> [Then a lord laughed there and "By these lights!" said,
> "I hold it as right and reasonable to take from my reeve
> All that my auditor or else my steward
> Advise me by their accounts and my clerk's records.
> With *Spiritus intellectus* they took the reeve's books
> And with *Spiritus fortitudinis* I'll fetch it, whether he likes it or not."]

Not for the first time in the poem, Langland's agrarian writing addresses socially determinate conflicts and forces, even though the scale of representation is minute in comparison to Passus VIII.

The forces mediated in the quotation just above include the sharpened conflicts between lords and tenants after the great plague of 1348–49. Tenants (bond and free) as well as landless laborers sought to improve their conditions in the changed demographic circumstances while landlords resisted such attempts using both local forms of power and national legislation.[166] Langland's laughing lord refers to the former. The reeve was normally an unfree tenant of the lord who was made responsible for organizing work, labor services, and the collection of the lord's rents and fines. As Skeat observes, the reeve's "rolles" provided a very detailed account of receipts and expenses.[167] J. L. Bolton describes such rolls as having two parts. The face of the roll "dealt with cash transactions, recording receipts from rents, fines, the sale of produce or any other source, disbursements for labour in seed corn, and the sum left which ought to be paid over." On the back, "very detailed grain and stock returns were made, showing the quantities of crops grown, how they were disposed of, whether to the household or to the market or to another manor to pay servants in kind, the numbers of stock, how many calves or lambs had been born, how many sold and so on."[168] And of course the detail was also part of a disciplinary structure for extracting the lord's livelihood from tenants. We have come into a country far from the Pentecostal community where the Holy Spirit made Piers "my procuratour [agent] and my reue," responsible for receiving just restitution essential to the life of charity in the community (XXI.258–61), for a harvest rooted in Christ's gifts (XXI.317–32). But in this distant country which we have now entered, the language is both familiar and made strange. Langland has been cultivating us to discern just how strange our daily, literal discourses may be, how we see allegorical modes and allegorical vision. The letter kills, the spirit gives life, and God sends fit ministers of the New Testament not in the letter but in the spirit ("sufficientia nostra ex Deo est: qui et idoneos nos fecit ministros novi testamenti non litterae, sed Spiritus: littera enim occidit, Spiritus autem vivificat" [2 Cor. 3:6]). "No 'death of the soul' is more aptly given that name than the situation in which the intelligence which is what raises the soul above the level of animals, is subjected to the flesh by following the letter [carni subicitur sequendo litteram]." It is, Augustine continues, "a miserable kind of spiritual slavery to interpret signs as things, and to be incapable of raising the mind's eye above the physical creation so as to absorb the eternal light" (Ea demum est miserabilis animae servitus, signa pro rebus accipere et supra creaturam corpoream oculum mentis ad hauriendium aeternum lumen levare non posse).[169] But in the distant country, perhaps ravished by fortune "into the land of longyng," with the prodigal Wille (XI.164–85), we too may forget how the letter can kill, and we may forget our apprenticeship in allegorical modes of writing and hermeneutics. So one would forget the key to Christian allegory, the one who makes meaning from history and redeems time, who with "A gobet [mouthful] of his grace" can "bigynne a tyme / That alle tymes of my tyme to profit shal turne" (V.99–101).[170]

In the speech of the lord who speaks after the "lewed vicory," Christian speech has been emptied of Grace's allegory, while Christian virtues have become whatever maximizes seigneurial dominion and material profit. Clerical skills are de-Christianized and transformed into a technology for strengthening the lord's power over tenants and resources through "my clerkes writing" (XXI.459–62). This integration of clergy with increasing levels of exploitation ("efficiency," from the perspective of the owners) was combined with their role in composing ideological legitimizations of current structures of power and wealth in a traditional Christian vocabulary. This kind of integration was intrinsic to Christian "clerks" in the Middle Ages and the Reformation but had been sharply criticized at the beginning of the poem (Prol. 85–94). That passage reminds us of an important part of the work done by the person the lord refers to as "my styward" (XXI.461):

> And summe aren as seneschalles and seruen other lordes
> And ben in stede of stewardus and sitten and demen.
>
> > (Prol. 93–94)

> ———
>
> [And some assist lords as seneschals
> And serve as stewards and sit and judge.]

The steward held the lord's courts, where he made judgments on tenants and laborers. Because such clerks obey the lord who employs them, their writing will not remind him that *Spiritus fortitudinis* had nothing to do with coercive violence and everything to do with spiritual joy and strength in the face of injustice and adversity (see this infused cardinal virtue at XXI.289–96a). Clerks who are the lay lord's servants will not direct him to the substantial treatment of this virtue by St. Thomas Aquinas in the *Summa Theologiae* (II-II.123–38). Aquinas explains that fortitude (or courage) contributes to sustaining people in a virtuous life in the face of difficult impediments which could overwhelm their will to do well. The virtue is most perfectly displayed in the Christian martyrs, who maintain justice, truth, and the love of God in the face of persecution and death (see esp. II-II.123.1–3, 121.1, ad 3). Langland has shown us such fortitude in the death of St. Thomas of Canterbury who "Amonges vnkynde cristene in holy kirke was slawe [slain], / And alle holy kirk honoured thorw that deyng [through that dying]" (XVII.274–76). But, of course, the lord's own genealogy is that of the knightly killers of Becket in a cultural formation where *Spiritus fortitudinis* was de-Christianized. Langland's attack on such appropriation of the clergy in the Prologue has common ground with the *Twelve Conclusions of the Lollards* displayed during Parliament in early 1395. For there the authors described such merging of "the temporal and the spiritual" as the attempt to serve two masters (see Matt. 6:42), which begot a "hermaphrodite or ambidexter."[171]

Appropriately, the lay lord in the contemporary community is followed by a king. He turns out not to be the king initially divided between Conscience and Mede in Passus II–IV, since that figure was persuaded to support attempts at reformation under the guidance of Conscience and Reason in Passus IV. On the contrary, this lay sovereign has no interest in such reformation. He chooses to follow the lord in the reinvention of the cardinal virtues. His focus is *Spiritus iusticie*, the seed Conscience had just described as "The cheef seed that Peres sewe [sowed]," a seed essential to justification in Christ, to the fulfillment of the new covenant, to salvation (XXI.405–6, 182–98). In the Pentecostal community we saw that this seed leads people to be "trewe / With god," to practice justice and equity without any capitulation to the socially powerful (XXI.297–308). As Aquinas had argued, justice is the habit whereby a person with a constant and stable will renders to each person her due ("ius suum").[172] As we saw, the Christian community received this virtue from the Holy Spirit. But in and under this king, justice becomes what sustains his unqualified domination of the "commune" and "lawe." The latter is explicitly subjected to his will (XXI.465–70). Adopting traditional organicist imagery, the sovereign represents himself as the head of the social body ("ye ben bote membres and Y aboue alle") and also head of the law. Maintaining that whatever he wills is by that fact just, his position approaches that ascribed to Richard II when he was deposed as a tyrant in 1399.[173] Reiterating his headship of the community, he adds the extraordinary claim that he is "youre alere hele," a phrase that lays claim to healing, even salvific powers (XXI.469–71). Skeat glossed *alere hele* as "the health (or safety) of you all" and rightly linked this to an earlier line in the same passus where Conscience used the word *hele* to signify "salvation" or "spiritual health" (XXI.388).[174] Langland is showing us a secular organicism which *jettisons* St. Paul's attention to the basis of solidarity, of charity in mutual care: "we being many, are one bread, one body, all that partake of one bread" (1 Cor. 10:17; see too 1 Cor. 12 with XXI.227–89). The sovereign's relations with the church are assimilated to this model of nascent absolutism. The king appropriates conventional medieval language in which the armed elite is the defender of the Constantinian church.[175] Earlier in the poem, such language was used by the knight and Piers in their attempt to organize agrarian production in contemporary England (VIII.23–34). Now the king declares that he himself is "cheef helpe" of the church and its defender (XXI.467, 472). He does so without even mentioning Christ, the Holy Spirit, or Piers, without so much as a glance at the soteriological narratives of Passus XVIII–XXI. In these contexts such an omission should be particularly striking. It casts a salutary light on neo-Wycliffite models of reformation such as that put forward by Liberum Arbitrium in Passus XVII. Reformation of the church by the king and lay elites would involve the exorbitant increase in royal power, something about which Wyclif himself was perfectly happy, as would be Henry VIII.[176]

The king in Passus XXI identifies all extractions he makes from the community as justice: he sees himself as owing nothing to anybody. Justice is thus reduced to an act of unilateral dominion over "alle" (XXI.474). He is the embodiment of those whom Jesus commanded his disciples not to imitate, namely, the kings of the Gentiles who lord it over their people, predatory authorities called benefactors by their victims but identified as tyrants by Jesus (Matt. 20:23–28; Luke 22:24–27; Mark 10:42–45). Nowhere in Passus XXI did the Holy Spirit advocate the need of the church of Christ for such an armed, regal defender. On the contrary, the missionary church, the church of the martyrs, carried no carnal weapons and did not depend on them. Nevertheless, clothed in the language of the virtues, this king presents himself as a defender of the faith, of "holy kyrke and clerge" (XXI.467, 472). As self-proclaimed defender of the church and king of the community, he assumes that whatever he takes from church and community must manifest the infused virtue of justice, "*Spiritus iusticie*" (XXI.473–74). This transformation of the meaning of justice persuades him that he is never in debt to anyone. He thus considers himself exalted above his fellow Christians who pray every day, at Jesus's instructions, "forgive us our debts [*dimitte nobis debita nostra*], as we also forgive our debtors"

(Matt. 6:12). He does not consider that he must fulfill the condition at-tached by Christ to his pardon, a condition mediated by Piers: "*Redde quod debes*" (XXI.182–90). So he insists that he can confidently receive Holy Communion ("Y may boldely be hoseled [receive communion] for Y borwe neuere" [XXI.475]). In this almost demonic confidence, the king illustrates how someone could receive Communion "not discerning the body of the Lord" (1 Cor. 11:17–34). He has *unhinged* the divine gift of justice from the theological virtues, from the infused cardinal virtues, and from the narratives of redemption (XVIII–XXI). In the modern Christian commu-nity, we seem to witness either outraged rejection of "godes body" with its covenant of restitution (XXI.383–85) or proud confidence of entitlement to communion in the body of Christ.

Conscience's response to the lay sovereign is distinctly troubled, but it is also strangely de-Christianizing. Hence it is oddly collusive with the king. This is what he says:

"In condicioun," quod Consience, "that thou the comune defende
And rewle thy rewme in resoun as riht wol and treuthe,
Than haue thow mayst al thyn askyng as thy lawe asketh."
(XXI.477–79)

["On condition," said Conscience, "that you protect the commonwealth
And rule your realm well with reason and truth,
Then have you all your asking just as your law asks."]

To observe de-Christianization here, as I have just done, may seem rather hyperbolic. But the comment is made in light of Conscience's own exten-sive Christological discourse earlier in the passus (XXI.1–199). There he interpreted the vision Wille received in the Mass, when "men yede [went] to offrynge," the vision in which the bleeding Christ was manifest in "Peres armes, / His colours and his cote armure" (XXI.1–14). When asked by Wille about the relations between the names Jesus and Christ, he offered a substantial life of Christ up to his commissioning of Piers in the Resur-rection and Christ's return "at domesday" (XXI.26–198). This account was immediately followed by a vision of the Holy Spirit "to Peres and to his felawes" which Conscience interpreted for Wille (XXI.200–212). We should also recall that it is Conscience who has just been dispensing the sacrament with "godes body thereunder" (XXI.383–90). Now a cloud of forgetfulness apparently obscures these central Christian narratives, doctrines, and practices from his attention. It is as though the force of the king's rhetoric has disoriented his knowledge. This renders him a *conscientia* without *scientia* essential to an instructor in Christian living, *scientia* he has displayed in Passus XXI just as in Passus III. In the present moment he is only capable of suggesting some distressingly vague mitigation to the king's tyranny and to his perversion of ethical language, namely, that royal power should be used in reason as right and truth demand, in defense of "the comune." But this is exactly how the king has described his practices. He did so while claiming inspiration from the teaching of *Spiritus iusticie* even as he discloses that the substance and teleology of the cardinal virtue has been abandoned. Conscience seems to have forgotten something else in his reply to the king. One of the qualities of *Spiritus iusticie* is "to correcte the kyng" if the latter does any wrong, to be a fearless judge of the powerful without any compromise (XXI.302–8). Has he also forgotten that he is "goddes clerk and his notarie" (XVI.192) rather than a mere adjunct of secular power? Apparently so. And this, Langland shows, is among the disastrous consequences of Constantinian Christianity. This showing also contributes to our growing understanding of the ironies in the neo-Wyclifite reformation of Constantinianism proposed by Liberum Arbitrium. Such a reformation, massively strengthening the centralizing power of the monarch and the wealth of lay elites, would subject church and Christian ethics even more uncritically to the new Constantine. This would move from the realm of critical speculation to historical event in sixteenth-century England, with Henry VIII, and then his daughter Elizabeth, as the new Constantine.[177]

Langland is also showing the difficulties encountered by Conscience in contemporary culture and its moral language. These are the difficulties Pride promised when he predicted Conscience would become unable to discern a Christian from a heathen and no merchant would be able to know whether his profits were gained with right, with wrong, or with usury (XXI.344–50). Such, in Langland's view, is the present cultural moment as he wakes and writes his vision (XXI.481). It might seem that he is exploring questions traditionally debated by late medieval theologians addressing the conscience. For example, in the *Summa Theologiae* Aquinas offers extensive discussion of synderesis, conscience, erring conscience, and erring reason. The difficulties that most seem to intrigue him concern determining whether an erring conscience binds and whether an erring conscience can excuse.[178] Aquinas's teaching on whether the erring conscience or reason binds and whether such error excuses us certainly throws up fascinating cases—for example, if the erring reason or conscience dictates that belief in Christ is evil but the will nevertheless adheres to Christ according to Christian creeds. Aquinas determines that such an act is evil. This is because the will tends to Christian belief *as evil*, even though belief in Christ is good (*ST* I-II.19.5, resp.). Another example: if erring reason or conscience tells someone to have sexual union with another's spouse and the person's will follows this instruction, then this will is evil because such ignorance of the divine law is culpable ignorance. However, if the person's reason or conscience errs in *mistaking* another's spouse for her or his own spouse and the error arises from ignorance of circumstance, then such ignorance excuses. What seems an adulterous act in this case is not so, and the will is excused by a licitly rather than culpably ignorant reason or conscience (*ST* I-I.19.6, resp.). This is hardly as searching as the exploration Shakespeare gives us in *Measure for Measure* when Angelo goes to bed with a woman whose identity he mistakes. But one can see how such cases might be developed into more complex fables than Aquinas's examples. Langland does not pursue these in Shakespeare's modes, but he has composed an extraordinarily complex situation that goes beyond the bounds of Aquinas's discussions of conscience. Let us consider this further.

X

Langland is exploring a form of cultural revolution in which he believed himself to be immersed. He has just dramatized processes of de-Christianization engulfing those who are Christians. Think of the following: the people collectively reject the body of Christ; they reject Christ's forgiveness with its covenant; the brewer rejects the infused cardinal virtues and so their author, the Holy Spirit; the lord transforms the meaning of the virtues given by the Holy Spirit into antithetical forces; the king incorporates the language of the eucharistic sacrament and the infused cardinal virtues into alien, antagonistic practices under a new Constantinianism.

Writing at the end of the twentieth century, Pope John Paul II puts very well what Langland was envisioning:

> Dechristianization, which weighs heavily upon entire peoples and communities once rich in faith and Christian life, involves not only the loss of faith or in any event its becoming irrelevant for everyday life, but also, and of necessity, *a decline or obscuring of the moral sense.* This comes about both as a result of a loss of awareness of the originality of Gospel morality and as a result of an eclipse of fundamental principles and ethical values themselves.[179]

John Paul II reflects on the ways that Christians are caught up in such cultural processes: "In a widely dechristianized culture, the criteria employed by believers themselves in making judgments and decisions often appear extraneous or even contrary to those of the Gospel" (par. 88). Langland himself, writing in the later fourteenth century, is representing what he imagines as just such a moment—one that includes its own grounds for the pope's lament that "amid today's growing secularism" many people, including Christians, "think and live 'as if God did not exist'" (par. 88).

    Near the beginning of his own work, Langland showed a figure descending from Treuthe to complain that people in the contemporary world are utterly circumscribed by the social "mase" they inhabit:

> The moste party of this peple that passeth on this erthe,
> Haue thei worschip in this world thei wilneth no bettere.
>
>   (I.7–8)
>
> ———
>
> [Most of the people that pass through this earth
> Are satisfied with success in this world.]

The heavenly speaker tells Wille that modern Christians have set aside the tradition of the faith and the teleology these traditions inculcate: "Of othere heuene then here thei halde no tale" (The only heaven they think of is here) (I.9). The speaker turns out to be "Holy Churche" (I.72). I shall return to this juxtaposition of the modern pope and the medieval writer toward the end of this essay, but for the moment it suffices to recall Holy Church's judgment in relation to the situation Langland has unfolded in Passus XXI.

Both are congruent with what John Paul II called "growing secularism" (par. 88). No wonder that despite his encounters with Christ, the joys of Easter, and the promises of Pentecost, Langland represents the figure of the poet writing his vision with a heavy spirit (XXI.481; XXII.1–3).

For what Langland has just shown us about cultural transformation, political power, and the language of the virtues belongs to a history which was to trouble even Thomas Hobbes. Unhinged from their cultural role in building a virtuous community, the cardinal virtues now name practices that had been traditionally understood as vices, forms of life inimical to human flourishing. So, as we have just observed, Langland displayed the virtue fortitude (courage) as the name for a lord's violent exploitation of tenants, the virtue of justice as the name for voracious tyranny. There is a rhetorical term for such redescriptions: *paradiastole*. It has been illuminatingly studied by Quentin Skinner in his work on Hobbes. He shows that paradiastole was a technique in forensic speech designed to redescribe an adversary's claims to virtues such as justice in terms of adjacent vices.[180] But its cultural implications were not lost on historians and moralists. In his *Bellum Catalinae*, Sallust has Cato complain that "we have lost the true name of things. It is due to the fact that the squandering of other people's goods is nowadays called liberality, while audacity in wrong-doing is called courage" (8). Milton's Satan is a virtuoso in this particular form of paradiastolic speech as he lays claim to "courage" in *Paradise Lost* I–II, V–VI. Seneca too complained that we name our vices as virtues while "evil things present themselves to us in the guise of virtues" (11). In his account of paradiastole, Skinner argues that it was put to "increasingly provocative uses" in the sixteenth century (28). He offers copious and thoroughly engaging examples of such uses, none of which are actually more "provocative" than Langland's. Skinner also gives nice examples of objections against paradiastolic rhetoric and ethics by those he calls "conservative moralists" (28–31). It is in this context that he sets Hobbes's sustained and "systematic critique of paradiastole" (31). Skinner follows this critique through Hobbes's works to *Leviathan* (1651). There the fifteenth chapter is notable for the even greater pessimism with which he confronts "the dangers of using the device" (37). Writing after the civil wars, Hobbes brooded on the fragility of the polity, the malleability of moral language, and the material interests shaping scriptural hermeneutics. He saw good reason to maintain his voluntarism and argue that "private appetite is the measure of Good and Evil," a situation that can easily reduce us to what he considered to be the state of nature, the war of all upon all, the condition of "mere Nature" (37; see *Leviathan* chaps. 15 and 13). Skinner demonstrates that while Hobbes was "deeply troubled by the dangers of paradiastole," he insisted that "all existing attempts to neutralize the threat have fallen far short of the mark" (46).[181]

We can leave Hobbes at this point because his responses to political and linguistic forces he found anarchic and terrifying are not Langland's. Nor is his version of the "state of nature," the human person, and Christian faith within shouting distance of Langland's.[182] His attempts to invent some kind of discursive stability through a putatively geometric model of rationality together with his voluntarism, nominalism, and absolute centralization of power in the lay sovereign, including power over scriptural interpretation, are solutions to religious conflicts and civil disorder utterly alien to Langland. Perhaps, though, in some respects they are less alien to Marsilius of Padua and some aspects of fourteenth-century philosophical theology.[183]

Despite obvious theological and ethical disparities between Langland and Hobbes, following Skinner may help us see how Langland has introduced paradiastolic speech to identify a profound challenge to Christian-Aristotelian ethics and its language of the virtues. Skinner unfolds a history whose relevance seems not to have been noticed by those who write on Langland and the later Middle Ages, or by those who tell grand narratives of the intellectual and cultural history of modernity. Yet in the gripping episodes which conclude Passus XXI, continued into Passus XXII, Langland discloses the significance of tendencies he discerned in his culture by dramatizing paradiastolic speech and ascribing it to the lay ruling elites. This classical discourse is open to a different rhetorical tradition, that of biblical prophecy. So Isaiah hears God object to what sounds very like the paradiastolic language of Langland's lord and his king in Passus XXI: "Woe to you that call evil good, and good evil: that put darkness for light, and light for darkness: that put bitter for sweet, and sweet for bitter" (Isa. 5:20). But this does not lead into the specificity of Langland's dramatization of the lay elites and the tradition of the virtues quite as illuminatingly, I think, as does the classical material Skinner discusses.

Indeed, in the poem's final passus, Langland suggests how no way emerges to "neutralize" (in Skinner's vocabulary) the paradiastolic subver-

sion of the virtues and the language in which we learn them. This passus
actually begins without any recognition of Christian resources for resisting such subversion as we encounter the simulacrum of another cardinal
virtue: Temperance in the guise of "Nede." In such contexts Wille's misery
is completely understandable (XXI.481; XXII.1–50). His hunger is as
spiritual as it is carnal (XXII.1–3). Besides witnessing the triumph of
paradiastolic speech in those who govern society, the "lewed vicory" had
observed the same triumph "among the peple." For he, like Langland, discerned the way *Spiritus prudencie* (the cardinal virtue of prudence given by
the Holy Spirit) had become the term for describing what was traditionally
known as the vice of "gyle" (XXI.455–58; cf. II.179–96). This perversion,
the priest rightly observes, is bound up with the way "the comune" now
prioritizes the making of profits, "wynnynge," over pursuing justice and rationality as defined by Christian tradition (XXI.451–53). Furthermore,
Wille has also witnessed the whole community refusing to receive the Eucharist, "bred yblessed and godes body therunder" (XXI.385, 391–402). In
his need he now encounters a personification named Nede (XXI.4–50).
This figure has proved to be among the most enigmatic in the poem. Some
scholars intepret him as a representative of Langland's theology of poverty
and need; others see him as a harbinger of Antichrist.[184] Having addressed
Langland's theology of poverty elsewhere at length, here I wish to concentrate on Nede's teachings on the cardinal virtues, especially the one
with which he claims identification, "*Spiritus temperancie,*" the infused virtue of temperance.[185]

Nede directs the wretched Wille to the vision of the previous passus.
He also asks why Wille has not excused his form of life by invoking *Spiritus temperancie,* just as the tyrannical king and others had excused theirs by
invoking cardinal virtues in their self-legitimation (XXII.4–9). He does
not offer any overt criticism of the turn to paradiastolic speech in these
precedents. So R. M. Adams responds to Nede's invocation of such antecedents as having "something like the quality of the proverbial dead
mackerel in the moonlight: it both shines and stinks."[186] Even if one were
to hear irony in Nede's voice, the invocation does not sound good. Nor can
it be much help to Wille who has not been challenged to justify himself or
his life in the vision to which Nede refers. He had certainly been challenged many passus and many years before. In Passus V he had encountered Reason and Conscience as he wrote satirical poetry in London,

wandering in remembrance and eschewing manual labor as befitted a lit-
erate clerical person. Reason and Conscience had questioned him sharply
about his way of life and its place in the community. Wille had defended
his nomadic life, pointing out that he begged his daily bread "Withoute
bagge or botel," in return offering prayers (V.10–52). He separates himself
from those who begged until their bags were crammed full, a group fiercely
attacked in *Piers Plowman* (Prol. 42; IX.98–104, 153–75). He thus also
separates himself from friars whose mendicancy was, as Langland maintained, dialectically united with a massive accumulation of material and
political resources. But despite this restraint, this apparent practice of temperance governed by his daily need, Wille's self-justification was rejected by
Reason and Conscience. They were troubled by the unanswerability of
Wille's life to any traditional vocation in the community (V.12–21, 26–34,
89–91).[187] And with good reason, as it turns out. For in the community
founded by the Holy Spirit in Passus XXI there are apparently *no* mendicant vocations.[188] Grasping the objections of Reason and Conscience
(which are emphatically not those of people trying to impose the Statute
of Laborers on *lewed* working people), Wille had abandoned his self-
justifications. In a deeply moving prayer of hope and faith (theological
virtues encountered again in Passus XVIII and XIX), he repeated and followed the directions of his inner teacher "to the kyrke" (V.92–108). But
in Passus XXII Nede is trying to persuade Wille that had he invoked
the virtue of temperance he would have seen he needed no such conversion, no such repenting prayer for God's grace to redeem wasted time so
that "all tymes of my tyme to profit shal turne" (V.93–101). Nede is also
oblivious of Wille's recent encounter with Christ (XIX–XX) and the Holy
Spirit (XXI). His rhetoric, directed against Reason and Conscience in
Passus V, encourages us to ask what even constitutes the virtue of temperance in Nede's discourse.

Nede understands Temperance in only one way: as a guide to those living by the conventional medieval teaching that in extreme need all things
become common goods.[189] Guided by *Spiritus temperancie*, the needy "hath
no lawe no neuere shale falle in dette" (XXII.10). So this cardinal virtue,
like the others reconfigured in paradiastolic speech, becomes a means to set
aside "the obligation of 'redde quod debes,' the doctrine of restitution," proclaimed by the risen Christ.[190] His claim is akin to the king's at the end of
Passus XXI. The king could boldly receive Communion because he is con-

vinced he never borrows but only takes whatever he wants and that such tyrannical dominion is legitimate, indeed, is justice (XXI.465–76).

It is helpful to recollect Aquinas's explanation of Christian teaching invoked by Nede, including the doctrine of temperance. Aquinas explains why everything became common in states of urgent need during his study of justice in the *Summa Theologiae*. Obligations to the poor and needy are a matter of natural law ("ex naturali jure").[191] Instead of "no lawe" (XXII.10), instead of setting temperance over the other virtues (XXII.23–34), Aquinas would encourage Wille to reflect on Nede's proposals in the light of justice and the particularities of his situation. This is what Reason and Conscience did with such delicacy and force in Passus V. As for the virtue temperance: Aquinas makes it very clear that temperance is *not* a virtue exclusively, or even primarily, concerned with the destitute. It is a virtue ordering our concupiscent appetites, our natural desires for the great pleasures of sex, food, and drink, with right reason. Temperance especially orders our sensual, tactile pleasures toward our true flourishing, but it also concerns all the needs we have in living a good life as embodied beings. In fact, Aquinas includes a substantial study of sexuality, virginity, and marriage in his account of temperance.[192] Turning back to the brief description of the infused virtue of temperance in Passus XXI, we find that it was given as a means of ordering our "kynde" in our relations to goods, wealth, language, clothing, and provocations from other people (XXI.281–88). There is no suggestion that this virtue flourishes only, or even especially, among the mendicant poor.[193]

The comparison with Aquinas helps one grasp the peculiarities in Nede's version of Temperance. Langland is showing us a transformation of another cardinal virtue as it is unhinged from the contexts established by Grace and Piers: the making of a Christian community of mutual love with resources flowing from the person and work of Christ (XXI.289, 319–34). We should also recall Aquinas explaining how without the presence of prudence (the cardinal virtue perfecting reason) we will simply lack temperance (*ST* II-II.141.1, ad 2). Furthermore, he explains that in any ranking of the cardinal virtues, temperance is below prudence and justice and fortitude. This is because prudence perfects reason, whereas the other cardinal virtues perfect the appetite powers (insofar as these participate in reason). Justice is in the *will* (the rational appetite) and so approaches nearer reason than temperance and fortitude, which are, respectively, in the concupiscible and irascible part of the soul (*ST* I-II.61.1, resp.).[194] Nede's version of Temperance is an utterly diminished travesty of the virtue we find in Aristotle's *Nichomachean Ethics*, Aquinas, book II of Spenser's *Faerie Queene*, and Milton's *Masque Presented at Ludlow Castle* (or *Comus*). Such diminishment contributes to Langland's explorations of the possibility that the modern church might have become a polity unable to provide contexts in which the gifts of Grace in the cardinal virtues are intelligible to Christians. Paradiastolic speech is a particularly overt symptom of this, but, as Nede illustrates, the discursive consequences also have subtler manifestations.[195]

After Nede's rebukes, Wille falls asleep to receive the work's final vision (XXII.51–386). Immediately he sees Antichrist attacking the field so recently cultivated by Piers with the gifts and guidance of the Holy Spirit. In human form, Antichrist uproots their plants and cultivates human needs (XXII.52–57). This profound image encourages us to think of the malleability of needs and the way that in the culture represented by Mede (II–IV) they can tend to infinity. Aquinas describes this with great lucidity in his account of market relations, trade, and the pursuit of accumulating profit. Immersion in a culture driven to pursue exchange not to provide the necessities of life for the community but for financial gain ("propter lucrum") will make its subjects develop a boundless desire for wealth which tends to the infinite ("quae terminum nescit, sed in infinitum tendit" [*ST* II-II.77.4, resp.]). In multiplying our so-called *nedes* (XXII.55), Antichrist teaches us to forget the word *enough*. This is the modern form of what is called "the world" by the "pris neet [prize ox] of Peres plouh, passynge alle othere" (XXI.262–66), the evangelist John. For example, he ascribes to Christ the following language: "If the world [*mundus*] hate you, know ye that it hath hated me before you" (John 15:18); "I am not of the world" (*non sum de hoc mundo*) (John 8:23); "I pray not for the world" (*non pro mundo rogo*) (John 17:9).[196] And in what were read as his epistles he wrote against the love of "the world" (1 John 2:15). Yet in the Prologue to *Piers Plowman* we were told that the poet's vision is "Of alle manere men, the mene [poor] and the riche, / Worchyng [working] and wandryng as this world ascuth [asks us]" (Prol. 20–21). In John's context this is a troubling observation, but it will take the whole poem to unfold it in light of the divine vision of love. "*Deus caritas*" (God is love), observes Holy Church in the next passus (I.82), quoting John, who also wrote, "For God so loved the world as to give his only begotten son" (*sic enim Deus dilexit mundum, ut filium suum unigenitum daret*) (John 3:16). While he affirms this, John commented on Antichrist as one "who denieth that Jesus is the Christ" and "denieth the Father and the Son," one who "dissolveth Jesus" (*qui solvit Iesum*) (1 John 2:22, 4:3). Such certainly is Antichrist's aim in *Piers Plowman*.[197] In the face of the "world" and Antichrist, one might expect Christians to deploy the resources poured into the church by Christ and the Holy Spirit with Piers as Grace's "plouhman my procuratour [agent] and my reue" (XXI.256). One certainly wonders what might be the outcome of Conscience's erring attempt to turn the church into a fortress, how "inside" and "outside" might have to be reconfigured against that model. But whatever Langland does with these issues, one might expect some staging of an allegorical battle.[198]

Under the sign of Antichrist and the contemporary world, Langland pours forth visions of rampant individualism, desperate hedonism, panic, and the complete abandonment of Christian narratives so recently and so powerfully dramatized (XVIII–XXI). The risen Christ spoke some words that were traditionally taken to promise the church's indefectibility: "behold I am with you all days, even to the consummation of the world" (*ecce vobiscum sum omnibus diebus usque ad consummationem saeculi*) (Matt. 28:20). How does Langland envisage the life of this promise under Antichrist's attack?

In one perspective, the whole poem has been an exploration of this question, from the Prologue on. But now the inquiry is taken up in circumstances that seem distinctly unpropitious. As Antichrist's forces attempt to uproot "the crop of treuthe" (XXII.53–55), we are forced to reconsider a crucial part of the model of the church as a fortress designed by Kynde Wit and Conscience. It turns out that the language of "within" and "without," of defended castle and external threat, is misleading. What had been imagined as "within" is now shown to be also and simultaneously "without" (XXII.58–73). Langland names certain groups of Antichrist's energetic followers: friars, monks, a hedonistic lord, and a king (XXII.58–73). But this is only the beginning of Langland's final representations of the church under the actions of "a fals fende Auntecrist" (XXII.64). So it would be premature to determine the relations between this vision and the earlier commentaries on the contemporary church by Reason (V.140–79) and by Liberum Arbitrium (XVI–XVII). Premature to determine the scope and force of Christ's promise of the church's indefectibility. For Passus XXII evolves in a series of attacks in which the constitution of Antichrist's army is gradually unfolded by the seven capital sins. Now they are no longer distracted by being drawn toward repentance as in Passus VI–VII. But despite their apparent triumph over "all folke" formed in the modern church (XXII.64), they meet with some opposition. This is once again led by Conscience. Piers and the Holy Spirit who had been so present in the making of the apostolic church in Passus XXI continue to be absent. Nor is there any talk of a legitimate vicar to stand for Piers in the contemporary church.[199] On this sequence I now want to concentrate.

Langland sets it in postplague England where "fewe" seemed to survive the Black Death and its return in 1361 (XXII.110: well over 40 percent of the people died during the plague of 1349).[200] Conscience had expected such terror to induce conversion, but this is another of his errors and one I shall address below (section XI). For the moment suffice it to note that the response to the massive rates of mortality from the plague is not conversion but a desperately hedonistic turn to the goods of fortune. This recapitulates on a collective scale the earlier story of Wille's own renunciation of moral questions in despair and his own collapse into hedonism, ravished by Fortune "into the lond of longyng and loue" (XI.164–85; XXII.110–20, 143–55). As he moves to the collective scale, Langland is drawing traditional accounts of sin toward the figuration of a society experiencing de-Christianization. And if medieval society was a Christian society, the one so powerfully described in Duffy's account of what he calls "traditional religion" in *The Stripping of the Altars*, de-Christianization of society will be *within* the church, even if it is a fortress church. If so, some reconfigurations of church and world will belong to such a process. In dramatizing ruminations in this domain, Langland makes a significant move as he considers the part of Antichrist's forces led by Covetyse (XXII.121–42).[201]

In the earlier sequence of the seven mortal sins, Langland had paid great attention to Covetyse as he explored the pervasiveness of commercial practices that were considered vicious in traditional Christian ethics (VI.196–307). Although Covetyse found the language of restitution unintelligible (VI.234–38), he was led by Repentance at least to identify his involvement in usury as sin (VI.239–307). But in Antichrist's army there is no glimmer of sin and no will to repent. On the contrary, there is a total commitment to overwhelm "Conscience and cardinal vertues," to deploy all the guile and deceit of the market, all the tricks of language, "glosynges and gabbynges," all that was traditionally known as avarice, greed, and simony. So it is especially striking that Langland locates the hierarchy of the contemporary church in this very part of the army assaulting "al the crop of treuthe" (XXII.53–57). "Simony" is the name for the commodification of spiritual gifts, for the establishment of a financial market in the offices and powers of the church. Widely attacked and much lamented in medieval culture, it represents the union of the contemporary "world" with the church, the church with the "world."[202] Here, woven into this union, legitimizing this union, Langland places the pope and the prelates of the modern church. The pope joins with Simony to make prelates and to make them "holde with Auntecrist" (XXII.127–28).

Why does Langland present this extraordinarily provocative alliance of the pope, the alleged successor of Peter, the modern Piers, with Antichrist? Langland's answer is specific. Pope and prelates nowadays belong to networks in which covetousness and simony are so normalized that any challenge to them is construed as an attack on the very identity of the church. Nor were such construals by the hierarchy and its defenders mistaken. For the church was inextricably bound up with these networks and the interests they form. That is, at least, the direction in which Langland's judgment was confirmed by the hierarchy's own insistence that challengers to its "temperaltees" (XXII.128), its temporal possessions and the political force that went with these, were heretics. The defense of ecclesial temporalities was thus unequivocally assumed by the current guardians of the church's identity to be a core component of the faith. Such assumptions were evident in the earliest papal attacks on Wyclif's teaching (1377), before he had formulated eucharistic heresies, as well as in the later Blackfriars Council (1382). One of the propositions condemned as *heretical* at Blackfriars was the argument that "it is contrary to holy scripture that ecclesiastical ministers may not have temporal possessions."[203] So there can be no doubt that both the papacy and the leaders of the English church in Langland's time were adamant that defending the material foundations of the church as a major landholder and political power was essential to the defense of Christian faith and the church of Christ. It is this identification of faith, church, and the maintenance of temporal power in the contemporary social formation that Langland sees as a mark of Antichrist.

The heavenly figure who discloses herself as Holy Churche (I.72) had complained that Mede is as familiar in "the popes palays" as she herself (II.4–24). Many strands in the poem's early passus confirm this judgment as they display the church's permeation by the forces of the market, from the commodification of sacraments and Christ's pardon to the interpretation of scripture and clerical education.[204] These highly critical strands certainly belonged to a reformist agenda that was a distinct and permanent part of orthodox ecclesial traditions, as I observed in the preface to this book. But in identifying the contemporary church's commitment to "temperaltees" with Antichrist and in identifying the contemporary papacy and prelates with Antichrist, Langland goes *beyond* the boundaries of orthodox reformism.[205] The removal of material and temporal power from the church, together with its legitimizing theology, would have transformed the late medieval church, its hierarchy, its priesthood, and clerical relations with the laity, including those such as Hawisia Mone, Walter Brut, and the priest William White (burned to death in 1428).[206] Such a transformation would have entailed what James Simpson calls "cultural revolution." But in no way would such a reformation beyond orthodox reformation have required distinctively Lutheran inflections of the theology of justification.[207]

Perhaps, however, any such move beyond reformism must have depended on a Wycliffite ideology and merged with it. Fine scholarship by Pamela Gradon and Anne Hudson has given us some of the most nuanced and learned accounts we have of this difficult question insofar as it concerns Langland.[208] Certainly Langland has both Reason and Liberum Arbitrium develop extensive critiques of the modern church earlier in the poem. These include moments that by the late 1370s and 1380s would smack of Wycliffite ideology (XVI.242–85; XVII.51–64, 73–124, 204–38). In preaching "tofore al the reume [realm]" (V.114), Reason turns to religious orders. He combines traditional satire on their luxurious material life and their aristocratic haughtiness with the threat of expropriation by "the kyng and his consayl" (V.143–72a). Later Liberum Arbitrium recalls the donation of Constantine touched on in the preface in discussing the term *Constantinian Christianity*:

> Whan Constantyn of his cortesye holy kirke dowede
> With londes and ledes, lordschipes and rentes,

An angel men herde an hye at Rome crye,
"*Dos ecclesie* this day hath ydronke venym
And tho that haen Petres power aren apoysened alle."
(XVII.220–24)

———

[When Constantine out of his courtesy endowed Holy Church
With lands and peoples, lordships and incomes,
Men heard on high an angel cry at Rome:
"*Dos ecclesie* has this day drunk venom
And poisoned are all who have Peter's power."]

In the preface I commented on Langland's understanding of Constantinianism and its subordination of church to contemporary political power, with Christian teaching becoming the ideological cement of the current social formation. But Liberum Arbitrium does not leave matters with the angel's lament about such poison. He calls for "medecyne" to counteract the "venym" of "possession" in the church. This medicine is to be the disendowment of the church by lay elites:

Taketh here londes, ye lordes, and lat hem lyue by dymes
Yf the kynges coueyte in Cristes pees to lyuene.
For if possession be poysen and inparfit hem make,
The heuedes of holy churche and tho that ben vnder hem,
Hit were charite to deschargen hem for holy churche sake
And purge hem of the olde poysen ar more perel falle.
For were presthode more parfyte, that is, the pope formost
That with moneye maynteyneth men to werre vppon cristene—
Ayen the lore of oure lord as seynt Luk witnesseth,
Michi vindictam, &c.—
His preyeres with his pacience to pees sholde brynge
Alle londes into loue and that in lytel tyme;
The pope with alle prestes *pax vobis* sholde make.
(XVII.227–38)

———

[Take their lands, you lords, and let them live by tithes
If the kings desire to live in Christ's peace.
For if possession is poison and makes them imperfect,

The heads and their subordinates of Holy Church,
It would be charity to relieve them for Holy Church's sake
And purge them of the old poison before the peril grows.
For were the priesthood more perfect, that is, first of all the pope
Who maintains men with money to war upon Christians
Against our Lord's teaching as Saint Luke testifies;
Vengeance belongeth to me,
His prayers with his patience should bring to peace
All lands into love and that in little time;
The pope should make *pax vobis* with all priests.]

In her essay "Langland and the Ideology of Dissent," Pamela Gradon composed an intellectual history offering a meticulous set of cautions to the propensity in commentary on Langland to bring many of his views under the alleged influence of Wyclif.[209] Gradon does some important de-coupling of Langland and Wyclif based in broad knowledge of Christian traditions. But in her analysis of the proposal for disendowment quoted above, she concludes that Langland "echoes" Wyclif's position condemned by the pope in 1377.[210] Given the centrality in Wyclif's ecclesiology of his demand that lay elites use their material powers to disendow the church, this conclusion is plausible. But it is worth recalling that in the 1350s the authorities of Oxford University were complaining about a scholar who "at the devil's own prompting publicly determined in the schools against the possessions of the church, damnably asserting to be lawful for founders of churches to take away goods dedicated to God and the church on account of the abuses of clerics, and to transfer and apply them directly to seculars and knights."[211] Margaret Aston traces such views, certainly beyond reformation acceptable to the church, from the 1350s to the "Lollard disendowment bill," probably proposed in 1410 (49–56). She finds that the mixture of politics (financing the long war with France; heavy taxation; popular opposition to taxation, most powerfully embodied in the great rising of summer 1381) and religion was "not initially altered by Wyclif's contribution" to the arguments about the church's temporalities. She finds that at least one of the heresies and errors condemned at the Blackfriars Council in May 1382 was a very familiar "heresy": "That temporal lords may at will take away temporal goods from habitually offending churchmen" (52). Langland's Liberum Arbitrium was clearly drawing on the same traditions as Wyclif in the same political contexts and offering exactly the same material payoffs to lay elites and king: "Taketh here londes, ye lordes." Yet Liberum Arbitrium strikingly claims that such action will be shaped by the theological virtue of charity, that is, a virtue infused by God and leading the graced person to God, a goal far in excess of our nature.[212]

And it is this understanding of charity as demanding the disendowment of the church by the lay sword which marks a distinctive convergence with Wyclif's theology.[213] But if, as Gradon says, Liberum Arbitrium "echoes" Wyclif in this domain of reformist ideology, can such charity be the same virtue unfolded later with such extraordinary scope from the tree of Charity in Passus XVIII, through the lives of Christ, including his manifestation as the Samaritan, into the great oration on human salvation and divine love in the harrowing of hell (XIX–XX)? One might assume that this must be so, especially given Liberum Arbitrium's authority as "Cristes creature" well known in "Cristes court" (XVI.167–68), the one who guides Wille to the tree of Charity, "Cristes oure fode" (XVIII.14). Yet Liberum Arbitrium had also explained to Wille that "holy churche" must be understood as "Charite." This charity, to which I shall return, is "Lif in loue," making a "loue-knotte of leute and of lele byleue" (love knot of loyalty and true belief) (XVII.125–29). Such a model of charity, Christian faith, and church does not map very congruently onto the Wycliffite one of armed and coercive reformation by an elite of lay Christians against many groups of fellow Christians. After all, Christian ethics, at least for Langland in this most Christocentric of poems, will have to be disciplined by the visions of Christ's practice in the Incarnation and his evangelical precepts. How do we see him in the armed elite, a chivalric knight?

We see him as an extraordinary, corrective parody of such a figure in Passus XIX–XXI. He appears as the Samaritan of Luke 10:25–37 sitting on a mule and riding swiftly to joust in Jerusalem. Langland defers the joust for a dazzling passus in which he narrates the story of the Samaritan rescuing Semyvief, the half-alive figure of humanity assaulted and abandoned in the wilderness. In this narration he incorporates its rich tradition of allegory, exploring central themes of the theology of divine grace, sacraments, church, and human agency.[214] After this the Samaritan teaches Wille about faith in the Trinity, to which Wille has been sharply dismissive, and explains how the only sin against the Holy Spirit, the only sin that will alienate humans from divine love, is "unkyndenesse" (XIX.80–334). On Palm Sunday Wille receives a vision which elaborates the figure of Christ as Charity the Samaritan knight riding barefoot on an ass to joust in Jerusalem. With Faith's help he learns that Jesus will joust to free humanity. But his armaments consist not of the signs of knightly power but only the "armes" of the agriculturalist Piers, "*humana natura*," human nature in its utter vulnerability and fragility (XX.1–25). So Langland moves to the narratives of crucifixion and the triumphant liberation of imprisoned humanity from hell by Christ revealed in his divine life. Appropriately enough, it is in hell that we encounter the technologies of the contemporary elites' forms of war, demonic technologies whose final end is figured in the confrontation with the light and voice of Christ (Passus XX). Once more, on Easter Sunday during Mass, Wille has a vision of Christ as crucified conqueror, still in the "armes" of the plowman but now "so blody" and with Christ's own "croes" (XXII.1–14).[215]

These figurations and narratives of Christ together with their theological ethics belong to a composition of Charity which takes us beyond the Constantinian reform of the church produced by Wyclif and Liberum Arbitrium. Invoking the armed lay power to reform the church in an act of coercion and describing this act as the theological virtue of "charity" is gradually placed as quite inadequate to Langland's theology and its unfolding of the virtues centered on Christ. This critical placing of Liberum Arbitrium's version of reformation finally includes another dimension, a simpler but forceful one. The end of Passus XXI and much of Passus XXII display the lay elites (lords, king, knights) as part of the church's troubles rather than a medium for the kind of reformation for which Liberum Arbitrium would hope. So it will turn out, as we follow Langland's explorations, that the distinctly Wycliffite moment of reform in Passus XVII will be superseded. It belongs to the dialectical processes that constitute *Piers Plowman* and has to be interpreted as such. And perhaps I should venture a comment on this characteristic dialectic, one which introduces, explores, and situates Wycliffite ideology of disendowment by the armed elite.

In a rather rough nutshell: Langland creates a dialectic which is rooted in a logic of disputation, of restless argument. Multimodal, dramatic, lyrical, and adventurous, it moves by exploring a range of positions and their consequences. This process draws readers into all the moments that constitute it while simultaneously demanding that we do not isolate the particular moment from the wider process. This is a dialectic of minute particular and totality. Contexts are crucial. True enough, in such a long poem often committed to disrupting narratives (until they center on Christ) we are often tempted to extract a moment and *substitute* this for the wider process in which it lives. This is a particularly strong temptation in *Piers Plowman* because some of the moments are dramatized so powerfully, expressed in such vigorous rhetoric, that they may seem to claim a certain autonomy. So, for example, some readers have been tempted to read the pardon of Passus IX (or its earlier version in B VII) in isolation from the long exploration of sin with human and divine agency in the soteriological narratives of Passus XVIII–XXI. Or some have been tempted to take Trajan's self-description as Langland's view on the salvation of non-Christians, isolating it from the carefully corrective elaborations in Passus XVII and Christ's own ecstatic but nuanced oration on salvation in Passus XX, in the harrowing of hell. Or some have been tempted to produce unqualifiedly Franciscan readings of the poem, even construing the author as a Franciscan apologist, by abstracting the work's Franciscan moments from their dialectical contexts.[216] In Langland's distinctive dialectical form, critically explored and superseded moments are not simply abandoned to be forgotten. For they too, in their very supersession, remain constitutive of the total dialectical movement. Langland's characteristic way of foreshadowing and echoing, of juxtaposing and recollecting episodes, has been exquisitely described by Elizabeth Salter.[217] These ways belong to a dialectic in which superseded stages are recognized as such and raised to a higher form which enfolds and illuminates what it supersedes. Does Langland's dialectic have a teleology? Yes, most certainly. It is the divine vision glimpsed in the encounters with Christ and the Holy Spirit, glimpsed too in the tree of Charity and by Abraham (Faith) and Moses (Hope).

While any account of Langland's extraordinarily dynamic, adventurous dialectic will be schematic and itself always in need of supersession, I hope that the "bittere bark" I have offered (XII.145–48) may help us see how the work treats the moment in which Liberum Arbitrium advocates coercive disendowment of the church by powerful lords and lay sovereigns.

Certainly the moment is one of prophetic wrath against the modern church for its immersion in the modern world. And it seems appropriate that such wrath should generate an idea of reform which converges with that increasingly wrathful reformer, John Wyclif. Yet while accepting the account of this convergence in work by Gradon and Scase, I think that even here we need to note some important differences. For Wyclif elaborates an exorbitance of monarchic power with a commitment to the centralization of power and law. The expropriating king is God's vicar; it is he who allegedly bears the image of Christ's divinity while the priest ("sacerdos") bears the image of Christ's humanity.[218] In light of this monarchic ideology, with the king appointing priests, it is hardly surprising that Wyclif should become a hero in the mythology of the magisterial reformation in sixteenth-century England, the morning star ("stella matutina") who anticipated the new enlightenment.[219] Henry VIII's proclamation of himself as supreme head of the church, displacing the pope, his dissolution of religious orders, his appropriation of their extensive material resources, and his making of a monarchic church—all this was foreshadowed in Wyclif's political theology.[220] And perhaps this is how Robert Crowley read *Piers Plowman* as he decided to publish it in the reign of Edward VI. He aligns the work with "John Wicklefe, who also in those dayes translated the holy Bible." He celebrates its prophecy concerning "the suppression of Abbayes," now fulfilled by "the iuste iudgment of god, whoe wyll not suffer abomination to raigne unpunished," and he picks out the passage we have been considering, observing that "possession poysoned the church." Perhaps most significantly he fails to discern Langland's critical display of paradiastolic speech by the lord and king at the end of Passus XXI. If the poem was to be appropriated by the magisterial reformation, Langland's own complex dialectic would have to be ignored. Then one could simply identify the author with the call to lay elites: "Taketh here londes, ye lordes" (XVII.227). And with the "morning star" of the English Reformation.[221]

And yet in the final two passus of the poem Langland presents a vision of contemporary Christianity which supersedes Liberum Arbitrium's medicine for curing the church from Constantinian poison.[222] What Gordon Leff wrote about Wyclif's plan for "the spiritual regeneration of the church" is congruent with Liberum Arbitrium: "By making its implementation depend upon the lay power he turned an indefinite aspiration into an immediate programme: in place of the prophetic expectations of the Franciscan Spirituals and Joachists, which he explicitly rejected, he put political action."[223] But from the close of Passus XXI to the end of Passus XXII, Langland makes it remorselessly clear that the political agents imagined by Liberum Arbitrium, with their paradiastolic version of cardinal virtues and lust for dominion (XXI.459–76), share the same ideological and material commitments as the papacy, prelates, and friars now so unequivocally aligned with Antichrist. In Passus XXII those figuring forth the lay powers continue to fight against Conscience's correct understanding of the virtues (XXII.69–73). They also advocate the corrosive individualism which Chaucer's Arcite sees as normative in courtly life and its forms of competition. Arcite reminds his cousin Palamon that promises of fraternal solidarity simply dissolve in the face of competition:

> And therfore, at the kynges court, my brother,
> Ech man for hymself, ther is noon oother.
> 　　　　　(*Knight's Tale*, *CT* I.1181–82)

Of course, Arcite is a worshipper of pagan gods, especially Mars, but through him Chaucer is certainly ruminating on contemporary court culture and ethics.[224] Langland's lord belongs to the community of Christians, members of the body of Christ, but his assumptions are the same as Arcite's: "vch lyf kepe his owene" (XXII.90–92). Langland also chooses to emphasize that in the king's court, at his council, Conscience is beaten ("knokked") by the forces of covetousness: good faith is expelled and falsity triumphs. Simultaneously in the center of justice, "Westmunstre halle," wit and wisdom are overwhelmed by "many a brihte noble." Covetousness, capital sin, controls the commanding heights of lay power and justice. Inevitably in such a society, the powers of commodification, here represented by Simony, "jogged til a justice and iustede in his ere / And ouertulde al his treuthe with 'Taek this on amendement'" (jogged towards a justice and jousted in his ear / And tilted over his integrity with "Take this to make things right") (XXII.129–35). Skeat's comment on this figure is as memorable as it is perspicuous: "Simony runs a tilt at the justice's ear, and by a crafty whisper of a bribe overturns all his ideas of truth and justice. He accompanies this offer of money with the words—'take this [deed, and at the same time this money] on amendment'; meaning, 'surely you can amend this.'" Skeat also picks out the way "jogged" alludes both to riding at a leisurely pace, to *joust* with the *justice*, and to nudging someone.[225] The specifically ecclesiastical courts, represented by "the Arches," are transformed by the same forces so that the sacrament of marriage, like the sacrament of penance, becomes a commodity. Once this sacrament,

the union of Christ and the church, becomes fully subject to market exchanges, the church makes divorce possible (XXII.136–39). Just as merchants and their confessors can no longer discern usury from licit profit
(XXI.349–50), once divorce is as buyable as marriage discerning licit
from illicit marriage will become a difficult business. This all, of course,
belongs to Langland's extended figuration of the Pentecostal community
becoming the polity in which the forces of Mede threatened to become as
dominant as they were pervasive (Prol.; Passus II–III). But in the earlier
passus there seemed a possibility that Conscience and Reason might insti-
gate a reformation from above, a reformation led by the Crown with Conscience and Reason drawing Christians to conversion initiated in the
sacrament of penance (IV–VI). Later on, as I have discussed, this reformation from above was transformed in Liberum Arbitrium's Constantinian cure of Constantinian poison, a cure which identified the church as
the source of "*omne malum*" (all evil) (XVI.273–85; XVII.125–238).

But toward the work's ending it is made clear that what had been envisaged as agencies of reform in the polity, the elites and the institutions
they deploy, can no longer be considered in this light. Even less can they
be represented as Liberum Arbitrium and Wyclif had done: agencies
of evangelical reformation and cultural revolution in the church. Conscience's cry that he now falls because of imperfect priests and prelates
confirms Liberum Arbitrium's ascription of major responsibility for the
current condition of Christianity in England to the clergy (XXI.228–29;
XVI.231–85). But his call to lords and king as agents of charitable, coercive
reformation has now been decisively superseded. It remains in the work as a
memory of a very plausible delusion, itself the product of top-down fantasies of reformation. Ideologies of magisterial reformation, whether in
Wycliffite or sixteenth-century England's version, are utterly discredited.
Their analogy might be the Leninist vanguard party: a recipe for deceit,
the legitimization of endless violence against unreformed elements, and
the centralization of cultural capital in the revolutionary elite. Conscience
spoke truthfully in Passus IV when he told the reforming king to set aside
a top-down coercive model. In its place he evoked one dependent on "the
comune help" together with the assent of "alle youre lege leders [liege-
men]" (IV.176–78). Out of this model comes the understanding that reformation without conversion in the community will come to no good end.
Hence the turn to the collective sacrament of penance led by Repentaunce

(VI.1–2).[226] Whatever failures emerge from this attempt, we have to remember that it gathers a community praying to Christ and the Virgin Mary for "grace to go to Treuthe," drawn by Hope's horn, "*Deus tu conuersus uiuificabis nos*" (O God, you will turn and bring us to life) sounding words of divine blessing, "*Beati quorum remisse sunt iniquitates et quorum tecta sunt peccata*" (Blessed are they whose iniquities are forgiven, and whose sins are covered), accompanied by the communion of saints singing, "*Homines et iumenta saluabis; quemadmodum multiplicasti misericordiam tuam, deus*" (Men and beasts thou wilt preserve, O Lord: O how hast thou multiplied thy mercy, O God) (VII.151–57).[227] This attempt to achieve a nonviolent reformation is a good outcome to Repentaunce's prayer to Christ for grace to amend our "mysdedes" and for "mercy to vs alle." Repentaunce's beautiful prayer enfolds a version of salvation history: from God's goodness in creation through the fall transformed into "*felix culpa*" (happy fault) through divine love reconciling the world to God in Christ (Incarnation, Crucifixion, harrowing of hell, Resurrection) and joining God to humanity (VII.119–50). This is the disclosure of an ontology of peace in the history of the Son of God and humankind.

XI

In fact, the attempt to impose spiritual and moral reformation by violence is among the strands of medieval Christianity that Langland addresses. This tradition tended to represent itself as mirroring God's ways. For example, early in *Piers Plowman* Langland shows a natural power of the soul, Reason, dressed "ryht as a pope" and preaching to the realm of England. He recalls the great plague of 1348–49, with its successors and a famously destructive tempest of January 1362.[228] Plague and tempest, he asserts, were "for puyre synne." In the storm, trees "were poffed [puffed] to the erthe" as symbols of the Last Judgment. Plague and tempest are presented as encouragement that "we sholde do the bettere" (V.111–22). As Pearsall notes, "The orthodox ecclesiastical view was that such disasters were God's punishment of man's wickedness."[229] The idea was that we will do "bettere" if we are terrorized, and the assumption was that this idea was shared by God. So God is rather like a murderous version of the grammar teacher Studie (XI.120–21). Such thinking undoubtedly represents a prominent strand in some conventional Christian images of God and discipline. But it is far closer to Blake's Urizen or his Nobodaddy than to the Samaritan figuring the Son of God in Passus XIX or to the theology of Christ's oration on divine love and identification with humankind in Passus XX. And what, after all, is Langland's consummating image of what it is to "do the bettere"? It is Christ's ministry as healer and liberator of suffering humanity (XXI.124–39). Even if Reason, dressed up as a pope, forgets this, forgets the life of Christ in his zeal to frighten people into doing "bettere," Langland gives the reader of his complete work no reason to follow such a reason.

Yet its model of reformation, by means of fear and coercion, is a prominent presence in the tradition Langland inherited, as Pearsall states. Indeed, in section III above, I considered some of Langland's reflections on this in his dramatization of the conflicts in Piers's "half-aker" (Passus VIII). The context of that discussion was the limitations of Piers's "olde" plow in the light of Pentecostal politics and his "newe" plow together with the implications of these figurations for the church. What I want to recall from that discussion is the language in which Piers seeks to impose coercive jurisdiction on behalf of governing elites (Statute of Laborers, knight, king, "kynges justices").[230] Reformation has to be imposed on those who resist it, violence directed against them *for charity's sake:* "'Y preye the,' quod Perus tho, '*pur charite*, sire Hunger, / Awreke [avenge] me of this wastors" (VIII.169–70). This model of coercive reformation as charity is akin to the one projected by Liberum Arbitrium (XVII) and the wrathful Wyclif. The poet vividly evokes the charity in the forces Piers has invoked: Hunger "boffatede the Bretoner aboute the chekes / That a lokede lyke a lanterne al his lyf aftur, / And beet hem so bothe he barste ner her gottes" (battered the Breton about the cheeks / So that he looked like a lantern the rest of his life, / And he so beat both of them up he nearly busted their guts) (VIII.173–75). But as we followed this narrative in section III, we saw how Piers repents this mode of reformation, determining that it is incompatible with discipleship of Christ, the revelation and embodiment of Charity (VIII.211–18). Langland has Piers recognize that the will cannot be converted by violence and fear. Instead of a top-down model of coercive reformation, Christian politics should be informed by this perception: "hit are my blody bretherne, for god bouhte [bought] vs alle" (VIII.216). A perception confirmed in Christ's great oration from hell as he himself declares his identity with humankind: "we beth brethrene of o [one] bloed" (XX.417–18). Charity, then, involves the love of enemies (Matt. 5:38–48).

In such a light has Langland illuminated the reformation politics of Liberum Arbitrium and its rhetoric of charity. None of this undermines the force of Liberum Arbitrium's critique of the contemporary practices he addresses, or of his objection to the pope for maintaining "werre [war] vppon cristene" (XVII.233–35). The problem is the failure to grasp the forms and consequences of violence in his own model of reformation. They too, as history would disclose, entail "werre vppon cristene," and war in the name of charity.

The next moment in which Langland explores this cluster of theological and political issues is in the poem's final passus. It involves another example of an erring conscience. Once more we see an authoritative figure confronting apparently vicious practices among Christians. The figure is Conscience, "goddes clerk and his notarie," an act, in Langland's view, of Liberum Arbitrium (XVI.192–94; see 165–201). What he confronts is the turning of "alle folke" to "Auntecrist" (XXII.51–73), that is, a massive de-Christianization within the overtly Christian community. Conscience responds by calling the tiny remnant of those who defied Antichrist and his army. These are known as "foles" (1 Cor. 1:22–29), and Conscience invites them to join him in fortress Unity. At the same time, he invokes "Kynde" to defend the "foles" from Antichrist, for love of Piers the Plowman (XXII.74–79). There may be confusion in Conscience's invocation commensurate with the complex ambiguities in the word *kynde*. When Wit talked to Wille in Passus X, he took "Kynde" to designate the "Creatour" of all, one who loves every human soul "ylyke to hymsulve" (X.128–82). Elsewhere *kynde* often means what in modern English would be termed "natural," expressing a distinction from "supernatural" fundamental in St. Thomas's *Summa Theologiae*.[231] It was in this sense that we encountered Kynde Wit in section VII. There I discussed how Kynde Wit teaches Conscience to transform the open evangelical church of the Holy Spirit into a putatively defensible fortress (XXI.360–63). In this sense of *kynde*, it becomes easy to occlude the Christological dimensions gradually woven by Langland into the word as he discloses the transformation of humankind enabled by the kindness of divine love in the incarnation of Christ (XIX.48–336; XX.270a–475).[232]

Who or what Conscience intends to invoke by calling on "kynde" is not made clear in his brief statement. But the contexts should at least make us surprised that his invocation is unformed by the concentration on Charity, Christ, Trinity, and Holy Spirit from Passus XVIII–XXI. Is his attempt to defend the remnant of Christ's disciples being affected by the forces of de-Christianization he opposes? Is the culture of de-Christianization overwhelming his judgment? After all, in the earlier figurations of Conscience, Langland has him talking as a Nicene Christian on the Trinity and on the incarnation of God (III.344–62, 394–406a). More recently Conscience explained the relations between Christ and Piers and followed this with an extended account of the life and name of Christ (XXI.2–197), recognized the Holy Spirit at Pentecost (as Wille could not), and became constable of the church (XXI.198–212; XXII.214). In these contexts, and now with apparent catastrophe overwhelming Christian communities, it is striking that Conscience fails to pray to Christ whose work he had expounded so recently. While noticing what Conscience fails to do here is part of understanding his journey into error, we are not given enough to be confident about the dispositions ascribed to him at this point.

Nevertheless, by their fruits shall you know them, so let us consider the response to Conscience's invocation of Kynde. The "kynde" that hears and identifies with Conscience comes out of the planets bringing fevers, heart diseases, boils, tumors, madness, and other "foule eveles," including poxes and plague, which bring immediate death to many people (XXII.80–87, 97–105). This is the Saturn of Chaucer's *Knight's Tale* rather than the benevolent Nature of his *Parliament of Fowls*. Saturn was the planetary god responsible for resolving conflicts over sexual passions and the lust for dominion on earth and in the heavens. In Chaucer's tale, he celebrates his might in a poetry of grim power:

> "My cours, that hath so wyde for to turne,
> Hath moore power than woot any man.
> Myn is the drenchyng in the see so wan;
> Myn is the prison in the derke cote;
> Myn is the stranglyng and hangyng by the throte,
> The murmure and the cherles rebellyng,
> The groynynge, and the pryvee empoysonyng;
> I do vengeance and pleyn correccioun,

Whil I dwelle in the signe of the leoun.
Myn is the ruyne of the hye halles,
The fallynge of the toures and of the walles
Upon the mynour or the carpenter.
I slow Sampsoun, shakynge the piler;
And myne be the maladyes colde,
The derke tresons, and the castes olde;
My lookyng is the fader of pestilence."
   (*Knight's Tale*, *CT* I.2454–69; trans. 85)

———

["My heavenly orbit marks so wide a pattern
It has more power than anyone can know;
In the wan sea I drown and overthrow,
Mine is the prisoner in the darkling pit,
Mine are both neck and noose that strangles it,
Mine the rebellion of the serfs astir,
The murmurings, the privy poisoner;
And I do vengeance, I send punishment,
And when I am in *Leo* it is sent.
Mine is the ruin of the lofty hall,
The falling down of tower and of wall
On carpenter and mason, I their killer.
'Twas I slew Samson when he shook the pillar;
Mine are the maladies that kill with cold,
The dark deceits, the stratagems of old;
A look from me will father pestilence."]

Chaucer clashes this vision against the Neoplatonizing political theology of the Athenian ruler, Theseus. He does so as part of a profound exploration of political theologies and the emergence of theodicies much earlier than is habitually assumed in works of historical theology.[233] But what is Langland doing with his own display of Saturnine "kynde" descending from the planets?

He is reflecting on Conscience's tendencies to err and their potential consequences. The tricky relations between Conscience's invocation of Kynde and the horrible suffering this seems to unleash may be illuminated by Conscience's final observations in the poem. Responding to the consequences of another error he had made, Conscience begs Kynde to avenge him against those who argue against him (XXII.384). Conscience is again frustrated and angry, passion catalyzed by opposition from Christians within fortress Unity. Piers himself, in the labor disputes discussed above, had similarly expressed a wish to be avenged on those who resisted his juris-diction (VIII.169–70). He had summoned Hunger as a punitive and disci-plinary agent: Conscience summons an even more ferocious force. Like Piers he assumes that people can be terrorized into virtuous reformation.[234] But as in Passus VIII, Langland displays the distressing mistake in this con-ventional assumption. The outcome he depicts is not repentance and virtue but panic and rampant individualism. Conscience wonders whether those attacked by diseases, age, and death will be compelled to convert "and be parfyt cristene" (XXII.88–108). So he asks Kynde to halt his assault. This too recapitulates Piers's plea to the punitive force he had called. But there is now a crucial difference. Piers's plea was accompanied by pro-found, Christological reflections: those who oppose him are recognized as his brethren in Christ's blood, "for god bouhte vs alle" (VIII.213–18). There can be no separation of Christian ethics from the theology of re-demption through Christ's reconciling work. Conscience, however, offers no such reflections.

But once Kynde's attack ceases, Langland gives his own response to Conscience's musings about the relations between terror and conversion to "parfyt cristene." The people turn from panic to a committed hedonism (XXII.110–20, 143–60, 169–82). To them "holinesse" is now just a joke, "a jape" (XXII.145). This recapitulates in a collective mode Wille's earlier path from a despairing abandonment of his search for the virtues to a des-perate hedonism in "the lond of longyng" (XI.160–98; Luke 15:13). Once again Langland demonstrates his conviction that the will cannot be converted by force. Conscience still does not recognize this reality. Instead he again invokes terror to convert the de-Christianizing people, summon-ing Elde and Death (XXII.165–98). Yet once more Langland shows the responses generated by the "fere" alone:

> And Lyf fley for fere to Fisyk aftur helpe
> And bisouhte hym of socour and of his salue hadde
> And gaef hym goelde goed woen that gladde here hertes

And they gyuen hym agayne a glasene houe.
Lyf leuede that lechecraft lette sholde Elde
And dryue awey Deth with dyaes and drogges.

(XXII.169–74)

———

[And Life fled out of fear to Physic for help
And asked him for relief, and had some of his remedy
And gave him a good deal of gold, which gladdened his heart,
And was given in return a cure made of first class quackery.
Life believed medicine would delay Old Age
And drive away Death with prescriptions and drugs.]

People respond to such fear with the habits they already have. Instead of Christ and his sacramental legacy, they seek physicians whose salvation belongs to the market economy. These experts foster the fantasy that their "salve," their medicines, can set aside old age and death. Yet Christ as Samaritan had offered a very different model of healing when he rescued Semyvief, the half-alive man found in "a wide wildernesse where theues hadde ybounde" him (XIX.53–58). There Christ had eased the victim's wounds with wine, oil, and bandages and carried him to the church of the new covenant where he left resources for "his medicyne." The Samaritan explains that the wounds of Semyvief, the figure representing humanity, can only be healed by Christ's blood in the sacraments received in faith (XIX.48–95).[235] But while this central episode is recalled in the poet's narrative, it is simply forgotten by all the participants in Passus XXII, forgotten not only by a de-Christianizing people but also by Conscience, the constable of the contemporary church. For unlike Piers, Conscience seems still drawn to the most conventional ideas of control and reformation, ideas he seems unable to subject to Christological correction. Piers remembered, and this memory gave him distance from the immediate conflict with the laborers' subversion of his intentions. The plowman's memory was informed by the life of Christ, and this presence turned him from righteous indignation to identification with the laborers in Christ: conversion.

Had Conscience remembered as Piers had done, he too might have repented of his own wrath. Perhaps he might have recollected a passage from Ockham's *Breviloquium*. There Ockham writes of Christ:

When his disciples James and John wished to punish with death the contempt the Samaritans had shown to Christ by refusing to receive them, he rebuked them: "Do you not know of what spirit you are? The Son of Man did not come to destroy lives, but to save" (Luke 9:55). This is as if to say, "Though this contempt deserves death yet I will not inflict it; for I have not come, as passible and mortal man, to take away bodily life for any contempt or crime, but to give life." Hence also he visibly revived three dead persons, but did not punish any criminal with death or loss of limb.[236]

Jesus's disciples had not suggested summoning diseases and plagues from the planets, but they had offered something very similar: "Lord, wilt thou that we command fire to come down from heaven and consume them?" (Luke 9:54). So Conscience is reiterating the kind of ethos unequivocally rejected by Christ. He is also rehearsing the conventional view proclaimed by his close ally Reason in Passus V, one I considered earlier, namely, that a good prologue to a "sarmon" on reformation is to claim that the suffering caused by plague and tempest are simply punishment "fore pure synne" and a wonderful inspiration for individual and collective conversion (V.114–200). Some of the consequences of this version of seeking "Seynt Treuthe in sauacioun of youre soules" include advocacy of such violence as beating recalcitrant wives and beating those who resist so that they "be parfyt cristene" (XXII.108). This may be one of the violent outcomes of Reason and Conscience reflecting on Christ's gospel, perhaps a familiar enough one in Christian tradition. It was not Ockham's, and it was opposed by Walter Brut, by some of the Norfolk and Suffolk Wycliffites persecuted by the church's authorities in 1428–31, and in the 1395 Wycliffite presentation to Parliament.[237] More important in the present context, the model of reformation assumed here by Conscience and Reason is placed and superseded in Langland's Christocentric work.

Does Wille's own encounter with Elde and the approach of Death contradict the foregoing argument? Is Wille not finally converted by Elde's attack on his body and the fear of Death (XXII.183–216)? This passage is Langland's account of "the gifts reserved for age," the account ascribed to "some dead master" in T. S. Eliot's *Little Gidding*. There the teacher warns the poet of "the cold friction of expiring sense / Without enchantment" and "the rending pain of re-enactment" disclosing hidden

motives.[238] Langland's writing about Wille's encounter with Elde lacks
Eliot's haunting interiority, but it is far from being a simple exemplum of
conversion by terror. What Pearsall calls "this strange and marvelous interlude" includes a complex mixture of registers very far removed from
terror, even in its unflinching acknowledgment of loss upon loss:

> And of the wo that Y was ynne my wyf hadde reuthe
> And wesched wel witterly that Y were in heuene.
> For the lyme that she loued me fore and leef was to fele
> A nyhtes, nameliche, when we naked were,
> Y ne myhte in none manere maken hit at here wille,
> So Elde and [s]he hit hadde forbete.
>
> (XXII.193–98)[239]

———

> [And my wife took pity on the fix I was in
> And sincerely wished that I was in heaven.
> For the limb she loved me for and enjoyed feeling up
> (Especially at night when we were both naked),
> I could in no way make it do her pleasure,
> So had she and Old Age beaten it down.]

There is no trace here of the conventional obsession with the sinfulness of
marital sexuality enjoyed without the intention of procreation or by a
spouse's demand to pay the debt of sexual union. No trace of anxiety, let
alone guilt, at the prospect of a hostile judgment by a god who allegedly
shared the punitive obsessions of Roman and Protestant churches with the
too ardent lover of her or his spouse. In this tradition, those so described
were castigated as adulterers, a tradition affirmed by Chaucer's Parson. He
declares that if a married couple "assemble oonly for amorous love" they
commit "deedly synne" (*Parson's Tale*, *CT* X.942). He complains that many
married Christians do not believe this, since they think that whatever
"likerousnesse" (lustfulness) spouses enact together is not sin. But this is
"fals": "a man may sleen [slay] hymself with his owene knyf, and make
hymselve dronken of his owene tonne [barrel]" (X.858). In his *Institutes of
the Christian Religion*, Calvin continues this teaching, albeit less graphi-
cally.[240] Langland's writing about zestful marital sexuality and its termina-
tion goes against the grain of such traditions of Christian teaching with

their inability to envisage a union of affection, love, and sexual delight as part of the sacrament of marriage. Langland's writing in the passage is playful, even tender, and it evokes a transformation of dominant teaching and its assumptions. There is acknowledgment of loss but no denigration of what is lost (contrast Chaucer's Reeve, *CT* I.3864–82, 3886–98).

Wille's responses are very different from those around him because he has been on a pilgrimage of continual conversion, cultivating habits to resist the de-Christianization led by Antichrist. True enough, his journey involved wrath, despair, and a fall "into the lond of longyng" under the enchantments of the lust of the flesh (XI.160–85). He is always prepared to argue with anyone, whether Liberum Arbitrium or Abraham or Moses or Christ the Samaritan, and over anything, including orthodox teaching of the Trinity (which he had dismissed) and the names of Jesus.[241] But the process of disputation is as integral to his conversions (plural) as it is to Langland's dialectical work. We can think back to the early and profoundly moving conversion in Passus V. There Wille confesses, and not to any priest, how he has wasted God's gifts of time, but now infused with the theological virtue of hope, he prays for divine grace:

> So hope Y to haue of hym that is almyghty
> A gobet of his grace and bigynne a tyme
> That alle tymes of my tyme to profit shal turne.
>   (V.99–101)
>
> ———
>
> [So I hope to have from him that is almighty
> A mouthful of his grace, and begin a time
> That all times of my time shall turn to profit.]

Immediately after this, he goes to the church to worship God and kneels before the cross in penitential tears praying the "*pater-noster*" (V.102–8). Not only are there other moments of conversion, but his troubled search for the virtues has brought him to visions of charity, Abraham, Moses, Christ, and the Holy Spirit (XVIII–XXI). So when he is encompassed by the forces of de-Christianization and the apostasy of the church's hierarchy, religious orders, and people he has habits and resources which encourage choice against assimilation by such forces—acquired and infused habits. There is no way in which Langland implies that Wille's ability so to choose and the habits with which he chooses are the product of fear.

But does he not fear death? He certainly does (XXII.200). Is this not culpable? No. Human beings naturally fear death and turn from the loss of bodily life. Even Jesus Christ in the garden of Gethsemane shows fear, thus manifesting his full humanity. This is carefully explained by St. Thomas Aquinas in his treatise on Christ in the third part of the *Summa Theologiae*.[242] In his own "drade," Wille does not react with the panic and blankness overwhelming those around him. He calls on Kynde to deliver him from care and asks to be avenged on the forces dismembering his body, if that is Kynde's will (XXII.199–203). Who is this Kynde addressed by Wille, and what relation has he to the malevolent Saturnine forces Conscience summoned from the planets? And how does Wille's request to be avenged relate to Conscience's a few lines earlier and to Piers's in Passus VIII? I will first consider the question about Kynde.

Unlike the version of Kynde emerging from Conscience's invocation, this figure does not bring violence against anyone. He commands Wille to stay in "Vnite" till Kynde sends for him. Wille has expressed a desire for death, as well as fear (XXII.203, 200). But Kynde calls for patience and a further commitment to learning, whatever Wille's age and whatever the proximity of death: "'Lerne to loue,' quod Kynde, 'and leef [leave] all othere [set aside any other 'craft']'" (XXII.208). As for the means of subsistence, Kynde's answer echoes that of Christ's teaching against being "solicitous for your life, what you shall eat, nor for your body, what you shall put on" (Matt. 6:25; see 6:24–34). He tells Wille, "And thow loue lelly, lacke shal the neuere / Wede ne worldly mete while thy lif lasteth" (If you love loyally, you'll never lack / Clothes or earthly food as long as you live) (XXII.210–11). Wille accepts this counsel because it belongs to a long process of conversion upon conversion and a longing which included visions of Christ and the Holy Spirit. This process informs his obedience and gives him access to the "carte hihte [called] Cristendoem" which is composed by Grace to bring home "Peres sheues" (XXI.330–31; cf. XXII.212–13). So I am arguing that Wille's long and often erring apprenticeship in the resources of Christian narratives and virtues, an apprenticeship drawn by God's grace disclosed in Christ, has prepared him to invoke Kynde who is "Creatour," "Fader and formour of al that forth groweth, / The which is god grettest, bygynnynge hadde he neure / Lord of lyf and of lyht, of lisse and of payne" (Father and former of all that grows forth, / Who is greatest God, who never had beginning, / Lord of life and of light, of bliss and of pain) (X.152–55). Such was the answer Wille had received from Wit when he asked what "kynne thyng is Kynde?" (X.151). His will has been formed in the process that is the poem drawing him to his encounter with the persons of the Trinity: Christ, Holy Spirit, Father.

This brings me to the second question, which concerns the language of vengeance in Wille's invocation. It is significantly different from that of Conscience or the early Piers. For Wille does not seek vengeance against any other human being seen as an impediment to his projects of reform. He, tentatively, requests vengeance against the forces under which his body is disintegrating. Nor does Kynde simply reject the language: instead he tells Wille that if he wants such vengeance he is to go into "Vnite" and learn to love while he awaits Kynde's call (XXII.204–8). Furthermore, through a glass darkly, in an enigma, Wille's prayer for this vengeance, together with Kynde's response, hints at the resurrection of the body and its glorified reunion with the soul.[243]

XII

It seems worth offering some brief comments on the available paths Langland did not take in his sense of an ending. Talk of harvest in the context of Antichrist would have drawn many late medieval writers to concretize their narratives with some specific predictions about historical stages and persons. These could certainly involve convictions about imminent reformation. Such tendencies had been initiated and encouraged by Joachite treatments of the Apocalypse, with their rejection of Augustinian exegesis and their understanding of the millennium. Chapter 20 of the Apocalypse envisions the devil being bound for a thousand years during which the saints reign with Christ; after this Satan is loosed out of his prison for "a little time" (20:1–7). He seduces the nations, persecutes the camp of the saints and the beloved city: "And there came down fire from God out of heaven, and devoured" the nations whereupon the devil is cast into the pool of fire and brimstone (20:8–9). In the *City of God*, Augustine had explicitly opposed readings of this chapter by those he calls "Chiliasts" (in Greek) and "Millenarians" (in Latin, *miliarios*).[244] Despite some exegetical complexity and alternative interpretations, Augustine unequivocally determines that the thousand-year reign of the saints with Christ refers to the historical period initiated by Christ's redeeming work in the Incarnation, the work of binding the strong man (Matt. 12:29). This is the historical form of his kingdom or the kingdom of heaven ("regnum eius regnumve caelorum"), the church militant (*City of God* XX.7, 9). It includes the souls of the pious dead who are remembered at the sacrament of the altar and are not separated from the body of Christ, the church (XX.9). The brief release of Satan after the thousand years will be the last persecution immediately before the final Judgment. Inflicted by Antichrist, it will last for three years and six months (*City of God* XX.11, 13; Apoc. 12:6, 13:5; Dan. 12:7). This attack does not impede the reign of the saints with Christ (XX.13). Augustine's "Millenarians" included those who thought they could calculate the date of the imminent millennium, but Augustine dismissed such exegesis as ridiculous fables ("ridiculas fabulas," XX.7).[245]

Joachite exegesis and theology of history set aside Augustine's account of the thousand years and opened it out into a wide range of prophetic and millenarian visions looking toward the third *status*, that of the Holy Spirit.[246] Let us briefly recall some typical outcomes of this late medieval tradition, the path Langland did not take. Joachim himself had used his complex concordances and typologies to give him confidence about the unfolding of divine providence in sometimes striking detail. He declared that the emperor Henry IV was an Antichrist, the Saracens the sixth head of the red dragon of the Apocalypse, and the great Antichrist the seventh head who would emerge from a sect of heretics.[247] Characteristic Joachite modes are cultivated by the French Franciscan Jean de Roquetaillade (Johannes de Rupescissa).[248] His writings are inspired by what Marjorie Reeves nicely describes as "his own role as the interpreter of the cosmic future" in a divine gift to "uncover those secret things hidden" in the prophecies of scripture. He was convinced that "after great tribulations and several Antichrists the world would reach the Age of Blessedness, the apotheosis of history." Although Reeves finds that he does use "Joachim's concept of the third *status*" for this age, he "more often speaks in terms of the millennium," a literal thousand years of peace.[249]

Characteristic of such schemes is a "political programme of Last Things," and once again it is the mode, and its contrasts to Langland's dialetical thinking and sense of an ending, that interests me.[250]

In Roquetaillade's vision, one finds a concretization of persons and stages in world history as it enters its millennial stage. For example, Antichrist was born in 1337, is now rising (1349–66), and will reign from 1366 to 1370. His destruction in 1370 will bring in the millennium, which will last until the arrival of Gog in 2370. The root of contemporary evil is in Frederic II, a poisonous heretic from whom would come Louis of Sicily, the future *Antichristus magnus*. The emperor who had protected William of Ockham, Louis of Bavaria, had prefigured Louis of Sicily as *Antichrisus mysticus*. The Jews will worship the great Antichrist Louis of Sicily. But Roquetaillade's nation, France, will oppose Antichrist (a nice contrast with Langland's few "foles" to whom I shall return). In fact, the French are the great opponents of Antichrist, and in France the true pope will be protected. In the final battle the king of France, true pope, and rigorous Franciscans will triumph. The Holy Spirit will abound, "Antichrist will be destroyed and the whole world will submit in peace to the Vicar of Christ." In different works there are different details, so in the *Liber Secretorum eventuum* the English and Antichrist fight against the French. In this work Christ himself would strike down Antichrist around 1370, although the millennium would not begin until 1415. While in the slightly later *Vade mecum in tribulatione* the Western Antichrist would appear between 1362 and 1370, a new Nero, and the third *status* of the world would begin with the angelic pope and the king of France as Roman emperor who would destroy the tyrannical power of Mohammed. Reeves is right to describe Roquetaillade's prophecies as "Francophile," just as across the channel the makings of God into an Englishman were under way.[251] But neither in mode nor in ideology was this Langland's way. Nor his sense of endings.

There is, however, an earlier moment in *Piers Plowman* where Langland places a medley of such traditions and their rhetoric in an oration by Conscience. In light of the preceding analysis, I want to consider this moment and its relations to the poem's political ideology. It emerges during Conscience's struggles against the manifold forces of Mede which pervade and shape contemporary society. At this early stage of the poem (Passus II–IV), Conscience foreshadows Liberum Arbitrium's assumptions that necessary reformation of the polity will be top-down, depending entirely on

the lay sovereign. With the help of Reason, he intends to persuade the king
to enact the reformation by rejecting Mede rather than by trying to harness
her to Conscience.[252] He tries to show the sovereign that Mede is a dangerous ally who destroys kings. To demonstrate this he takes a story from
scripture. In chapter 15 of the first Book of Kings (also known as the first
Book of Samuel) we meet the account of Saul and the Amelakites. Conscience claims that King Saul spared the Amelakite king (Agag) and the
best livestock and garments "for Mede" (III.410). Because of "that synne,"
Saul and his son died, God bestowing the kingdom on his "knave," the
shepherd David (III.407–42). Conscience reiterates that Saul's motive was
"mede" and that God hated Saul because the king "coveytede" Amelakite
possessions and was "overcome thorw coveytise of mede" (III.417–32). So,
once again, Mede destroys kings. The passus ends with Conscience rightly
objecting to Mede's exegesis of scripture: she misconstrues a passage from
Proverbs to support her own practices (III.484–500). However, this exchange on the politics of exegesis does not leave Conscience unscathed.
For Conscience has just done the same thing with scripture as has Mede,
namely, misconstrued the text to serve his own polemical interests. Scripture makes it clear that the issue between God and Saul is not "mede" or
"coveytise of mede" (1 Kings 15:1–35). It is, rather, obedience to God's
commands. Saul has been told to destroy all Amelakites and their possessions. But while he destroyed all the "common people" and everything
that was "vile and good for nothing," he and his own people spared Agag
and the best possessions. He did *not* do this for "mede." He did so to offer
"a holocaust to the Lord": "the people spared the best of the sheep and the
herds that they might be sacrificed to the Lord" (15:12, 15). God, however, objects that whatever Saul's motives, he "hath not executed my commandments" (5:1). Samuel conveys this word to Saul, who insists that he
has acted according to the "voice of the Lord." Samuel informs him that
God desires not holocausts but "rather that the voice of the Lord should
be obeyed." It is better "to hearken rather than to offer the fat of rams"
(15:15–22). So *that* is the moral of the story. Saul's "sin" is disobedience
to a highly specific command of God, and for that disobedience he is
overthrown (15:22–24). Neither "mede" nor "coveytise" comes between
Saul and God.[253] Obedience to God's revealed will is, of course, a central
topic in Christian teaching. Aquinas devotes articles to it in the *Summa
Theologiae* and twice deploys Conscience's own text in his explication of

obedience.[254] It is relevant to the understanding of faith and is a central virtue in accounts of Christ's redemption of humanity: "He humbled himself, becoming obedient unto death, even to the death of the cross" (Phil. 2:8).[255] But Conscience sets aside the crucial theological directions of the text he misconstrues to fit his immediate struggle with Mede, even as he attacks the latter for doing the same. Treating scripture as if it has a wax nose is thus among the errors of Conscience, and it is from here he shifts into a mode which is millenarian, once more drawing on some fragments of scripture (III.437–83).

And once more we need to recall the preceding contexts. Conscience has been trying to reform a polity pervaded by Mede in which traditional virtues and distinctions are dissolved while even the sacrament of penance is commodified. In his attempt to persuade the king to impose the reformation he demands, Conscience appropriated the story of Saul and Agag. Now it emerges that the violent resolution to this narrative draws him on. The captured Amelakite king, Agag, was hewed "in pieces" by the prophet Samuel (1 Kings 15:33). Conscience picks this out along with the overthrow of Saul, for his "mede," and God's substitution of David. Exultantly Conscience moves from this violent moment to a millennial world in which Mede will have been liquidated. Indeed, any opponents to his reforms will be dealt with just as Agag who was butchered by Samuel. A new David will become world ruler and one Christian king will look after us all ("o cristene kyng kepe vs echone," III.442). Reform over the rule of Mede and over injustice will be secured. Love and Conscience will effect a revolutionary transformation of ecclesiastical, legal, and political forms. Any who resist this millennial peace, when swords are beaten into plowshares, will be executed. Jews will rejoice that Moses or the Messiah has come as the prophecy of Isaiah 2:2–5 is fulfilled. Conscience is confident that there will be a centralization of justice. The parcelization of sovereignty and law typical of most medieval social formations will be ended by some unspecified revolutionary agent: "Al shal be but o court and o buyrne [man] be iustice" (III.473–75). Will this "buyrne" be Samuel, the hewer of Agag into pieces? Perhaps, for Conscience has warned that in this millennium "riht as Agag hadde happe shal somme: / Samuel shal sle hym" (III.439–40). Peace, nonviolence, unchallenged centralization without militarization (swords into plowshares, no more wars, III.461a, 477a). Yet simultaneously Conscience affirms some remarkable continuities with contemporary England. The death penalty will be retained (III.458–62, 467, 477). The medieval church seems to survive in a recognizable form, since Conscience proclaims that priests and parsons will perform the current liturgy properly. No longer will they go hunting or hawking: if they do some anonymous authority will deprive them of their livelihood and perhaps kill them (III.464–68). In culmination to such an uninhibited revel in contradictions, the passage concludes with a portentous riddle promising the conversion of Jews and Saracens to Christianity. This issue is explored at some length by Liberum Arbitrium in Passus XVII, an exploration which takes seriously the need for the Christian church to abandon its commitments to war and return to the model offered by the martyr church, a model discussed earlier in this book. Conscience's riddle simply evades such issues. Scholars who claim to crack the code of the riddle from conventional grammar books and substitute a simple paraphrasable content simply miss the point of such riddling in this poem. The rhetoric is designed to suggest profundities and secrets revealed to the special one who speaks. Shakespeare was to display such rhetoric with characteristic critical force in Owen Glendower and later in Gloucester.[256] Langland's dramatic exploration of such voices is closer to Shakespeare's than to that of Jean of Roquetaillade or Joachim. In the overall processes that constitute his work, the apocalyptic and millennial foray by Conscience could, at the most charitable, be seen in some lines of T. S. Eliot in response to his own examination of apocalyptic rhetoric and modes:

> That was a way of putting it—not very satisfactory:
> A periphrastic study in a worn-out poetical fashion,
> Leaving one still with the intolerable wrestle
> With words and meanings.
> (*East Coker*, pt. 2, in *Four Quartets*)

But because this is one of the passages that has elicited most discussion among those seeking to draw the poet into affinity with Joachite prophecy and millenarianism, I will add a few more observations on it. Because the question concerns the kind of reformist Langland was, it belongs to the present study. As I have made clear in my discussion, placing that in the context of Joachite prophecy, Conscience is made to exhibit a millenarian vision that could have been stimulated by Joachite traditions, although non-Joachite apocalypticism was hardly rare in the later Middle Ages.[257] But this passage belongs to a dialectical process in which it is an exploratory moment, criticized and superseded. Its grounding in wrath at the resistance to his project of reform has been made clear, nicely symptomatized in the identification with Samuel chopping the enemy Agag into pieces. His apocalyptic mode generates the anti-Augustinian version of the millennium as an imminent eschatological peace within history, one governed by the kind of world emperor ("o cristene kyng") whom Jean de Roquetaillade expected to come from his own nation, the French.[258] The promise of such a Christian ruler dissolves the Christocentric liturgical context of Isaiah 2:2–5 (the first week of Advent), as does the retention of the death penalty for those deemed to transgress peace, including priests who go hawking or hunting.[259] The millennial eschatology here is actually shown to have displaced the Word made flesh, crucified and resurrected. It has displaced the work of Christ and the distinctly Christian virtues flowing from that work. However remote Joachim's eschatology may have been from versions cultivated by his admirers such as Gerardo of Borgo San Domino or Jean de Roquetaillade, it compromised, in the words of Henri de Lubac, "la pleine suffisance de Jésus-Christ."[260] It is such tendencies in medieval eschatology that Langland is exploring in Conscience's oration. By ascribing it to Conscience, he associates this millenarianism with a reforming zeal whose longings and frustrations are part of *Piers Plowman*. But as we have already seen, and as St. Thomas so carefully taught, Conscience is not infallible, and here he errs both in his version of the millennium and, especially, in the displacement of Christology I have just identified. This displacement will be beautifully corrected, at length, from Passus XVIII to XXI.

There is just one more observation I want to make about Conscience's millenarian fable. It is derived from that teacher we met misleading him in Passus XXI: Kynde Wit. He declares: "I, Conscience, knowe this, for Kynde Wit me tauhte" (III.437; cf. XXI.360). Kynde Wit has taught him to expect a millennium in which Reason (his colleague in Passus IV and V) will govern the polity (III.437–42). I have already discussed some ecclesial errors into which Kynde Wit will lead Conscience much later. There I focused on the consequences of mistaken trust in a purely natural power when the supernatural ends of humanity are at issue. As Aquinas observes, humans could achieve the good proportionate to their divinely given nature while in their unfallen state, but even then they could not reach the good surpassing that nature. In the fallen state we cannot even achieve the good proportionate to our nature, though we can do such good things as build houses, plant vineyards, and play cricket. So in both unfallen and fallen states, humans need a divine gift to help their natural powers if they are to will, know, and do the supernatural good bringing them to supernatural happiness, an end quite out of proportion to our nature.[261] These basic distinctions in Aquinas and in many strands of Christianity are congruent with Langland's theology, congruence powerfully illustrated in the narrative of Semyuief and the Samaritan who figures Christ (XIX.48–171).[262] And let us also remember Christ's warning that if Kynde Wit is given credence beyond his sphere of competence, he is likely to draw Wille into heresy and should be resisted (XIX.108–232). We, however, are neither locked into Conscience's millenarian moment under the guidance of Kynde Wit nor fixed into the rhetorical mode Conscience embraces in that moment. For we have to read it *as* a moment in a long, dialectical work. This means we must take seriously the disparities between the extraordinarily rich, sustained Christology and Trinitarian theology of Passus XVII–XXI together with the absence of such a focus in Conscience's millenarian passage. This absence, together with the complete absence of the relevant scriptural narratives and liturgy shaping Passus XVIII–XXI, encourages an incoherent political theology and equally incoherent representations of agency. So Langland's approach to Christian eschatology had more in common with Robert Holcot's comments in his widely read lectures on the Book of Wisdom than with Joachite traditions and millenarians.[263] Lecture 58 sets out from Wisdom 5:1: "Then shall the just stand with great constancy against those that have afflicted them, and taken away their labours." Holcot considers those who discuss the coming of Antichrist, Paul's "man of sin" (2 Thess. 2:3). Against modern predictions of eschatological events, Holcot insists that the advent of Christ is of uncertain time. Holcot is familiar with those late medieval anti-Augustinian traditions forecasting the coming millennium, and he observes that around the coming of Antichrist modern prophets have been led astray, seduced.[264] In taking this position, Holcot, like John Wyclif writing soon after him, was accepting the explicit teaching of the risen Christ: "It is not for you to know the times or moments [*tempora vel momenta*], which the Father hath put in his own power" (Acts 1:7).[265] This statement confirmed another, equally clear statement during his ministry: "But of that day and hour no one knoweth; no, not the angels of heaven, but the Father alone" (Matt. 24:36). This was not persuasive to those whose prophetic confidence had been inflated by Joachite exegesis and millenarianism. But, as I noted earlier, this was a familiar enough path that Langland chose not to take with its identification of times, moments, and historical agents. Like Ockham, his suspicion that the hierarchy of the modern church had become assimilated to the forces of Antichrist is independent of Joachism. In his late work *On the Power of Emperors and Popes*, Ockham aligned the pope with Antichrist (chap. 27). But Brian Tierney, in his commentary on Ockham's ecclesiology, rightly remarks that this argument bore "no traces of Joachimite fantasy."[266] No more did Langland's.

XIII

Also like Ockham, Langland has transformed traditional confidence in the indefectibility of the church. He did so to fit the ecclesiology emerging from his corrosive dialectical exploration of the modern church and its contrast with the church of the martyrs. The canonical text in the church's doctrine of indefectibility was the promise of the risen Christ to his disciples: "behold I am with you all days, even to the consummation of the world" (*ecce ego vobiscum sum omnibus diebus, usque ad consummationem saeculi*) (Matt. 28:20). Here I think it helpful to recall some reflections by Ockham. Christ's promise, he argued, offers absolutely no warrant for the hierarchy's claims to authority and its confidence in its own inerrancy. Famously enough, he came to the view that Christ's promise means that some Christian somewhere will always hold the truth disclosed in Christ even if the church's hierarchy (including the pope, of course) and most members of the church were to become heretics and apostates. As he wrote to his fellow Franciscans, now conforming to a pope Ockham judged to be a heretic, in the spring of 1334:

> I would think that the whole Christian faith, and all Christ's promise about the Catholic faith lasting to the end of the age, and the whole Church of God, could be preferred in a few, indeed in one; and I would judge that all other Christians erred against the Catholic faith, on the

example of the prophet Elias, who, though he believed that he was
God's only worshipper left [3 Kings 19:10], nevertheless did not at all
desert the true faith: though I do not doubt that in fact many "thousands
of men" and women "have by no means bent the knee" of their faith before Baal [19:18].[267]

Later, in the unfinished part 3 of his massive *Dialogue*, he returns to this
question. The dialogue's "master" quotes Christ's promise, "I am with you
all days, until the end of the world [Matt. 28:20]," and comments thus:

> Because of this it is not at all to be feared that because of the wickedness
> of one head there will ever be a general corruption or infection of all
> Christians, because such a corruption of Christians would conflict with
> the promise of Christ; but an almost general corruption of Christians
> would in no way conflict with that promise. Christ's promise would
> stand if, under one perverted or infected head of all Christians, all were
> infected except two or three.[268]

And in the next book of the same part, he writes:

> The law of eternal salvation given by Christ would not be in vain even if
> the great part of the faithful—indeed all except a very few, or except
> one—erred, not damnably but detestably, about it, even about an under-
> standing necessary to salvation; nor would the law have been given in
> vain even if all Christians except a few or one erred about it damnably,
> because the whole Christian faith could be perceived in one alone (as
> during the three days [Good Friday to Easter Sunday] the whole faith
> remained in the mother of our Redeemer alone).[269]

Ockham has absolutely no doubt that true faith disclosed by Christ could
survive among a very few dissenters. As Brian Tierney said, "In Ockham's
ecclesiology, the individual dissenter might well constitute the one true
church."[270]

This view comes close to John Milton's theology of dissent and its ecclesiology so beautifully figured through the angel Abdiel in *Paradise Lost*,
through the figure of the poet himself, and through the just individuals
and tiny groups of faithful in the last two books of the poem. Or, also

beautifully figured in his words published in the face of the restoration of
the monarchy and persecuting Church of England at the close of the second (April 1660) edition of *The Ready and Easy Way to Establish a Free
Commonwealth*:

> Thus much I should perhaps have said though I were sure I should have
> spoken only to trees and stones, and had none to cry to, but with the
> prophet, "O earth, earth, earth!" [Jer. 22:29] to tell the very soil itself
> what her perverse inhabitants are deaf to. Nay, though what I have spoke
> should happen (which Thou suffer not, who didst create mankind free,
> nor Thou next, who didst redeem us from being servants of men!) to be
> the last words of our expiring liberty.[271]

Because of the understandable presence of Wyclif in commentaries on
Langland, I should make it quite clear that the ecclesiology of Ockham
and Milton, however different, both centralize versions of evangelical liberty, and both are far removed from Wyclif's in at least one crucial respect
which is also relevant to Langland. Wyclif was sure that the true church
was composed only of the predestined: *ecclesia predestinatorum, congregatio
omnium predestinatorum*. Indeed, nobody could claim to be a member of
the true church, clergy, or laity without being known as predestinate. However, he also agreed with traditional Catholic instruction that nobody
knows whether they are predestinate (or reprobate) without a special revelation. This was hardly a coherent set of ideas on which to ground the kind
of ecclesial polity Wyclif projected.[272] And it as alien to Ockham's account
of the true church as it is to Milton's and Langland's.

Ockham offers a cogent account of why all Christians (women and
men, lay and ordained) have an individual responsibility to examine the
doctrinal claims of the hierarchy, what Catholics now know as their "magisterium," and to evaluate them. After all, Christ's truth may reside, as we
saw, not in the papacy or episcopacy but in a small group of dissenters or in
one layperson, such as Piers, in Passus VII (182–291). Paul's instructions
to test all things ("omnia autem probate" [1 Thess. 5:21]) could, according
to Conscience in his polemics against Mede, be abused (III.489–95).
What couldn't? But in his *Breviloquium* Ockham says that this text applies
to all Christians. It means that when teachers propagate Christian doctrine with the mystical sense of scripture, all Christians must "test, exam-

ine and probe to determine whether it is true or false, heretical or Catholic, or in the middle, neither Catholic nor heretical."[273] Ockham considers the question, "who is to judge whether the pope's assertion is true or false, Catholic or heretical?" The answer is that *any* Christian who knows the truth, whether "with certainty" or "by faith alone" or "by evident argument" or by "certain experience, if it can be known that way."[274] He stresses that "every Christian" must evaluate every papal claim about Christian doctrine. If anyone discovers that the pope errs in his construal of scripture, even in matters of apparently little importance to eternal salvation, then the Christian is obliged to judge the pope and oppose him. Sometimes the pope may make determinations of such complexity that only "experts" can know them to be erroneous or heretical. When this happens, the experts (theologians trained in the universities) must expose the pope's errors and resist his authority. But sometimes papal heresy is "so obvious even to the simple that even the simple should judge that he errs."[275] Even without touching on Ockham's often innovative and moving reflections on the *evangelical liberty* of all Christians, including liberty in the face of the church's hierarchy, it should be clear that his ecclesiology and ideas of hermeneutic authority presented a challenge to contemporary forms of ecclesiastical authority and order that went beyond any reformation within contemporary paradigms of orthodoxy.

The same should be said of Langland's ecclesiology as it emerges through a dialectical criticism sustained through the final stages of his work. He too finally located the indefectibility of Christ's church in a tiny dissident minority. This is the remnant, the group known as "foles." They alone resist the de-Christianizing forces of Antichrist which had *assimilated* the hierarchy of the church, including, explicitly, pope and cardinals together with religious orders and most laypeople from the king and lords to the brewer. Given the collective rejection of Christ's covenant and Holy Communion, participation in the body of Christ, this is perhaps not astonishing (XXI.381–402). One could recall Paul's letter to the Romans: "And Isaias crieth out concerning Israel: If the number of the children of Israel be as the sand of the sea, a remnant [*reliquiae*] shall be saved. . . . And as Isaias foretold: Unless the Lord of Sabaoth had left us a seed, we had been made as Sodom, and we had been like Gomorrha" (Rom. 9:27, 29; see Isa. 10:22, 1:9). Or in Isaiah's words: "For if thy people, O Israel, shall be as the sand of the sea, a remnant of them shall be converted [*reliquiae convertentur ex eo*]" (Isa. 10:22). Langland's "foles" pose the question of the remnant. As Augustine observed while preaching on Psalm 73, "We must try to understand here what the prophets meant when they said that *a remnant shall be saved* [*Reliquiae salvae fient*]."[276] For Augustine the whole of Psalm 73 is the voice of the remnant, while the promise of the psalm looks toward Christ in John 1:7: "the law was given by Moses; grace and truth came by Jesus Christ." However unpalatable to those wanting Langland to remain within the paradigms of orthodox medieval reformation, his remnant stands in the face of the Roman Church with its pope at Rome or Avignon. Let us recall the realities he envisions:

> Freres folewed that fende for he yaf hem copes
> And religious reuerensed hym and rongen here belles
> And al the couent cam to welcome a tyraunt
> And alle hise as wel as hym, saue onelich foles;
>
> . . . .
>
> Symonye hym suede to assaile Consience
> And presed on the pope and prelates thei made
> To holde with Auntecrist, here temperaltees to saue.
> (XXII.58–61, 126–28)

> ———

> [Friars followed that fiend, for he gave them cloaks,
> And religious orders reverenced him and rang their bells
> And all the convent came to welcome a tyrant
> And all his followers with him, with the sole exception of fools;
>
> . . . .
>
> Simony pushed him to assail Conscience
> And pressed on the pope that they make prelates
> Teamed up with Antichrist, to save their temporalities.]

We should not turn Langland's vision away from his continuing attention to the late medieval church: hierarchy and people are aligned with Antichrist. Christ's promise of the indefectibility of his disciples is honored in the remnant, the fools ("foles") who correctly identify the forces they encounter. In these circumstances we should also take seriously the fact that Wille, now one of the fools, has an exchange with the divine teacher of love, Kynde, which takes place without any form of ecclesiastic mediation.

Such too had been his long exchange with Christ the Samaritan, as were Julian of Norwich's contemporary visions and dialogues with Christ. After he has heard Kynde's reiteration of his love command, he answers the call to the "craft" of love before roaming through contrition and confession into Unity (XXII.212–13). Contrition requires no priestly presence, and none is mentioned. Does confession entail sacerdotal mediation? Late medieval orthodoxy maintained that in an emergency this was not necessary, but there must be the *intention* to perform sacerdotal confession.[277] Does Wille have such an intention? None is expressed. Perhaps he remembers his wretched experience with his own friar confessor (XII.13–36).

Be that as it may, this silence over intent is not insignificant in a context where the assertion or denial of the need for individual confession to a priest had become a contested area. Typical of this was the fifth heresy itemized in the Blackfriars Condemnations of 1382, namely, that if one was duly contrite all external confession was superfluous or useless.[278] William Thorpe gives an example of the conviction that if one wanted to make confession a layperson was perfectly well qualified to receive it, while sacerdotal confession was superfluous. In accord with earlier norms in the church, Thorpe stressed that only God can forgive our sins. If someone wills to repent, God will move her or him to recollect relevant sins inspiring sorrow, while the Holy Spirit will inspire the penitent with "a good wil and a fervent desir" to live well. God will illumine the contrite person with heavenly grace and confidence in God's mercy. Thorpe actually finds any claims that priests can "asoyle" (absolve) sins blasphemous, since, as we saw, God alone can absolve people of sin. Such blasphemy, he rightly indicates, is a medieval invention. As for confession, Thorpe transforms it into voluntary counseling for troubled people. The counselor can be any virtuous person, priest, or "secular man." Christ Jesus, he tells his archbishop, who had just threatened to have him burned to death as a Wycliffite heretic, died to make humans *free* ("fre"), whereas the modern church enslaves people by threatening them with damnation unless they obey the excessive "ordynaunces" it invented.[279]

As for Wille, he certainly journeys through contrition and confession in response to Kynde's counsel. But I see no reason to transgress Langland's silence concerning Wille's intentions here and to ascribe to him the search for a priestly confessor. He belongs to a small group of resistant, dissident fools. He is in the position of the earliest Christians or modern

Lollards: a tiny minority. The Constantinian church is withering away and its hierarchy is quite irrelevant now to these fools. And soon Langland will give us his final, devastating dramatization of the sacrament of penance in the contemporary church. This powerful episode gives Wille and his fellow travelers good reason for eschewing the institutionalization of confession. As we shall see.

Before that, Langland returns to Conscience's battle with the seven deadly sins (XXII.217 ff.; cf. XXII.69 ff.). Here priests do play a prominent role. They are agents in the forces of Antichrist. Once more they seek to undermine "goddes clerk and his notarie," Conscience (XVI.192). They display the same contempt for Conscience manifested by the brewer as they combine overwhelming love of money with a love of "goed ale" and blasphemous oaths (XXII.218–27; XXI.396–408). Conscience now makes an extraordinary confession in an extraordinary moment of recognition:

> Consience cryede, "Helpe, Clergie, or Y falle
> Thorw inparfit prestes and prelates of holy churche!"
> (XXII.228–29)

> [Conscience cried out, "Help, Clergy, before I fall
> Through imperfect priests and prelates of Holy Church!"]

Although these two lines confirm what Langland has already shown us about the composition of Antichrist's army, the significance of this kind of reiteration is striking.[280] For once again the passage emphasizes the scope of Langland's critical vision of the contemporary church, one that includes all forms of priesthood at all levels of the hierarchy together with the laity. Furthermore, the lines recall Conscience's somewhat smug dismissal of the skills provided by "clergie" to Christians, a dismissal he now seems to regret without actually acknowledging his own role in producing the absence of adequate learning among "prestes and prelates" (XV.175–84).[281]

Conscience's cry to Clergie for help is now met with extremely harsh irony. Answering to the call for priests with "clergie," Christian learning, come representatives from what have been revealed to be the forces of Antichrist: friars. "Freres," Langland had written, "foloewed that fende for he yaf hem copes" (XXII.230). The accumulation of "copes" symbolizes one of the poem's central ironies in its treatment of friars and the church's institutions. Let us recall that through the friars the church (led by the thirteenth-century papacy) had institutionalized a life of absolute poverty with mendicancy in a state of perfection which imitated the form of life allegedly followed by Jesus Christ. But the institutionalization had unintended consequences which Langland's work pursues in detail. Elsewhere I have followed Langland's dialectical critique of Franciscan ideology, and here it suffices to identify just one strand of his exploration.[282] The institutionalization of poverty, of need, leads to the accumulation of papal privileges, power, and wealth. Much conventional antimendicant writing, from William of St. Amour and Jean de Meun, subjects this split to a moral attack: hypocrisy.[283] Langland of course includes this but in a wider context. The friars are not simply vicious Christians, hypocrites, but are also seen as those who are the product of institutional factors. The church, or rather the papacy, determined to institutionalize holy detachment from worldly goods in friars. But such institutionalization necessarily led to palpable attachment to material goods. The friars' "copes" represent the reification of the state of collective voluntary poverty, their covering.

At first, Conscience rejects the friars' offer "to helpe" because he discerns their inadequacy as confessors following the demands of the new covenant.[284] It is appropriate that the personification Nede supports Conscience's initial rejection of the friars by identifying their need as one for material goods distorting their relations with penitents who come to them as confessors. He observes the consequences of their apparent poverty, their official lack of "patrimonye," that is, a regular form of livelihood. Their institutionalized mendicancy draws them to flatter those they absolve, directing their ministry to the rich who will provide them with a good (material) life (XXII.232–41). Despite the different inflections, Chaucer uses the same models in his figuration of the friar in the *General Prologue* to *The Canterbury Tales*:

> Ful wel biloved and famulier was he
> With frankeleyns over al in his contree,
> And eek with worthy wommen of the toun;
> For he hadde power of confessioun,
> As seyde hymself, moore than a curat,
> For of his ordre he was licenciat
> Ful swetely herde he confessioun,

And plesaunt was his absolucioun:
He was an esy man to yeve penaunce,
Ther as he wiste to have a good pitaunce.
For unto a povre ordre for to yive
Is signe that a man is wel yshryve;
For if he yaf, he dorste make avaunt,
He wiste that a man was repentaunt;
For many a man so hard is of his herte,
He may nat wepe, althogh hym soore smerte.
    (*General Prologue*, *CT* I.215–30; trans. 25)[285]

———

[Highly beloved and intimate was he
With County folk within his boundary,
And city dames of honour and possessions;
For he was qualified to hear confessions,
Or so he said, with more than priestly scope;
He had a special licence from the Pope.
Sweetly he heard his penitents at shrift
With pleasant absolution, for a gift.
He was an easy man in penance-giving
Where he could hope to make a decent living;
It's a sure sign whenever gifts are given
To a poor Order that a man's well shriven,
And should he give enough he knew in verity
The penitent repented in sincerity.
For many a fellow is so hard of heart
He cannot weep, for all his inward smart.]

Here too the ideology of mendicant poverty generates material needs which are fulfilled around the sacrament of penance, itself a commodity in a society where "al is for to selle" (*Wife of Bath's Prologue*, *CT* III.414). Chaucer and Langland are exploring some of the same processes in the ecclesial polity they inhabit and using some of the same traditions of discourse to do so. Their modes, of course, differ and so, perhaps, do the outcomes.

    Nede's advice to Conscience is that those who embrace what Aquinas and convention called a state of perfection ("status perfectionis") in a life of individual and collective poverty should be made to turn the formalism of their life into reality.[286] Since they claim to have chosen the "chele and cheytyftee" (cold and misery) of poverty, let them "chewe as thei chose." As Nede says this, we will remember Langland's own powerful representation of those whose poverty is not a privileged, freely chosen form but a devastating daily reality (IX.70–97). Like his author, Nede opposes the friars' appropriation of the "cure of soules" which belongs to parish priests, an opposition which is also opposition to papal privileges. In their claims to the state of perfection in absolute poverty, let them "lyue by angeles fode" (XXII.237–41).

In the face of this profoundly antiformalist irony, Conscience laughs (XXII.242). But laughter can be an impediment to careful reflection, and so it proves to be here. For Conscience immediately reverses his decision to turn away friars and instead welcomes them: "welcome be ye alle / To Vnite and holi churche" (XXII.242–43). This is the beginning of his final and most catastrophic error. The constable of the church, still without Piers, decides to welcome a group he has just seen in the vanguard of Antichrist's army. Has he become like the blind leading the blind toward the ditch of de-Christianization (Matt. 15:14)? Perhaps part of the problem is that he has yet once more taken "kynde wit" as his teacher in his rumination on friars (XXII.268). As we have already been shown, a natural power unaided by divine grace is likely to generate errors when it determines issues related to humans' supernatural end, to salvation in Christ. Be that as it may, Conscience at first seeks to mitigate his error by inviting friars to reform their practices and to limit their numbers, just as kings limit the number of those receiving "wages" in war (XXII.245–72). Without strenuous allegorization, a model of reform drawn from contemporary organizations of war profits may not be the most propitious model for those who claim to be in a state of perfection. Such profits, after all, have already been associated with Mede in an earlier argument before the king whom she advises not to appoint Conscience as constable (III.232–57). But whatever difficulties may lie in this model, Langland's own dialectical exploration of mendicant orders and Franciscan ideology presses beyond Conscience's welcome to the friars and his suggestions for their reformation. Here he is moving in the same direction as John Wyclif. In *De Blasphemia* (1381), Wyclif notes that the Franciscans' only foundation ("fundamentum") is a papal determination and that they should no longer exist.[287] Conscience, however, still assumes that a reformation of the friars is possible. So he invokes "Frere

Fraunceys and Domynyk" as models of holiness and instructs contemporary friars to live "aftur youre reule" (XXII.246–52). Nevertheless, he also proposes a reform that actually contradicts Franciscan espousal of poverty and voluntary mendicancy as essential elements in their embrace of perfection. This reform is presented quite blandly: friars should accept food, clothing, and other resources so that they lack nothing ("yow shal no thyng lakke," XXII.248–49). The blandness reflects Conscience's failure to grasp the ideological and historical identity of mendicant orders, especially Franciscan traditions. At this stage he does not grasp how his proposal subverts their distinctive identity and their sense of superiority to monks in the ladder of holy poverty. He is unaware that his reform would reduce friars to the same state of life as monks or even parish priests. It would be transformation, root and branch. As yet, Conscience neither realizes this nor does he realize the need for such a transformation. But the extended engagement he is about to have with friars will educate him and he will return to his proposal. But with understanding of its ramifications.

Meanwhile, Langland forces Conscience and his readers to witness the disastrous consequences of this invitation to the friars. First of all, we are shown the resistance to the idea that friars should abandon their leading role in late medieval universities together with their ambition to appropriate the parish priests' cure of souls and its material foundations. In both spheres of ambition, Langland ascribes the mendicants' motives to the deadly sin of envy (XXII.273–96).[288] Momentarily, Conscience seems to rescind his invitation to the friars, turning instead to the parish priest they seek to displace in the confessional. The parish priest administers a "scharp salve," demanding that "Peres pardon were ypayd, *redde quod debes* [pay what you owe]" (XXII.304–8, XXI.182–94). Conscience too had tried this in the previous passus only to be confronted by a rebellion culminating in the people's rejection of Christ's covenant and the Lord's Supper (XXI.381–408). Christians wanted the sacraments but without any change in their lives. So penance would remain merely formal. Such was the outcome of the institutionalization of mandatory annual penance and Eucharist that emerged from the Fourth Lateran Council in 1215 ("Omnis utriusque sexus").[289] And Langland's return to this scene in Passus XXII confirms this nexus. Once again the people reject the evangelical law ("*redde quod debes*") and demand the replacement of the parish priest by a confessor "that softer couthe plastre," one who would make penance a more pleasant experience (XXII.309–15). Perhaps the people, like the reader, recall Mede's confessor in Passus III (38–67). Perhaps penance should be displaced by therapy for gratifying the client who, after all, pays for the commodity. The friars seem able and willing to offer such a service. One of these friars is named "frere Flatrere" (XXII.315).

Conscience remembers Piers's legacy from Christ. Forgiveness demands that the person to be forgiven change his or her life and tries to restore the broken bonds of community (XXII.318–21). But yet once more Conscience displays marked instability. Despite his memory of Christ and Piers, he immediately reverses his decision:

> "Y may wel soffre," sayde Consience, "sennes ye desiren,
> That frere Flaterare be fet and fisyk yow seke."
> (XXII.322–23)

> ──────

> ["I may as well agree," said Conscience, "since you desire it,
> That Friar Flatterer be fetched and treat you sick."]

A few lines earlier, Nede had reminded Conscience that because the friars identify themselves as truly poor, in the Franciscans' case lacking any civil rights to the property they held, friars "flatere, to fare wel, folk that ben riche" (XXII.234–35), as we saw in the confession of Mede (III.38–74a). Conscience is told the name of the friar who wishes to displace the parish priest: "frere Flaterere." But he has become such a poor reader of the allegory he inhabits that he cannot grasp the significance of a personification whose meaning is written all over its face. Nor can he heed the explicit warnings he has been given (XXII.234–35, 315, 323). So we are being shown a church under the leadership of constable Conscience stumbling from error to error and quite forgetful of the central Christian narratives (XVIII–XXI), a church with Piers long since absent and a hierarchy aligned with the forces of Antichrist. If Conscience is "the site of truth," Langland is showing how vulnerable and fragile God's precious gift may be when immersed in a cultural revolution involving de-Christianizing powers.[290] He makes his final error in defense of the institutionalization of penance in what he thinks is Christ's church. Unfolding this final error will bring to a close Langland's dialectical exploration of this sacrament and the church in which it had been central and made mandatory since 1215.

XIV

But first Langland displays, yet once more, the full participation of lay elites in the church's assimilation to the world that runs after Antichrist. For the last time he confirms how deluded was the Wycliffite idea, grasped by Liberum Arbitrium, that lay elites would be appropriate agents of reform. This confirmation is replete with significance for the magisterial reformation of the sixteenth century. Once Conscience has assented to set aside Christ's own demands to the pardon he brings humanity, the friar receives the enthusiastic support of the lay elite. A lord sends a letter to the bishop, who assents to the arrangement whereby the friar appropriates confessional work and income of the parish (XXII.324–29). The coziness between lay lord and bishop is grounded in the material realities of Langland's church. Many benefices were the property of lords and of lordly ecclesiastics, making parish priests their employees while they themselves extracted substantial proportions of parishioners' compulsory tithes given to support the parish ministry.[291] And of course bishops and abbots were grandees in the House of Lords. No wonder that the *only* bishop who opposed Henry's appropriation of the church was Bishop Fisher of Rochester, the martyr St. John Fisher in Catholic tradition.

Yet despite the agreements between constable Conscience, lay lords, and bishops, Langland figures one final source of opposition. He personifies Peace as the porter who asks the friar's name. Hitherto known as Friar Flatterer, the religious mendicant now names himself in even more sinister and famous terms. He declares the identity Conscience has conspicuously failed to discern. The friar's fraternal companion ("his felawe") names him "sire *Penetrans-domos.*" As all commentators note, this name is a traditional component of antimendicant discourse taken from St. Paul: "For of these sort are they who creep into houses [*ex his enim sunt qui penetrant domos*] and lead captive silly women laden with sins" (2 Tim. 3:6).[292] In this tradition, a profound allegorical dimension was found in "houses" (*domos*): both the material house from which mendicants extracted their material needs and the inner house which was "groped" by confessors. Both Langland (XXII.383) and Chaucer use this word to describe the search of mendicant confessors. Chaucer deploys it in his brilliant story of the groping friar told by his summoner (*CT* III.1918–41, 1948–73, 2121–55). There the friar's creeping into houses and consciences leads him to grope a pseudopenitent's "towel" (anus) in search of material profits, hidden treasures. He is rewarded with a very material parody of the voice of the spirit that "breathed where he will and thou hearest his voice" (John 3:8). Langland's inflection of "penetrans domos" (they creep into houses), is, however, set in a rather different context, mode of writing, and theological focus. Langland's Peace recognizes the tradition to which "sire *Penetrans-domos*" belongs. Unlike Conscience, he can still read allegory. So he wants to turn him away. But he cannot act against constable Conscience whose courteous spokesman, "Hend-speche," commands Peace to welcome Friar Flatterer, the self-declared "sire *Penetrans-domos*," together with "his felawe." These mendicant confessors will convert sinners who will then kiss Conscience (XXII.348–53). The latter reiterates his welcome to the friars, those warriors of Antichrist and the modern papacy, while now condemning the parish priest who had tried to administer penance according to evangelical demands (XXII.348–61). In doing so, of course, Conscience condemns his own earlier attempt to persuade Christians to follow the commands of Christ to pay to Piers Plowman's pardon from Christ, "*Redde quod debes*" (XXII.381–95). So Langland discloses that the conscience of the church is being assimilated by forces whose goal is to subvert the gifts of Christ and the Holy Spirit, to invert the crop of truth and make "fals spryng" (XXII.53–57; XXI.335–40). In this moment, Conscience lacks any perception of his errors and their consequences. Perhaps being constable of the Constantinian church makes even "goddes clerk" (XVI.192) forget what he once knew so well and could once articulate so eloquently.

Langland's account of what follows is a quite astonishing representation of the sacrament of his church on which he had bestowed the most attention in his work. Mandatory for all Christians, it was central to the church's version of justification and sanctification, while its refusal was conventionally represented as the primrose path to the everlasting bonfire, as *Jacob's Well* delighted to witness.[293] But now Langland displays the confessor turning both the sacrament of penance and masses into commodities in which Christian counsel is displaced: he "gloseth ther he shryueth" (smooth-talks his shriving) (XXII.362–68).

True enough, in one sense we have seen this all before. The poem's Prologue and third passus were replete with images of the church's incorporation in contemporary markets together with dramatization of the consequences. Exegesis of scripture, sacrament of penance, sacrament of orders, and sacrament of marriage were all shown in commodified forms making the church the world and the world the church. But then, as the poem began its journeys, one could imagine that we were encountering abuses which were being satirized in a familiar incitement to a traditional model of reformation. Now, however, at the poem's ending, we are no longer invited to imagine this. Nor should we be able to imagine it. The work's dialectic has shown, time and again, the resilience of such "abuses" and the ineffectuality of numerous attempts at reform. The processes we have been following in Passus XXI–XXII show us the *making* of what we encountered in the Prologue and from Passus II through Passus IX. We now see just how the Pentecostal community could become the church of those earlier passus. And we see this without any signs of any agents willing and capable of reformation. On the contrary, Langland compels us to contemplate a new vision which condenses the outcome of his dialectical exploration of the sacrament of penance in his church.

Under the ministry of the clerical elite, the sacrament is shown to dissolve contrition. The confessor "gropeth" Contrition until Contrition "hadde clene foryete to crye and to wepe / And wake for his wikkede werkes as he was woned bifore" (had clean forgotten to cry and weep / And to stay awake for his wicked deeds, as he once did). The sacrament of penance has thus become an *impediment* to repentance. The author's comment is that the confessor's therapy has drawn contrition to abandon contrition, which is the necessary "souereyne salue" (sovereign salve) for sinners seeking divine forgiveness (XXII.363–72). This observation recalls the risen Christ's command to Piers which makes remission of sins, pardon, inseparable from repentance and conversion of life. It is congruent with Aquinas's statement that contrition contains the whole of penance as the foundation to a building supports the whole edifice (*ST* III.90.3, ad 2). But Langland has an even more devastating representation of this sacrament.

Conscience calls for Contrition. He continues to assume the model of the church he accepted from Kynde Wit, a walled fortress keeping the bad people outside. So he tells Contrition to guard the gate (XXII.376). His model still seems to prevent him from recognizing that the forces of de-Christianization are *within* fortress church as well as in the world *outside*.[294] Nor does he acknowledge his own errors and his role in the current disasters. An impenitent constable of the church in this situation is an especially resonant image of its state. He had commanded peace to welcome "sire *Penetrans-domos*," and Peace now informs him of what he himself has failed to observe. However much he now invokes Contrition, in fact, Contrition will not come. We have been shown exactly why, and Peace now encapsulates the completion of this movement in a resonant image:

> "He lyeth adreint," saide Pees, "and so doth mony othere;
> The frere with his fisyk this folk hath enchaunted
> And doth men drynke dwale, that they drat no synne."
> (XXII.377–79)

> ["He lies drowned," said Peace, "and so do many others;
> The Friar's enchanted these people with his treatments
> And gives them sleeping potions so they fear no sin."]

The sacrament of the church so central in Langland's work and his church has finally enchanted Christian people. The church's elite, its magisterial teachers and ubiquitous judges in trials for heresy and inquisition, has turned the sacrament of penance into an opiate, a sleeping pill.[295] The consequences are that the moral recklessness we have been witnessing now becomes a chain of habit: "they drat [fear] no synne" (XXII.379). These words conclude Langland's dialectical exploration of the sacrament of penance in the modern church. They are his final evaluation of its teleology.

Because I am not convinced that the scope of this evaluation is adequately acknowledged in much scholarship on *Piers Plowman*, I will add a brief recollection of Catholic theology on the sacrament brought into such serious question. All sacraments and their salvific effects, it was agreed, flow from the passion and resurrection of Christ.[296] The sacrament of penance conveys justification and sanctification to the penitent. It interweaves the virtues of justice and charity (*ST* III.85.1–4, 86.4 and 6). Aquinas agreed that God can pardon sins without the mediation of a priest, and God does not bind his power to sacraments in such a way that he cannot bestow their effects in another way. Nevertheless, he insists that the virtue of repentance is essential to divine forgiveness (*ST* III.86.2 with III.64.7, III.68.2). This accords with Langland's depiction of Christ's pardon (XXI.182–98). It was a commonplace in late medieval teaching in whose light we see the trajectory of the sacrament of penance in *Piers Plowman*. In the culmination of Langland's dialectic, we encounter Christian tradition and its institutions participating in the forces of de-Christianization, working against the conversion which is repentance. In this last word on the sacrament of penance, *all* the participants are overwhelmed by amnesia. They *all* forget what the poem has just treated with dramatic, lyric, and theological brilliance: the redemptive reconciling work of Christ, the one who shows why Holy Church could affirm so wholeheartedly, "*Deus caritas*" (God is love) (I.82; 1 John 4:7–16). Conscience, "goddes clerk and his notarie" (XVI.192), must be included in this *all.* Not only because his errors contributed to the subversion of the church over which he is constable. But more especially because he fails to invoke, let alone apply, the visions of Christ and Trinity pervading the previous four passus (XVIII–XXI). This loss of divine vision, the forgetfulness of revealed knowledge he had recently taught Wille (XXI.1–210), is explicitly bound up with his enmeshment in the contemporary church's version of repentance and its institutionalizations of the forms of divine grace promised by Christ. This enmeshment is the source of the difference between the Christocentric Conscience of Passus XXI and the blundering amnesiac of Passus XXII. In the former, his attention is entirely given to the visions and teaching of Christ, as befits "goddes clerk and his notarie." From that attention he is able to interpret the "shewing" Wille has received and to teach Wille what he asks about the life of Christ. Long before this, Holy Church had lamented that contemporary people have no sense of any heaven other than this world (I.5–9).[297] But now we are being forced to recognize the decisive role of the church in bringing about this very situation: "The moste party of this peple that passeth on this erthe, / Haue thei worschip in this world thei wilneth no bettere" (Most of the people that pass through this earth / Are satisfied with success in this world) (I.7–8). Langland's obsession with the sacrament of penance comes from a profound conviction that the hope for humanity given by Christ is inextricably bound up with one precondition, namely, individual and collective acknowledgment of sin with the willingness to "pay / To Peres pardoun the plouhman *Redde quod debes*" (pay / To Piers the plowman's pardon *Redde quod debes*), to join with Wille in confessing, "That Y haue ytynt tyme and tyme myspened" (That I have wasted time and time misspent) (XXI.182–90; V.92–101). If we will not acknowledge our error, our participation in evil, then, individually and collectively, we are truly lost. In such a choice we reject the astonishing gift in which time may be redeemed and a new beginning made possible:

> So hope Y to haue of hym that is almyghty
> A gobet of his grace and bigynne a tyme
> That alle tymes of my tyme to profit shal turne.
> (V.99–101)

———

> [So I hope to have from him that is almighty
> A mouthful of his grace, and begin a time
> That all times of my time shall turn to profit.]

What a grisly irony that the church should develop a sacrament which enchants its members into the oblivion of such hope and the covenant to which it belongs: de-Christianization led by the church.

This returns me to my earlier mention of an encyclical by John Paul II in 1993, *Veritatis Splendor* (The Splendor of Truth). When one juxtaposes the modern pope and the work of the late medieval writer I have been studying, something quite unexpected emerges. I think this is worth considering briefly for what it helps bring out about Langland's vision of church and society. To John Paul II, the modern Western world manifests "growing secularism," with many people living and thinking "as if God did not exist," a view very close to Holy Church's in *Piers Plowman* (*VS*, 88; *Piers Plowman* I.5–9). The pope maintains that today "even the attitudes and behavior of Christians" are shaped by the "dechristianized culture" they inhabit (*VS*, 88). If some version of faith is affirmed, it tends to be split off from "morality" and the decisions of daily life (*VS*, 88, 106). Like Langland and many medieval theologians, the pope addresses the problem of an erring conscience. He writes about the way conscience can become "almost blind from being accustomed to sin" (62, drawing on St. Bonaventure and St. Thomas). Here one might think that John Paul II will produce an account of church, conscience, and people in the face of "dechristianizing" forces which will converge with Langland's. But this does not happen, and the way it does not intrigues me. It also helps one focus on the surprising particularities of Langland's concluding vision.

The modern pope has one major source of confidence that Langland does not share with him. John Paul maintains that in the face of the forces of "dechristianization" and "secularism," forces able to blind conscience in "even the attitudes and behavior of Christians," there remains "a great help for the formation of conscience" (*VS*, 64; see too 88 and 106). What might this be? It is "*the Church and her Magisterium*" (64; original emphasis). That is, the actually existing Roman Church, with its contemporary "Magisterium," can transcend, without qualification, the forces of "dechristianization" that have, according to the pope, so thoroughly transformed Christians. John Paul continues: "In forming their consciences the Christian faithful must give careful attention to the sacred and certain teaching of the Church. For the Catholic Church [i.e., the Roman Church] is by the will of Christ the teacher of truth" (64, quoting from *Dignitatis Humanae*). Unerringly, it fulfills the will of Christ, however incorrigibly its members err. The Roman Church can help conscience "avoid being tossed to and fro by every wind of doctrine proposed by human deceit (cf. Eph. 4:14) and helping it not to swerve from the truth about the good of man, but rather, especially in more difficult questions, to attain the truth with certainty and to abide in it" (64).

Little could be further from Langland's vision of the Roman Church and its "magisterium."[298] Little could be more alien to the ecclesiology emerging from his great work. Nowhere does Langland even hint, let alone affirm, that the contemporary church, led by the pope in Rome (or Avignon), is "a great help for the formation of conscience." Nowhere does he suggest it can be relied on to "attain the truth with certainty and to abide in it." No more, of course, does the Ockham who has appeared in this essay, a theologian addressing those he was confronting as heretical popes and hierarchy. Any attempt to fit the outcomes of Langland's exploration of his church into a modern orthodoxy (such as John Paul's) or a late medieval orthodoxy (such as those of Langland's Archbishop Courtenay persecuting Wyclif and his fellow travelers) will demand a reading so against the grain of the text as to make the text's specificities quite irrelevant.[299]

Langland's work shatters the Constantinian church so powerfully attacked by Liberum Arbitrium. But he refuses the solution favored by Liberum Arbitrium, Wyclif, and the magisterial reformers of the sixteenth and seventeenth centuries. That is, reformation under the power of lay sovereign and elites. As we have seen, this rejection follows from the poet's

ruthless display of the immersion of these elites in the paradiastolic rhetoric, practices, and lust for dominion that were so inimical to Langland's understanding of Christian discipleship. He thus rejects another Constantinian solution to the failings of the Constantinian church identified as
such by Liberum Arbitrium. He also rejects, with Liberum Arbitrium, the
church's version of mission that became Christendom, a church inextricably bound up with the structures of dominion, power, and exploitation.
Such a church could present England in 1377 as the special heritage of
God, the holy Israel with a king specially beloved by God, with Prince
Richard "sent to England by God in the same way that God sent his only
son for the redemption of the chosen people."[300] A few years later, we can
see the elaboration of such ideology under Henry V when a priest represents the king as a knight sent from heaven by God to save the church and
realm. God's special grace is manifest in victorious war against the French
and in his killing of Wycliffites. In his sharp sentence against these heretical Christians "by which they are given to fire and death," Henry V is a new
Joshua who has lifted the shield of faith by killing Lollards "and especially
their captain [Oldcastle] who was recently burned." In another sermon, the
same priest figures church and realm as "our ship" which has been saved by
Henry V.[301] Such is Constantinian Christianity, and Henry V was indeed
welcomed as "a new Constantine" by the church's elite.[302] In such a church
secular power and the means of salvation are bound together, temporalities
and spirituality interwoven. No wonder, then, that the archbishop of Canterbury, executed by the rebels in 1381, should also hold the office of chan-
cellor, called by Wyclif the most secular office in the kingdom ("secularissi-
mum regni officium").[303] Not surprisingly, Langland thinks that the
hierarchy of the church is drawn to participate in the forces of Antichrist
by its commitment to "temperaltees" (XXII.126–28).

XV

And so, instead of a Constantinian reformation to reform a Constantinian
church, Langland, like Ockham, turns to a theology of the "foles," the
fools. They constitute a tenacious opposition to the forces of Antichrist
whom they discern without confusion and without terror (XXII.53–68).
They understand the collusive comfort offered by the lay sovereign and

royal council composed of priests and laity. Understanding it, they curse this institution at the heart of the Constantinian church. Do such fools represent any institutional solution to replace the magisterial reformation prepared by Liberum Arbitrium and John Wyclif? *Certainly not.* Is this a failure in Langland's political theology and ecclesiology? *Absolutely not.*[304] Langland deliberately eschews any institutional solution to his devastating critique of the contemporary church and the history of its making. Just as did Ockham.[305]

Eschewal of institutional solutions, such as reformation under Crown lords and magistrates, is a logical outcome of Langland's work. True enough, he lacks Ockham's innovative theology of evangelical freedom or Milton's powerful account of Christian liberty in his *De doctrina christiana* (I.27). As Arthur McGrade wrote of Ockham's appeal to "the gospel as a law of freedom [*Lex evangelica est lex libertatis*]," this "treatment of evangelical liberty clashes sharply with the hierocratic ideal of comprehensive direction of man's spiritual life from above."[306] But this lack does not prevent a thorough subversion of any "hierocratic ideal" calling for "comprehensive direction of man's spiritual life from above." Nor has it prevented an equally thorough subversion of contemporary ecclesial institutions. As we have seen, even the sacrament of penance had first of all proved to be an inadequate means of catechetical instruction, leaving penitents completely puzzled as to how to go on with the Christian life:

> Ac ther ne was wye non so wys that the way thider couthe
> But blostrede forth as bestes ouer baches and hulles.
>
> (VII.158–59)

> ———
>
> [But there was no one so wise that he knew the way there,
> But blundered forth like beasts over valleys and hills.]

Instead of leading to completion in the Eucharist for which it was meant to be essential preparation, it leaves its subjects blundering around, lost from "the way" (VII.158–71). And, of course, that way is Christ: "Y am *via et veritas* and may avauncen alle" (X.255; see John 14:6). Furthermore, Langland represents the institution of the church's reconciliation between humanity and God as having become a sacralized commodity reconciling priests and laity to the current practices of the world's markets. And finally, as we have just observed, the form of penance becomes a means for the complete reconciliation of penitents with their sins "for a litel sulver [silver]," an enchanting drug freeing all from any reflection on sin and its consequences (XXII.362–79). Langland's unfolding of this sacrament characterizes his treatment of ecclesiastic forms and authority, his troubles with the historical institutionalizations of the gifts of Christ and the Holy Spirit in the Pentecostal community. Even attempts to imitate Christ's poverty as a state of perfection culminated in an institutionalization of voluntary mendicant poverty which generated power, privilege, wealth, and dominion for friars who became a special arm of the papacy.[307]

In fact, Langland's poem constantly attends to the unintended and ironic consequences of the institutions established in the Constantinian church. Everywhere he finds reified forms which are, at best, parodic simulacra of the Pentecostal church with its *allegorical* edifice and evangelical leaders, Holy Spirit and Piers the Plowman. These leaders, most significantly, lead by immediately *absenting themselves* from any determinate structures in the polity. Neither Langland's overall vision nor the particularities of his ecclesiology give a trace of anything remotely like Pope John Paul II's "Magisterium," let alone his unqualified confidence in the existence of such an office and its apparently total transcendence of the "dechristianized" culture it inhabits. Indeed, nothing in Langland's dialectic encourages us to expect any such institution and authority in this life, an institution so unscathed by its material foundations and cultural contexts. On the contrary, his restless dialectic addresses many ways in which the church's institutions are woven into social relations of dominion, power, and temporalities. He often shows the commitment of contemporary popes and the church they lead to forces he finally evaluates as Antichrist's. The poem constantly submits the self-descriptions and self-legitimizations of the modern church to a critical realism which is especially well suited to disclose reifications where sacralizing forms and actual practice have become split apart, often in grotesque contradictions.

This critical process is theological and literary. As St. Thomas taught, doctrine comes to us inseparable from its mode of discourse: "Notandum autem, quod ex modo loquendi datur nobis doctrina."[308] Langland's *modi loquendi* encourage a searching exploration of features that to many mid-seventeenth-century English revolutionaries would be attacked as *formalism*. There one of the objects of scrutiny would be the magisterial reformation in the inflection it took in the Church of England (especially under Archbishop Laud and King Charles) and then among Presbyterians: "New *Presbyter* is but old *Priest* writ large."[309] What links Langland's critical realistic dialectic with later attacks on the magisterial reformation by various Protestant groups, represented in the previous quotation by John Milton, is a refusal to accept that the outcome of the church's history in current forms of ecclesiastic polity, doctrine, and liturgy manifests God's will.

In Langland's era, the kind of orthodox self-defense at issue is well illustrated in the work of a friar, Roger Dymmok's *Liber contra XII errores et hereses lollardorum*.[310] His defense of ecclesiastical temporalities and opulence is as unashamed as it is orthodox. Dymmok acknowledges the striking differences between the modern and the early church. The difference was used by Waldensians, Wycliffites, and others to castigate the contemporary church as a lamentable fall.[311] The friar defends temporalities and dominion in the modern church as a sign of divine presence in the church's history of increasing wealth and power. There is simply no longer any need for the old ways of apostolic poverty and purely spiritual power to pervade the church, since this would not benefit the authority and power of the church today (40–51). Dymmok's work is an excellent example of the church's defense of Constantinian Christianity. In fact, he explicitly celebrates the Donation of Constantine and asserts that Constantine was divinely inspired in making it (40). And now priestly power is above that of the angels, because priests consecrate the Eucharist and effect the remission of sins (54–59). Any challenge to the Roman Church, whether to its material wealth or to its sacramental doctrine, would be a challenge to lay sovereign and elites. This would herald social anarchy. Church and lay elites are bound together by God in a shared culture (90–91, 147–49, 153–54; part 10 contains a defense of Christians involved in killing, attacking strands of Christian nonviolence and pacifism in Wycliffite theology). Such Constantinian Christianity has substantial common ground with the magisterial Reformation and its attack on Anabaptists, including nonviolent Anabaptists. I think of the crucial Elizabethan Act of Supremacy, severing the English Church from Rome. It was called an act "restoring to the Crown the ancient jurisdiction" over the ecclesiastical and spiritual state. It abolished "all usurped and foreign power and authority, spiritual and temporal." It demanded that every ecclesiastical officer and every temporal officer should declare in their "conscience" that Queen Elizabeth was "the only supreme governor of this realm . . . as well in spiritual or ecclesiastical things or causes, as temporal."[312] In the 1562 (1563) Articles of Religion, Article XXXIV is devoted to the traditions of the church. These are to be determined "by common authority," and nobody acting through "private judgement" is allowed to break such "traditions and ceremonies of the Church." Whoever challenges such "common order" in the church simultaneously "hurteth the authority of the Magistrate." Article XXXVII concerns "Civil Magistrates." It is affirmed that the lay sovereign "hath the chief power in this Realm of *England*," power over causes "Ecclesiastical or Civil." I appreciate that the English sovereign displaced the pope, who now "hath no jurisdiction in this Realm of England" (Article XXXVII) and proclaimed that "the Church of *Rome* hath erred, not only in their living and manner of Ceremonies, but also in matter of Faith" (Article XIX). But it is not insignificant that Dymmok dedicates his book to the king as a new David who had been raised up by God to defend the church from heretics and heresy (5–6).[313] Toward the end of section XIV above, I sampled similar sentiments in the Parliament of 1377 and in a sermon by one of Henry V's priests. As Jeremy Catto has shown, "In all but name, more than a century before the title could be used, Henry V had begun to act as the supreme governor of the Church of England."[314] Any grand narrative that seeks to take in the later Middle Ages and the Reformation needs to address such continuities across the great divide, although most have failed to do so.[315] Be that as it may, Langland's work explores and rejects Constantinian versions of political theology and its ecclesiologies. He knows the medieval versions intimately, and in his critical responses he challenges what will become their embodiment in the magisterial Reformation.[316]

XVI

Langland does not quite end his work with the church's sacrament of penance turned into the wine of delusion. He ascribes to Conscience a response. Despite the eschatological dimensions of Passus XXII, this response is quite free of the frustrated, wrathful, and utopian apocalypticism of Passus III (437–82, discussed in section XII). It is also freed from the model of the church as fortress. Instead, Conscience takes up language used to describe the evangelical work of the Holy Spirit and Piers in the Pentecostal community. He promises to become a pilgrim: "Y wol bicome a pilgrime / And wenden [walk] as wyde as the world renneth [reaches]" (XXII.380–81). This echoes the way the Holy Spirit "wente / As wyde as the world is with Peres to tulye [till] treuthe" (XXI.332–33). Conscience's universal pilgrimage is a search for the plowman commissioned by the risen Christ and led by the Holy Spirit (XXI). There is not a whisper about the church needing a pope elected by cardinals and somehow succeeding St. Peter with Piers as the putative vicar of Christ. We have, after all, just been shown the pope alive and well but aligned with the forces of Antichrist. Ockham's conclusion too.[317]

Conscience hopes that Piers the plowman might destroy Pride and end the church's mistaken attempt to institutionalize need and absolute voluntary poverty as the supreme state of perfection (XXII.380–84).[318] His search for this most elusive figure is certainly not the search for an institutional solution within a reformed hierarchical church that maintains continuities with the late medieval church. Such a comfortingly reformist solution is not Langland's. If anything, his conclusion would encourage sympathy with Wycliffite views that after Pope Urban VI nobody should be pope, a view well enough known to be condemned as a heresy at Blackfriars in 1382.[319]

Conscience's final three lines include a phrase which could be a regression to his earlier disastrous invocation of planetary powers to terrorize erring humanity into a godly life: "Now Kynde me avenge" (XXII.384). For Conscience to regress into error even as he gains new insights and sets out as a vulnerable pilgrim would not be inconsistent with the way Langland thinks. We have seen how he cultivates modes that give one few resting places, however epiphanic these may be. If Conscience is regressing, he might be identifying with biblical images of the saints carrying two-edged swords, "To execute vengeance" (*Ad faciendam vindictam*) among those who rebel against God (Ps. 149:7–9). We will remember how he had rather enjoyed the story of Samuel chopping Agag into pieces, an act explicitly offered as one of vengeance (III.439–40 [1 Kings 15:33]). But he may have now understood the futility and moral error in his invocation of Kynde as a planetary force which brings plagues and other diseases, nature in a thoroughly fallen world. If so, he might be invoking the figure of Kynde who has just taught Wille to continue learning how to love when Wille appealed to him for vengeance against old age and death (XXII.199–211). This final insistence echoes Holy Church's teaching in Passus I, and Elizabeth Salter plausibly relates it to Julian of Norwich's insistence, toward the end of her own great vision, that God's meaning is Love, his revelation Love, and his motive in disclosing this revelation is Love, and the sole content of his teaching Love.[320] "*Deus caritas*" (I.82). And perhaps such a reading accords better with what seems like the poem's final figuration of conversion.

For Conscience's final longing is for Piers the plowman, and his final cry is for Grace to whom he had once sung, with Wille, "Veni Creator Spiritus" (XXII.385–86; XXI.210). This "*creator spiritus*" is of course the Holy Spirit so eloquently celebrated in the discourse of Christ the Samaritan in Passus XIX. There the Holy Spirit was intimately associated with acts of *kindness* without which humanity cuts itself off from divine life (XIX.96–228). Perhaps Conscience's shift from a cry to Kynde for vengeance to a cry for Grace is part of another conversion to the God who has been revealed in Christ the Samaritan and Christ's embodiment of divine *kindness* in his great oration on his solidarity with humanity while emancipating humans from the prison of hell (XIX.360–475).[321] This final invocation of the Holy Spirit is made with a decision to become a pilgrim. As Skeat noted, a pilgrim "determined to wander wide over the world till he shall find Piers the Plowman."[322] This description brings out some resonant ideas in the ending and the processes which precede it. Conscience's pilgrimage entails a commitment to evangelical mobility foreshadowed by the Holy Spirit and Piers (XXI.332–33; XXII.381). Foreshadowed too by Wille who left his little cottage ("cote") in Cornhill to become a seeking wanderer, unenclosed by walls, institutional structures, or status (V.1–108; X.1–13, 56–62; XV.1–4; XX.1–5; XXII.1–5). It is also foreshadowed in Liberum Arbitrium's model of the church of the martyrs and his call for a nonviolent evangelical mission. This is far removed from Constantinian models, whether those of late medieval orthodoxy proclaimed by Dymmok or those of their Wycliffite adversaries and the magisterial Reformation of the sixteenth century. No need for temporalities, for dominion, for coercive jurisdiction, for a wealthy and well-fortified church. No need to take responsibility for maintaining the current regime in its structures of power and status. No need and actually no power to control the world's competing material and political forces. No need to join with King Henry IV and Archbishop Arundel in fighting "sedition and insurrection" allegedly inseparable from Wycliffite "conventicles and confederacies." No need to fight this threat to lay and ecclesiastical power with fire: *De heretico comburendo* (1401) stipulated that those the church handed to the lay power as incorrigible should be burned to death so that "such punishment may strike fear to the minds of others."[323] The few fools, the wanderers, have no fantasies of social or ecclesial control, no lust for dominion.

Indeed, we may remember Wille asking a gripping question: "What is holy churche, chere [dear] frende?" (XVII.124). The answer he receives from Liberum Arbitrium at this point has nothing to say about temporalities, power, and the need to shore up the current political regime. It is charity, a form of life shaped by love, fidelity, honest relations with others: love of God with love of neighbor (XVII.124–43). And in such a church those known as bishops will not live in palaces but be mobile teachers enchanting people to charity rather than enchanting them to reckless abandonment of Christian ethics through the sacrament of penance (XII.239–94; cf. XXII.363–79). And perhaps this lesson had continuities with the map offered by the layman Piers to the lost pilgrims in Passus VII. His ethical guidance culminated in the promise that if Grace so granted, this journey would disclose a vision of Treuthe in the searcher's own heart where Charity will make "a churche" nurturing others (VII.254–60a). This is a church fit for fools.[324]

Furthermore, we should note that as Conscience abandons the role of constable to become a pilgrim who will search for Piers the plowman, his decision highlights a decisive fact that seems to have escaped his attention as he tried to rule fortress church. The fact is this: Piers has been absent from the Roman Church where he had been displaced by the pope, cardinals, religious orders, and priests following Antichrist in Passus XXII. This church had substituted the opiate of its sacrament of penance for charity and cardinal virtues. We should not mitigate Langland's own emphasis: Piers has to be searched for beyond the actually existing papal church from which he has become absent. What are we to understand by Piers's absence? What are we to understand by Conscience's search and by Wille's own hidden place with the fools ("foles") in "Vnite" also known as "holi church" (XXII.213–16, 74–75)?

In her fine introduction to *Piers Plowman*, Salter discussed the "frequent vanishings and appearances[,] ... the rapid comings and goings" of Piers the plowman, and she associated these with an increasing "revelatory capacity: his 'materializations' will therefore be incalculable, since they are divinely controlled and *intimations* of truth to the struggling dreamer." She links this approach with one ascribed to the experience of contemplatives by Langland's contemporary Walter Hilton: "all such feelings come to them [contemplatives] in that state *as it were unwarily*, for they come or they wit it [before they know it], and go from them or [before] they wit it, and they cannot come thereto again nor wit not where they should seek it ... for they have not yet no homeliness with them, *but suddenly go and suddenly come*." She sets the treatment of "Langland's loose-woven fabric of procedures," which offer "a way of capturing something of a kaleidoscopic vision of truth."[325] This is a fruitful figure for thinking about the dislocations of narrative in the poem and the theological models they compose. Langland's dialectical processes continually drive the reader from anything that might seem a resting place even, or perhaps especially, from the most revealing encounters with one in whom "dwelleth all the fullness of the Godhead corporally" (Col. 2:9). For Langland agrees with Augustine, who in preaching on John's Gospel (John 14:1–3) observes that while humans live at a distance from God they are prepared for beholding the divine countenance by faith which purifies the heart (Matt. 5:8). In this situation, Augustine remarks, "Let him [Christ] remain concealed that faith may be exercised." For this exercise is actually "the longing of love" which is the preparation of the mansion promised by Christ (John 14:1–3).[326] Elizabeth Salter, Walter Hilton, and Augustine give us a language well suited to identifying a characteristic mode of writing in *Piers Plowman* and its theological implications. It helps us grasp the role of absence, of "vanishings" in the work and why Salter should claim for this a "revelatory capacity." There is a further dimension here which Salter's quotation from Hilton evokes: the searcher's lack of control in a process constituted by gifts. Hilton remarks on the unpredictable moments of presence, "as it were unwarily," and their equally unpredictable withdrawal. So the contemplatives "cannot come thereto again nor wit where they should seek," a characteristic experience of Wille in *Piers Plowman*. Never can the human control the gift, master the presence of the divine vision. Nor, in Langland's attention to the consequences of such a reality, will a faithful church have anything to do with projects of control and dominion.

Salter described Piers as offering "intangible leadership," and later Anne Middleton provided a congruent observation which seems to be particularly relevant to the ending of *Piers Plowman*. According to Middleton, "One can never again *find* Piers, still less seat him securely in a position of leadership."[327] This is an excellent formulation, and I will gloss it in terms of the present study and its consideration of the ecclesiastic polity that emerges from the critical dialectic of *Piers Plowman*.

We cannot find Piers because through his absence Langland is teaching us something central to his understanding of authority in the church and authority of the church. Bound up with his understanding of such authority is his understanding of claims to apostolic succession in the papacy. Piers, and what he represents, is beyond us, beyond our institutions, beyond our reformations, and certainly beyond our control. The fact that some may claim the origins of the contemporary papacy are to be found in Piers and the apostolic church emerges as either a fantastical delusion or an ideology sacralizing papal power and temporalities.[328] Either way, Langland casts such modern claims in the ironic light shed by the vision of Antichrist's forces in Passus XXII, forces that include the church's hierarchy. Piers is thus obviously and hilariously quite alien to papal elections by cardinals satirized in the Prologue and later (Prol. 128–38; XVII.233–38; XXI.413–23, 428–46a). In his presence-become-absence, he is a figure to draw readers to the Christ who appears "in Peres armes" and gave Piers power to mediate the new covenant (XX.6–25; XXI.182–90, 383–90). He works in the poem both as image maker and iconoclast. He is simultaneously mediatorial gift and one who resists reification and attachment to himself. As such, nobody can, in Middleton's words, "seat him securely in a position of leadership." For he resists all attempts to claim him as a figure legitimizing contemporary authority and office in the church. He is not the stuff from which "magisterium" arises, nor is he remotely a figure who would encourage such an idea, let alone its embodiment. Langland offers an unwelcome lesson to his church as well as to the magisterial Reformation where *Piers Plowman* was published as a herald.[329] The lesson is that Christians must learn to live without any version of "magisterium" in the modern church, one that provides what Pope John Paul II describes as "certain teaching" to those blinded by "dechristianization" and a consequent *"decline or obscuring of the moral sense."*[330] We must abandon any assumption that we can have a securely seated authority. All condensations of authority in the ecclesial culture figured forth by Langland will only lock us into the "mase" of Mede and the amnesia lamented by Wille's first teacher, Holy Church, before she herself becomes as absent as Piers (I.3–9; II.53–55). Perhaps even the sacrament of penance will have to lose its current institutional forms and find ones more congruent with the theology of such absences.

Let us return to the aging Wille in the poem's ending. In obedience to a divine admonition, he remains somewhere in the church, somewhere in Unity, still seeking to learn the one "craft" absolutely necessary for human beings: "Lerne to love" (XXII.204–11). Wounded with age and threatened by death, he seems to have been ordered to follow another wounded person, Semyuief, the half-alive man rescued by Christ the Samaritan and taken into the allegorical "grange" to be healed by the Samaritan's gifts (XIX.48–79; Luke 10:25–37). But that "grange," shadowing forth the Pentecostal community of Passus XXI, has become the late medieval church led by those Langland aligns with Antichrist and draws "alle folke" to him (XXII.51–64). How is Wille to learn such a "craft" of love here, and from whom can he learn? The answer is twofold. First, the divine admonition he receives is independent of ecclesial mediation. Second, he will join the group of fools ("foles") I have already discussed, that small, dissident remnant who resisted the forces of Antichrist. After this resistance, unmediated by ecclesiastics or the church, they are called by constable Conscience to stand together in unity. Totally independent of papal church and lay elites, they now seem to constitute "Vnite holi churche" (XXII.56–68, 74–77, 204–5). Furthermore, these "fools" escape classification in terms of the modern church's fundamental and hierocratic division between clergy and laity. But whatever they are, they have received the resources to withstand the forces dominating their cultural moment and the resources to manifest the "craft" of love (XXII.61–73, 204–13). They display no residue of Constantinian Christianity and its aspirations, no signs of any papal or magisterial consolidation of hierocratic authority.

As I have argued, they represent Langland's own eschewal of institutional solutions, an eschewal shared by the post-1328 Ockham. In *Piers*

Plowman this is a logical conclusion of the work's critical and realistic dialectic. A church of fools will neither have its own apparatus of violent jurisdiction nor seek to sacralize that of the king of England and his dynastic wars. Such a church will not take control for policing orthodoxy or sacralizing the current social order against, for example, the mass rising of people below the level of gentry in 1381. A church beyond Constantinianism will not be a part of the will to power that devastates the hearts of humans in the lust for dominion pervading the earthly city. To continue in this Augustinian mode: such a church will be like pilgrims in a foreign land. They make use of temporal things in their journey but are not attached to them, not trying to accumulate them. On the contrary, these pilgrims, fools indeed, will not increase the load of temporalities they carry on their way. They do indeed make use of any peace in the earthly city, but they do so as pilgrims and captives awaiting the fulfillment of the promise of redemption in Christ and the gift of the Holy Spirit already given.[331] Such a church points beyond orthodox medieval models of reformation and beyond the institutional networks of the late medieval church. It points toward the end of Constantinian Christianity. That church had, in its clerical and lay leadership, been discerned as participating in the forces of Antichrist.

In this vision, what becomes of the indefectibility of the church, promised by Christ (Matt. 28:20)? And what becomes of its unity (XXI.328; XXII.75, 204)? Langland's answers to these questions are oblique but perfectly discernible. We have seen how Ockham understood the church's indefectibility. We recall how, for example, in his letter to the Franciscans he maintained that "the whole Church of God could be preserved in a few, indeed in one." He thinks of Elijah and reminds his readers that although it seemed that Elijah was alone there were still, hidden from the prophet's perception, "many thousands" who have not bent the knee of faith to Baal.[332] Such is the experience of the angel Abdiel in *Paradise Lost* (V.772–907; VI.1–55). And something like this will be the experience of each fool who chooses to resist the multitudes of those aligning themselves with Antichrist. However serious the crisis in the papal church, and both Ockham and Langland thought it extremely serious, however serious the crisis in the Reformation churches, and Milton thought them to be extremely serious, evangelical faith will be preserved and Christ's promise kept ("behold I am with you all days, even to the consummation of the world" [Matt.

28:20]). And so, Langland's fools: this is one consequence of the end of Constantinian Christianity. Its end will force Christians to rethink and reimagine what "church" might be or become in such changed circumstances. Doubtless this will be confused and agonizing. As Karl Barth asked many centuries later as he reflected on the shattering of the "great Constantinian delusion": "What can a few Christians or a pathetic group like the Christian community really accomplish with their scattered witness to Jesus Christ?" Not far from Langland's closing questions. But then even one of the horses pulling the harrow given to Piers by Grace had declared that the church is still under construction, its dedication deferred. Thus Augustine, harrowing Psalm 29, remembering what the "Constantinian delusion" obscured.[333]

As for the question I posed about unity at the beginning of the previous paragraph: Langland's work, especially its ending but certainly not only its ending, demands that the conventional models of unity will have to be rethought, reimagined, and superseded. Meeting this demand will belong to Conscience's new search for Grace (XXII.386). Unity will have to be reconfigured against the grain of traditions shaped by Constantinian Christianity. I have illustrated those traditions mainly from later fourteenth- and fifteenth-century texts. There we saw how unity entailed the church's sacralization of the current political order, its hierarchies and wars, while the lay sovereign defended what were called the "liberties" of the church, its privilege and temporalities. The Crown's defense of the church included its killing of those the church judged to be Christians who were its incorrigible adversaries, those judged as heretics. As an example of the celebration of the Donation of Constantine, I mentioned the work of a Dominican friar dedicated to Richard II in 1395: Dymmok's *Liber contra XII errores et hereses lollardorum*. But in the days of Ockham, an English Carmelite theologian had similarly celebrated this donation and tied it in with the temporalities of the church as the most beautiful illustration of the divine blessings poured into the Constantinian church. John Baconthorpe, unlike Langland's Liberum Arbitrium, sees no "poison" in the donation but a declaration of the way ecclesial temporalities were of divine institution. The Constantinian settlement enabled the church to surpass heresies and to establish Christian unity. In the donation and its consequences, the church "formerly poor and small like a mustard seed, grew into a great branching tree [Matt. 13:31–32] on whose boughs the pope and ecclesiastics, like birds of the air might nest."[334] With the end of Constantinian Christianity, this model of unity will cease to be hegemonic and perhaps even cease to be intelligible. At least to the "fools."

For from the endings of Langland's poem we can glimpse a very different model of unity. Unity now resides in the gathering of fools obedient to divine admonition and the counsel of Conscience, a thoroughly fallible conscience. As unlike the unity of a Pseudo-Dionysian and Neoplatonic metaphysical hierarchy as it is unlike the unity of papal apologists or Henry VIII, such a unity will demand individual decision and responsibility. It will entail a decision to oppose the unity composed by Antichrist's forces. It will be a unity that from the perspective of Antichrist's followers, with their friars, cardinals, and pope, will seem a bizarre schism, a tiny, dissident sect of fools. Antichrist is a tyrant (XXII.60), and probably such fools would come to be among those who would be "defamed" and "suspected" as making "unlawful conventicles and confederacies," holding and exercising "schools" and informing people "to sedition and insurrection," people who would be handed to the lay powers "to be burnt" in a public place. Thus *De heretico comburendo* in 1401.[335] In his depiction of a few fools openly opposing the multitudes who follow Antichrist, Langland shows his agreement with Ockham's view that "it is more commonly the multitude that is in error." Indeed, Ockham argues that the common view "that one should not go against the multitude, smacks clearly of heresy."[336] Three centuries later John Milton, in *Areopagitica*, would remind readers anxious about conflicts between Christians in the 1640s, "The Christian faith . . . was once a schism."[337] Langland too was trying to develop a model of unity which would not preclude arguments and actions that challenge the reigning hegemony and consensus in the church. Unity must not be reified, fetishized as it was in so much orthodox Christian discourse of the Middle Ages and the magisterial Reformation. Elizabethan language legislating against Presbyterians or Brownists or others opposed to the current version of Constantinian Christianity echoes the repealed *De heretico comburendo* with an unacknowledged irony. So, for example, in 1593 an act is passed against the "perils" of disunity caused by "wicked and dangerous practices of seditious sectaries," by those who gather together in "conventicles, or meetings under colour or pretence of any exercise of religion contrary to her majesty's said laws and statutes." This was directed against Protestants.[338] Instead of such a model of unity,

Langland's work encourages us to unpack the language of unity to discern the practices in which it is immersed. How could this be pursued?

One could, for example, see the role of this model of unity in the conviction and punishment of those classified as heretics in late medieval England. Hawisia Mone, from Loddon in Norfolk, had been arrested by Bishop Alnwick of Norwich for maintaining views such as the following: "the pope of Rome is fadir Antecrist, and fals in all hys werkyng, and hath no poar [power] of God more then any other lewed [unlearned] man but if he be more holy in lyvyng . . . and he that the puple callen the pope of Roome is not pope but a fals extersioner and a deseyver of the puple." Or this, on the sacrament of penance: "confession shuld be maad oonly to God" while "sufficient penance for all maner of synne is every persone to abstyne hym fro lyyng, bakbytyng and yuel doyng." On the universal priesthood of believers: "every man and every woman beynng in good lyf oute of synne is as good prest and hath as much poar of God in al thynges as any prest ordred [ordained], be he pope or bisshop." She had not only thought such things but gathered with like-minded Christians in her house in Loddon. She was forced to acknowledge practices she must now agree to abandon if she was not to be killed in the maintenance of ecclesial unity:

> Y, Hawisia Moone, the wyfe of Thomas Moone of Lodne of your diocese, your subject, knowyng, felyng and undirstanyng that before this tyme Y have be right hoomly and prive with many heretikes [now forced to apply the hierarchy's language about herself and the fellow-Christians gathered in her house], knowyng thaym for heretikes, and thaym Y have receyved and herberwed in our hous, and thaym Y have conceled, conforted, supported, maytened and favored with al my poar—whiche heretikes names be these, Sir William Whyte, Sir William Caleys, Sir Huwe Pye, Sir Thomas Pert, prestes, John Waddon, John Fowlyn, John Gray, William Everden, William Bate of Sethyng, hys wyf, William Wardon, John Pert, Edmond Archer of Lodne, Richard Belward, Nicholas Belward, Bertholomeu Monk, William Wright and many others— whiche have ofte tymes kept, holde and continued scoles of heresie yn prive chambres and prive places of oures [the home of her and her husband, Thomas], yn the whyche scoles Y have herd, conceyved, lerned and reported the errours and heresies which be writen and contened in these indentures.[339]

Of the people Hawisia mentions, John Waddon, Hugh Pye, and William White had already been burned to death in Norwich, and William Caleys would be burned to death in Colchester (1430). She, with her fellows, follows the church's language, promising to return "to the oonhed of the Churche" (142). That is, to the church's version of unity enforced by coercive jurisdiction. This included public punishments such as floggings, humiliating processions, imposed fasting, imprisonment, and, as we have noticed, fire.[340] Unity, certainly, of a kind. Yet Hawisia's own abjuration, into her persecutors' script, does sketch a version of Christian unity, albeit one opposed to that of "the Churche of Roome," "holy Churche" (142). It outlines the model of the church as a freely chosen gathering of Christians in the houses of particular families. Hawisia's home becomes a place of Christian study ("scoles of heresie yn prive chambres and prive places of oures") and the solidarity of Christian fraternity ("Y have conceled, comforted, supported, mayntened"). Here one was "right hoomly" with others. Here too women could teach and be recognized as teachers, at least in Norfolk. For example, Margery Baxter of Martham refers to Hawisia Mone as the wisest woman in teaching ("sapientissima mulier in doctrina," 47).[341] It is no coincidence that these house churches mirror accounts of house churches in the letters of St. Paul.[342]

Nor is it at all unjustified, in the context of the Roman Church's model of unity and coercive jurisdiction administered through the lay power, that Wyclif should have wondered how Jesus Christ would be received in contemporary England. Suppose Christ came as a pilgrim, perhaps such as Conscience intends to be at the end of *Piers Plowman*; or suppose he came as an unknown prelate ("prelatus incognitus"), such as the figure of Piers for whom Conscience searches, if a "prelate" then certainly "incognitus" and a layperson, never ordained within the system of ordination maintained by the late medieval church. Suppose too that Christ behaved as he had done in his earthly life. Wyclif is sure he would be excommunicated by the Roman curia, and unless he recanted the truth he proclaimed, he would be burned to death as a heretic.[343] Wyclif recalls that Christ was executed as a heretic, and he thinks it very likely that "our prelates" condemn many as heretics who in God's judgment are nothing of the sort. In acting thus our prelates whether actually reprobates ("presciti") or sinning mortally are the heretics. Only those who follow Christ's law are catholic Christians, and only those who refuse to live a life trying to serve this law are heretics.[344] So the currently dominant model of "unity" will have to be abandoned. It exacerbates the likelihood of scapegoating in a manner that recapitulates the politics of the Crucifixion, scapegoating evocatively analyzed by René Girard.[345]

But if the unity of the church is manifested by rebellious, dissenting fools, in what does it reside, and how could one recognize it? To use language from prewar congregationalism in the seventeenth century, how do we identify "Christ's true visible political church"?[346] Langland's answer to Henry Jacob's question is that the church is where "foles" (like Wille) are learning "to love" in obedience to divine admonition. Such a love, the poem has insisted, is inseparable from a commitment to the justice encapsulated in the demand made by Christ, "*redde quod debes*" (XXII.207–11; XXI.182–87). In the figure of the Samaritan, Christ had also taught that the one unforgivable sin against the Holy Spirit is *unkindness* to one's fellow creatures (XIX.113–230). Along with these identifiable practices of justice and charity, we will recognize the fool's church by its opposition to the hierarchical, powerful, affluent Constantinian church so devastatingly criticized by Liberum Arbitrium and so prominent in Antichrist's army. If neither pope nor lay sovereign is head of the church, Christ's putative viceregent on earth, who is the head of the fools? It is Jesus Christ (Col. 1:18; Eph. 5:23), entered "into heaven itself, that he may appear now in the presence of God for us" (Heb. 9:24). The legacy of his work, Langland showed, was poured into history by the Holy Spirit in the Pentecostal community. From there, as we saw, the Holy Spirit and Piers become absent. Or, at least, their presence becomes indiscernible to Conscience and those in the church where he was constable. Piers, as I have shown with help from Elizabeth Salter and Anne Middleton, becomes a mediator of the divine vision in a manner that is antithetical to any imaginable medieval pope. It would have been easy for Langland to treat the situation in Passus XXII as one requiring the deposition of the delinquent pope (or popes, since 1378), to join in the discourses catalyzed by the Great Schism.[347] We followed passages of neo-Wycliffite reformation within Langland's work but saw this finally set aside for a range of good reasons there is no need to rehearse. As I have argued, like Ockham, Langland also eschewed any institutional solutions to his critical dialectic of the church and contemporary Christianity.

But perhaps the eschewal begets some further questions, although they may not be ones Langland articulated explicitly. Certainly Sarah

Beckwith and William Revere, responding independently to my commentary in this section of the essay, have both asked tough questions which I will try to address. I do so because these are very relevant to Langland's own explorations. How, they asked, do Langland and Aers, his admiring commentator, envisage the continuity of such a church of fools? How would one become apprenticed in the intellectual and moral habits that enable us to become flourishing human beings directed to the divine end revealed by Holy Church, Piers, and Christ? One might well remember that blissful moment on Easter Sunday when Wille called Kitte, his wife, and Calote, his daughter, to join the community, ringing bells "to the resureccioun" and the emancipation Christ has brought from sin and fear (XX.467–75). Can the group of fools in Passus XXII perform such worship, as communitarian and liturgical as it is individual and existential? Ruminating on such questions, I turn to "the church of God that is at Corinth," the church served not by Piers but by Paul (1 Cor. 1:1–2). What a mess! Contentions, shameful litigation to pagan judges, Christians defrauding Christians, nascent antinomianism, incest, excommunication, class divisions at the heart of the Lord's Supper (see 1 Cor.). Is Christ divided, Paul asks incredulously (1 Cor. 1:13)? Surely charity, the gifts of the Spirit, and unity go together? They do indeed. But once upon a time Paul had assumed that the unity God demanded entailed persecuting those who seemed divisive forces in the community. He had relished the killing of the rebellious fool Stephen (Acts 7:54–59). As he was to confess: "beyond measure, I persecuted the church of God and wasted it" (Gal. 1:13). But a vision of Christ in glory identifying himself not with the godly persecutors but with the persecuted forced an often agonizing transformation of his understanding of God's always faithful but strange and unpredictable ways (Rom. 9–11). So he became a fool and an evangelist of the gospel's foolishness to "the weak things of the world," to "the base things of the world and the things that are contemptible." For, so he had come to see, these "hath God chosen: and things that are not, that he might bring to nought things that are" (1 Cor. 2:14). Can such ruminations answer the kind of questions put by Sarah Beckwith and William Revere? Perhaps not, or at least not yet. For my Corinthian ruminations do remain rather far from any designs for an ecclesial polity, whether one assumed by papal apologists in the Middle Ages, by St. Thomas Aquinas, by the hierarchy of

the late medieval church in England, by magisterial reformers in the sixteenth century, or by the Erastians who formed the Church of England.
Langland, however, is quite clear that the fools in his final passus do not lack
the memory and even the voice of divine love: "Lerne to loue" (XXII.208);
"let us love one another: for charity is of God . . . God is charity" (1 John
4:7–8; quoted by Holy Church to Wille in Passus I.82). True enough,
their calling and discipleship does lack the order glimpsed in the Pentecostal community, its agrarian organizations (allegorical and social) and its
range of divine gifts. At least it seems to lack all this. But does such a
judgment forget a strange presence in the group of fools? Wille himself,
now one of the fools, asks a question which, I think, encapsulates the ones
put by Beckwith and Revere: "what craft be beste to lere?" (XXII.207).
What apprenticeship in the virtues do I now need? The answer, one I have
just rehearsed, is too familiar for strangeness. But it may still be a frustrat-
ing one for those seeking apprenticeship in a "craft" where the very fabric
that enables any sustained and orderly life seems catastrophically un-
woven. Here is the familiar answer from the hidden source of life: "Lerne
to loue . . . and leef all other" (XXII.208). No wonder Wille feels obliged
to remind his divine teacher that he is an embodied soul, the kind which
Piers Plowman was written to nourish: "How shal Y come to catel so, to
clothe me and to fede?" (How shall I earn a living, to clothe and feed myself?) (XXII.209). Wille's question pervades the poem as its author strives
to discern and hold the divine vision in a time of trouble. But the answer
he receives is, yet once more, as uncompromising as it is familiar: "And
thow loue lelly, lack shal the neuere / Wede ne worldly mete while thy life
lasteth" (If you love loyally, you'll never lack / Clothes or earthly food as
long as you live) (XXII.210–11). In its laconic way, this recapitulates central strands in Jesus's teaching (Matt. 6:24–34; John 6:22–35; Luke
12:13–34). This is an exemplary act of trust, of faith drawn by love. Wille
commits himself to follow the divine counsel even though he cannot yet
see what will be the specific embodiment love could take in this unpropitious historical moment. An abandonment of received institutional forms
and their hierarchies of authority (currently in the service of Antichrist) is
now appropriate. And perhaps it is helpful to recall Paul's letter to the He-
brews. Faith is celebrated as "the substance of things to be hoped for, the
evidence of things that appear not." This virtue is shown by Abraham who

"obeyed to go out into a place which he was to receive for an inheritance. And he went out, not knowing where he went" (Heb. 11:1, 8).

But I do want to emphasize that the last thing Langland encourages here is a reification of such a moment in salvation history. Any such reification would, without irony, seek to institutionalize a particular divine encounter into a putatively holy anarchism, a dogmatic iconoclasm abstracted from Langland's own dialectical union of iconoclasm with image formation and veneration: "Arise and go reuerence godes resurreccioun / And crepe to the croes on knees and kusse hit for a iewel / And rightfollokest a relyk, noon richore on erthe" (Arise, and go reverence God's resurrection, / And creep on your knees to the cross and kiss it as a jewel / And most rightfully as a relic, none richer on earth) (XX.470–72). Far from being any fantasy of institutionalized anarchism or solipsistic individualism, the moment in which fools are gathered against the late medieval church's version of Constantinian Christianity belongs to a thoroughly particular and contingent process, one I have tried to follow in this essay. Langland has taught us not to abstract any particular moment for analysis without careful attention to its place in the totality of processes to which it belongs, a moment both constituted and constituting. The God disclosed in Langland's poem reveals sacred narratives in the minute particulars of life just as the latter will finally become intelligible within the grandest providential narratives.

So we are not called to abstract and institutionalize the moments dramatized at the end of Passus XXII, for these belong in the dialectical processes through which the poet displays his understanding of God's ways with humanity and humanity's ways with God. The eschewal of institutional solutions and formations by the inspired fools in Passus XXII has thoroughly particular contexts and justifications. It belongs to the processes I have sought to follow. It does, however, have a tendency, a drawing beyond the poem's ending, an ending, after all, which is the initiation of a search for Piers the plowman under the invocation of the Holy Spirit. My name for the direction in which Langland is moving with the "foles" and the present absences is *congregationalism*. Perhaps the direction is toward the kind of congregation emerging in the house church of Hawisia Mone in Loddon and reemerging during the English Reformation both in opposition to the magisterial Reformation and in opposition to the restored Roman Catholicism of Mary Tudor (1553–58).[348]

XVII

There are three questions I wish to address in the conclusion to this essay. The *first* comes from what seems a common assumption in commentaries on *Piers Plowman*. Am I denying that Piers the plowman finally represents the Roman Church's theory of an unbroken succession from St. Peter to the contemporary pope elected by the church's cardinals? The answer is unequivocal: yes, and for the reasons given above in section XVI. I have shown something very different from a display of continuity from an apostolic origin to the contemporary office of pope and its encumbents with their plenitude of power, coercive jurisdiction, and temporalities. Instead of such continuity we have found a striking emphasis on the *absence* of Piers, a figure now displaced in the Roman Church's hierarchy. His absence has not been held in this church like the empty tomb, or even as an empty chair, to remind the church of its hidden source of authority "an heyh [high] vp into heuene" (XXI.191). No, on the contrary, it has been palpably filled. This Langland shows through his representations of a delinquent hierarchy whose final alignment with Antichrist is a condensed symbol of what we encountered from the Prologue and Passus II on. The ideology of Petrine succession, with its apologetics for contemporary papal power, so vehemently argued by Giles of Rome's *On Ecclesiastical Power* and so profoundly assumed in Roger Dymmok's *Liber*, this ideology is thoroughly discredited in Langland's work.

The *second* question could be phrased like this: does the dialectic of absence and presence exemplified in Langland's treatment of Piers have devotional implications? I think it does. Following Elizabeth Salter's analysis of Piers, I suggested that the absences she describes so eloquently were informed by an Augustinian understanding of the way God draws humans to the divine vision. This way involves an education in faith where God seeks worshippers who acknowledge that "God is a spirit" and who worship God "in spirit and in truth" (John 4:23–26). Augustine illustrated his meaning in a striking discussion of the encounter between the risen Christ and Mary Magdalene in John's Gospel: "Touch me not, for I am not yet ascended to my Father" (John 20:17). This "noli me tangere" greatly troubled Margery Kempe, a classic practitioner of conventional late medieval devotion to the humanity of Christ, especially to the Passion.[349] She has been contemplating the events of the Passion with her habitually detailed identification, comforting the Virgin Mary with "a good cawdel [drink]" and staying with her to the time when the resurrected Christ visits his mother. After this meeting Jesus asks his mother's permission to visit Mary Magdalene. His encounter with Mary follows the Gospel's narrative. In response to Jesus's "Towche me not," Mary replies, "A, Lord, I se wel ye wil not [do not wish] that I be so homly [familiar] wyth yow as I have ben aforn," and Margery observes that Mary "mad hevy cher" (took on a sorrowful expression). Jesus, however, promises Mary that he will never forsake her and sends her to tell the disciples he has arisen. Margery sees Mary obey "with gret joye," and she expresses her own "gret merveyl" at this. For, she says, had Jesus said "Towche me not" to Margery, "hir thowt sche cowde nevyr a ben mery" (she thought that she never could have been merry). Indeed, whenever she hears these words spoken in any sermon, "as sche dede many tymes, sche wept, sorwyd, and cryid as sche schulde a deyd, for lofe and desir [as if she would have died of love and desire]." This is a conventional form of devotion in Langland's church.[350]

Augustine preaches on the text that troubled Margery. He sees the episode as training in how "to discern things human and divine." When Jesus says, "Touch me not," he is "giving a lesson in faith to the woman." Mary had first mistaken the risen Christ for the gardener, and Augustine characteristically moves into an allegorical mode: "this gardner was sowing in her heart, and in His own garden, the grain of mustard seed." Why does he say, "Touch me not," and why does he say, "For I am not yet ascended to my Father"? And why did he tell the incredulous Thomas to thrust his hand into Christ's side (John 20:27)? Augustine dismisses misogynistic exegesis and goes on to unfold the "sacred mystery" in the text. Christ is drawing disciples, like Mary, to touch him "spiritually," to perceive his union with the Father and to set aside belief in his humanity "according to present notions," "carnally." For Mary, he says, was still weeping over him "as a man," not yet believing that he is the Son of God: "'For I am not yet ascended,' He says, 'to my Father': there shalt thou touch me, when thou believest me to be God, in no wise unequal with the Father." As for Thomas, "He saw and touched the man and acknowledged the God whom he neither saw nor touched."[351]

So Jesus is teaching that his disciples will have to overcome their resistance to the forms of faith and spiritual worship now required of them by the Resurrection and Ascension. Of course, much medieval devotion, in the traditions of the *Meditationes Vitae Christi*, Nicholas Love's *Mirror of the Blessed Life of Jesus Christ*, and Margery Kempe's *Book*, set aside such teaching and sidelined Augustinian theologies focusing on absence, on revelation that veils, and on contemplative detachment from the body *in* and *through* reflection on the Incarnation, Crucifixion, Resurrection, and Ascension.[352] And perhaps such setting aside was bound up with conventional teaching on transubstantiation and the multiplication of visions centered on the bleeding Christ, or parts of the bleeding Christ's body in the Eucharist.[353] The Dominican Roger Dymmok, whose defense of the English Church in 1395 has already been mentioned, exemplifies the kind of association I have in mind. In defending the church from Wycliffite criticisms, he moves from temporalities and power to the Eucharist. Dymmok affirms the church's teaching that Christ is present in his Galilean body once the bread has been consecrated and frequently appears in the consecrated Host. He rejects arguments that Christ's presence is figurative.[354] Wyclif had maintained that Christ is indeed present in the Eucharist, really present ("realiter"). But this is a spiritual presence, not one in which communicants will eat the body of Christ with their teeth but rather with faith: one communicates, one is nurtured by Christ, but one sees through a glass darkly, figuratively ("in aenigmate" [1 Cor. 13:12]).[355] Such teaching, denying that the bread's substance ceased to exist after consecration and denying the presence of Christ's Galilean body, was deemed heretical in the late medieval church. From 1401, persevering in such teaching was considered good reason for burning its adherents to death. Aquinas himself had, like Wyclif, affirmed Christ's presence in the sacrament and agreed that he cannot be seen in the sacrament since he is present in the mode of substance. However, unlike Wyclif, he insisted that Christ is present in his Galilean body: "not only the flesh, but the whole body of Christ, that is, the bones and nerves and all the rest" (*non solum caro, sed totum corpus Christi, scilicet ossa, nervi et alia hujusmodi*).[356]

Not only does Dymmok follow his Dominican master, as I observed, but he offers another thoroughly un-Augustinian and un-Langlandian assertion. He claims that Christ is always present in his Galilean body on the church's altars at the consecration *because he wanted his church to have his full bodily presence throughout history*.[357] So the lack inscribed in the strangeness of Christ's resurrection (the disciples don't recognize him, mistake him for the gardener or a strangely ignorant visitor to Jerusalem) and in Christ's ascension is simply overcome. Christians always have the Galilean body of Christ. Against the grain of the evangelical texts, the Resurrection does not create something strange, in history and not in history. Nor does the Ascension. So Dymmok and his church's orthodoxy overcome the *noli me tangere*, the *touch me not* that so perturbed Margery Kempe and troubled the conventional devotional forms she practiced so intensely. The church's priests are entrusted by Christ with the gift of continually making Christ fully present "bones and nerves and all the rest." Margery Kempe's understanding of this is fully articulated by Nicholas Love in the immensely popular *Mirror of the Blessed Life of Jesus Christ.* He emphasizes that the very body seen by the disciples at the Last Supper, "with hir bodily eye," was also the body present "vndur þat forme of brede" now displayed in the hands of the church's priests.[358] So Margery Kempe and other faithful Christians can set aside Paul's teaching that "though we have known Christ according to the flesh, yet now henceforth know we him no more" (*si cognovimus secundum carnem Christum: sed nunc iam non novimus*) (2 Cor. 5:16). But setting aside such teaching, however conventional in the dominant, pervasive forms of devotion in his church, is alien to the conclusions of Langland's work, and, so I have argued elsewhere, to his vision of Christian life.[359] Some people will receive the peculiar grace of such encounters with Christ as Wille has done (with Christ as the Samaritan or with Christ in "Peres armes" *before* the consecration of the bread and wine in the Mass [XIX; XXI.4–14]), or as Julian of Norwich recollects and strives to interpret in her *Showings.* But such encounters cannot be institutionalized. Nor can even the contexts in which such encounters might be given. We have been endowed with no such controls. The church and its hierarchy have been given no gift to control the giving of such gifts. And while Christ "yaf [gave] Peres pardoun" and promised the gift of forgiveness to those who seek to follow the demands of evangelical justice ("*Redde quod debes*"), Christ's ascension is emphasized in Passus XXI: "an heyh vp into heuene / He wente, and woneth there and wol come at the laste / And rewarde hym riht wel that *reddet quod debet,* / Payeth parfitly as puyr treuthe wolde" (on high up into heaven / He went, and dwells there, and will come at the end / And reward him right well who *reddet quod debbet* [pays what one owes], / Pays perfectly as pure truth wishes) (XXI.191–94). Far from promising the kind of presence on which Margery Kempe's devotion centers, Jesus tells his disciples, before the Crucifixion, "I will pray to the Father, and he shall give you another Comforter [Paracletum], that he may abide with you for ever." He promises, "I will not leave you orphans" but will come to you. Not, however, to remain in the Galilean body on your altars but through the Holy Spirit for whose presence he has prayed: "the Comforter [Paraclitus] which is the Holy Ghost [Spiritus Sanctus], whom the Father will send you in my name, he shall teach you all things" (John 14:16–26). So "when the Comforter [Paraclitus] is come, whom I will send unto you from the Father, even the Spirit of truth, which procedeth from the Father, he shall testify of me" (John 15:26). And that is just what Langland dramatizes in Passus XXI, as he moves from Christ's Ascension to Pentecost.

But "The Spirit breatheth where he will" (*Spiritus ubi vult spirat* (John 3:8), and in Passus XXI he builds "an hous" for Piers to put crops in but then disappears: he "wente / As wyde as the world is," taking Piers with him (XXI.317–33). So Piers's appearances cannot be institutionalized, cannot be guaranteed by human agents. He is with the Holy Spirit. In Langland's theology, Piers's absences disclose a dialectic of absence and presence beyond the control of humans, even if those humans are Christians in search of Treuthe, in search of Christ. Conscience grasps this in his final cry for the Holy Spirit and prayer for finding Piers as he becomes a pilgrim to go "as wyde as the world renneth" (XXII.380–86). He grasps and now represents the antiformalism, the iconoclasm at the heart of Langland's image making.[360] His dialectical literary modes and their ecclesiological outcome are inseparable. In his ecclesiology, so I have argued, we see not only the end of Constantine Christianity, but the withering away of its sustaining practices.

The *third* question I wish to address in the final part of this book is the following: what is the relation between the figure of Holy Church in Passus I and II, a figure who appeared earlier in this essay, and the vision of the late medieval church from Passus XXI.335 through XXII.379? Let us return to the "louely lady of lere [face] in lynnene yclothed" who appears to Wille in Passus I, names him, and asks him if he is asleep (I.3–5). Langland identifies the figure as descending from God whose will she mediates (I.3–67, 81–204). Frightened and dazzled, Wille cannot recognize her. So she discloses herself: "Holy Churche Y am" (I.72). Derek Pearsall and other annotators provide ample discussion of antecedents for this figuration.[361] Langland's ascription of heavenly authority to this figure is unequivocal, and she instructs Wille in a wide range of literary modes, including an exquisitely beautiful lyric on the divine love manifest in the Incarnation (I.146–70).[362] She explains to Wille that although he fails to recognize her, she is the church into which he has been baptized and made a "fre man" (I.72–75). She is thus a figure of the church proclaimed in the Nicene Creed, the "holy Catholic and apostolic Church."[363] Far from being immersed in the fabrics of the world's markets and lust for dominion, she descends from heaven to ask Wille if he has noticed the processes of de-Christianization already hinted at in the Prologue:

> Wille, slepestou? seestow this peple,
> Hou bisy thei ben aboute the mase?
> The moste party of this peple that passeth on this erthe,
> Haue thei worschip in this world thei wilneth no bettere;
> Of othere heuene then here thei halde no tale.
>
> (I.5–9)

———

> [Are you asleep, Will? See these people,
> How busily they move about the maze?
> Most of the people that pass through this earth
> Are satisfied with success in this world;
> The only heaven they think of is here.]

And to these processes the Prologue had shown the contemporary church belonged. But not at all as a critical presence. On the contrary, already we have seen how cardinals "preseumen in hemself a pope to make," how friars appropriate scripture "for profyt of the wombe," how secular clergy serve lay elites in their thoroughly material interests, how the sacrament of reconciliation is commodified, how what Langland confidently judges as *idolatry* is normalized in England's parishes (Prol. 136, 56–61, 62, 66–67, 95–124). Far from identifying with this church, Holy Church is made sharply distinct and laments the way Mede's forces pervade it, while Mede herself is now an intimate in the pope's palace (II.1–24). The figure from heaven tells Wille that he should *go to the gospel* (I.44). She does not send him to a priest or any other authority in the contemporary church. As soon as Wille grasps who is instructing him, he responds appropriately:

"Y knelede on my knees and criede here of grace / And preyede here pitously to preye for me to amende" (I fell to my knees and cried to her for grace / And begged her to take pity and pray I improve) (I.76–77).[364] She is indeed the true church, the "lemman" (lover) of Treuthe (II.20), the one whose evangelical knowledge elicits from Wille two pleas that are central to Langland's exploration of Christian's life in his own historical moment: a plea for appropriate faith in Christ and a plea to learn how he may save his soul (I.78–80).

After she has reminded Wille of God's supernatural ends for humanity and the way opened out by divine love, that "plonte [plant] of pees, most precious of vertues" (I.146–54), she makes us look once more at Mede's hegemony in the modern church. After that she commends Wille to Christ and leaves him, "lyggynge as aslepe" (lying as if asleep) (II.1–56). Never again does she appear. She is thus the work's first example of a revelatory gift. The presence of such gifts is soon withdrawn, leaving the recipient with an absence. But in such moments, in such gifts revelation *creates its subjects*. The ensuing absence fosters, as Augustine and Langland both taught, memory and faith. But because God's free grace creates free subjects, recipients of such gifts may meet their withdrawal with amnesia and denial. We are shown plenty of that in Passus XXI and XXII. And Holy Church in Passus I and II is like the risen and ascended Christ, like the apparently absent Holy Spirit and Piers. She escapes the control of those she emancipates ("fre man the made" [I.72–73]). She calls and draws Wille, but, like Piers, she cannot be turned into a human institution where her presence can be controlled, guaranteed. She belongs to a work in which the unveiling presence of divine visions is inextricably bound up with absence and hiddenness.[365]

As I have remarked, Holy Church is the poem's first manifestation of the forms in which revelation is received. But *Piers Plowman* begins *after* the decisive events dramatized later in the poem, the Christological, pneumatological, and ecclesial events of Passus XVIII–XXI. Out of those events came the Pentecostal community where Piers acknowledged that he himself could not build the house that the Holy Spirit desired for the crop of reconciled souls. Only the Holy Spirit, building with the legacy of Christ's Incarnation, could do this. And so he does. But as soon as this house, called "Holy Chirche," is built on the foundation of Christ's

Crucifixion and mercy, the Holy Spirit, with Piers, leaves (XXI.317–22). He leaves the church under the guidance of a layman, constable Conscience. In section IV of this essay I followed the story Langland unfolds, paying attention especially to its theological and ecclesial significances. Langland's disclosure that the Holy Spirit and Piers set out from the house as soon as it was composed brings him into whispering distance of the prophecy of the church's history told by the archangel Michael toward the end of Milton's *Paradise Lost*. After the apostolic ministry:

> Their doctrine and their story written left,
> They die; but in their room, as they forewarn,
> Wolves shall succeed for teachers, grievous wolves,
> Who all the sacred mysteries of Heav'n
> To their own vile advantages shall turn
> Of lucre and ambition, and the truth
> With superstitions and tradition taint.
>   (XII.506–12; see 469–551)[366]

However different their modes may be, Langland's vision is as subversive of Constantinian Christianity as is Milton's, as subversive of the magisterial forms of authority it performs. Langland's critical dialectic has only just gotten under way when Wille receives his vision of Holy Church. But when we reflect on this episode in the poem's totality, we see that it is a vision given to one who will join the fools ("foles") of the version of the church emerging after Constantinianism. Its lament about the contemporary church, pervaded by Mede, contributes to the work's disclosure of this modern church as a parodic simulacrum of the celestial figure.[367] As for Wille's perception of the celestial figure, he has done nothing to earn such a gift. On the contrary, he is rebuked for his amnesia, a fitting mark of the contemporary church introduced in the Prologue, one in which he wanders dressed up as a sheep, as a hermit "vnholy of werkes" (Prol. 1–4).[368] This does sound bad, rather like one of the "grievous wolves" Milton's archangel prophesies (see Acts 20:29), one of those false prophets in sheep's clothing who are inwardly "ravening wolves" about whom Jesus warned his disciples (Matt. 7:15). And yet this Wille turns out to have no ambitions in or for the Constantinian church and, drawn by grace, will become, in the end, one of the post-Constantinian fools in Passus XXII.

In fact, disciples of Christ are found in all sorts of places and vocations. Agricultural laborers like Piers the Plowman (Prol. 22–24; VII.182–282); anchorites and hermits "that holdeth hem in here [their] selles" (Prol. 27–32); people scattered among poor and rich, even once, in a distant past, a friar and, once upon a time, kings and cardinals, according to Liberum Arbitrium (XVI.340–74a). These all foreshadow the fools of the poem's ending, and all seem to practice discipleship in a manner independent of any ecclesiastic hierarchy directing their spiritual life, let alone of any identifiable magisterium deploying a legitimate coercive jurisdiction replete with worldly power.

While Langland discerns Christian discipleship in such individuals and groups, he also implies that individual spiritual disciplines, active and contemplative, guided by the Holy Spirit, may lead to the making of a church in the Christian's heart. This church within seems happier far and more faithful than any historical institution proves to be:

> And yf Grace graunte the to go in in this wyse
> Thow shalt se Treuthe sitte in thy sulue herte
> And solace thy soule and saue the fram payne
> And charge Charite a churche to make
> In thyne hole herte . . .
> (VII.254–58)

> [And if Grace grants you to go in in this way
> You shall see Truth sitting in your own heart,
> And solace your soul and save you from pain,
> And charge Charity to build a church
> In your whole heart . . .]

Here the devout layman Piers the plowman instructs lost Christians ("A thousand of men") who have just completed the church's sacrament of penance and immediately lost "the way." So much so that none of them knows how to carry on but "blostrede forth as bestes" (VII.155–60). Piers had preceded his promise of God dwelling in man with an explication of the path marked out by the Ten Commandments followed by an eloquent account of divine mercy as the "mote" (moat) of the heavenly mansion (VII.205–34). His outline of the church of God within the searching person is congruent with an earlier promise made by Holy Church. God is Love (1 John 4:8), she told Wille, and whoever seeks to embody truth in daily practice with a benevolent disposition to others gradually draws toward a convergence with divine life. In her language, a human becomes "a god by the gospel" (according to the gospel) (I.81–87).[369] In neither Holy Church's promise nor Piers's teaching does the joyful discovery of God within the human subject imply an isolated or solipsistic individual any more than it did in Augustine's *Confessions*. It is made very clear that the church *within* is *also* "to herborwe" (to provide refuge for) others, to offer nutritive communion, friendship with "alle manere folke" (VII.254–60). Furthermore, it should be recognized that such a church within is not only independent of any hierocratic institution overseeing this Christian life: it is quite antithetical to conventional hierarchies.

With this observation in mind, let us recollect a description of the church by Liberum Arbitrium. I have discussed his critique of Constantinian ecclesiology together with his ironically Constantinian proposal for reformation, a proposal finally superseded after subjection to a devastating narrative sequence in the poem's final two passus (see the preface and sections XIV–XV above). But he also evoked a very different model of church. Wille asks him, "What is holy churche, chere [dear] frende?" (XVII.125). His answer is summed up in one word: "'Charite,' he said" (XVII.125). However enigmatic the reply, his gloss on it shows that such a church is far removed from the contemporary ecclesiastical polity with its material powers and hierarchies of dominion. Liberum Arbitrium has in mind not such an institution, even if reformed by an armed elite, but rather a form of life freely chosen ("liberum arbitrium" is speaking). The latter is beautifully described as a "loue-knotte" in which people hold together in "o will," lending and selling with integrity, a memory of relations in the Pentecostal community founded by the Holy Spirit (XVII.125–29; XXI.213–61). No hierarchy and no conventional signs of divisions between laity and clergy can even be glimpsed in this model.

From Piers, Liberum Arbitrium, the celestial figure of Holy Church, and the Holy Spirit, Langland gives us hints and sketches of a church after the end of Constantinianism. These hints and sketches give us Langland's answer to the third question I asked in this section: what are the relations between Holy Church in Passus I and II and the work's vision of the contemporary church especially from Passus XXI.335 through XXII.379? The latter represents the contemporary Roman Church as a demonic simulacrum of the Pentecostal church of the Holy Spirit and Piers. It *obstructs* the visions of the risen Christ and the Holy Spirit. It *dissolves* the memory of doctrine taught so carefully by Christ the Samaritan and Christ the emancipatory orator in hell. It infuses Christians living in the Roman Church and obeying its mandatory sacrament of penance with an overwhelming opiate. This enchanting drug is represented by Langland as part of Antichrist's de-Christianization of church and polity. Perhaps Langland would have read with some sympathy Karl Barth's comments on secularization in his treatment of the doctrine of reconciliation:

> Secularisation is the process by which the salt loses its savour (Matthew 5:13). It is not in any sense strange that the world is secular. This is simply to say that the world is the world. It was always secular. There is no greater error than to imagine that this was not the case in the much-vaunted Middle Ages. But when the Church becomes secular, it is the greatest conceivable misfortune both for the Church and the world. And this is what takes place when it wants to be a Church only for the world, the nation, culture or the state — a world Church, a national Church, a cultural Church, or a state Church. It then loses its specific importance and meaning; the justification for its existence.[370]

But instead of a Constantinian church, triumphant in its worldly achievements so lovingly celebrated by Roger Dymmok, and instead of a representation of total de-Christianization, Langland leaves us with the church of a few fools. They would doubtless agree with the teaching of Robert Holcot, that fascinating Dominican theologian who died in the great plague: "The determination of conscience is more binding than the command of a prelate."[371] Langland shows us Conscience abandoning the modern church led by pope (or popes, in the present Schism) and cardinals, searching for the absent Piers, and crying out to the Holy Spirit. As he does so, the reader should recollect the hints and sketches of very different visions of the church that have emerged in the dismantling and wreckage of the Constantinian church and its putatively Constantinian reformation. Such emerging visions eschew institutionalization. All attempts to control divine ways and gifts are abandoned. The emergent visions point toward a strange church of fools who will not be drugged into oblivion of the reconciliatory gifts of God manifested in Christ, the Holy Spirit, and the martyrs. As for Langland's work, closing with a new pilgrimage, by one who now recognizes himself as a pilgrim and stranger (Heb. 11:13), one could well say of it what Julian says of her own *Showings*: "This boke is begonne by Goddys gyfte and his grace, but it is nott yet performyd as to my syght."[372]

NOTES

PREFACE

1. Pearsall's edition of the poem was published by Exeter University Press but was transferred in 2013 to Liverpool University Press, from which I received permission from Jenny Howard in September 2013. I am grateful to both Derek Pearsall and Jenny Howard. George Economou's translation is *William Langland's "Piers Plowman": The C Version* (Philadelphia: University of Pennsylvania Press, 1996). I am grateful to Jaime Marie Estrada and Jerry Singerman at the University of Pennsylvania Press for permission.

2. *The Vision of William concerning Piers the Plowman, in Three Parallel Texts: Together with Richard the Redeless*, ed. Walter W. Skeat, 2 vols. (1886; repr. Oxford: Oxford University Press, 1968), here see 2:xxi–xxiv. For the authorship issue, see George Kane, *Piers Plowman: The Evidence for Authorship* (London: Athlone, 1965); and Ralph Hanna, *William Langland* (Aldershot: Variorum, 1993). On the published version of *Piers Plowman*, see Charlotte Brewer, *Editing "Piers Plowman": The Evolution of the Text* (Cambridge: Cambridge University Press, 1996).

3. All quotations of *Piers Plowman* unless otherwise stated are taken from *Piers Plowman: A New Annotated Edition of the C-text*, ed. Derek Pearsall (Exeter: University of Exeter Press, 2008). I have constantly consulted *Piers Plowman: The C Version; Will's Vision of Piers Plowman, Do-Well, Do-Better, and Do-Best*, ed. George Russell and George Kane (London: Athlone, 1997). For the second version of the poem I have used *Piers Plowman: The B Version*, rev. ed., ed. George Kane and E. Talbot Donaldson (London: Athlone, 1988). As for dating the C version, I am persuaded by Walter W. Skeat in the nineteenth century and most recently by Ralph Hanna that "Langland completed his C version around 1390."

Ralph Hanna, *Introducing English Medieval Book History: Manuscripts, Their Production, and Their Reading* (Liverpool: Liverpool University Press, 2013), 156. In his edition, Derek Pearsall similarly surmises that this version of the poem was "not finished until soon after 1388" (*Piers Plowman*, 1).

4. See Eamon Duffy, *The Stripping of the Altars: Traditional Religion in England, 1400–1580*, 2nd ed. (New Haven: Yale University Press, 2005).

5. For recent grand narratives in which the medieval has a substantial role to play that does not include Langland, see, for example, Charles Taylor, *A Secular Age* (Cambridge, MA: Harvard University Press, 2007); Michael Gillespie, *The Theological Origins of Modernity* (Chicago: University of Chicago Press, 2007); Brad S. Gregory, *The Unintended Reformation: How a Religious Revolution Secularized Society* (Cambridge, MA: Harvard University Press, 2012); Thomas Pfau, *Minding the Modern: Human Agency, Intellectual Traditions, and Responsible Knowledge* (Notre Dame: University of Notre Dame Press, 2013).

6. Namely, Sarah Beckwith, James Simpson, Thomas Pfau, and Stanley Hauerwas.

7. Here see Thomas Aquinas's exposition on the Pater Noster, section 1066 in his *In Orationem Dominicam Videlicet "Pater Noster" Expositio*, in *Opuscula Theologica*, ed. R. A. Verardo, R. M. Spiazzi, and M. Calcaterra, 2 vols. (Rome: Marietti, 1954), 2:228; see, too, *Summa Theologiae* I.39.4, resp.; I.39.5, resp.; I.39.5, ad 3 and ad 4; I.41.1, ad 2. I refer to part, question, and article with part of the article: I use unless otherwise indicated the six-volume (4 vols. in 6) Leonine edition titled *Summa Theologica* (Rome: Ex typographia Forzani, 1894).

8. Thomas Aquinas, *The Literal Exposition on Job*, trans. Anthony Damico (Atlanta: Scholars Press, 1989), VI.28.

9. The best introduction to Langland's *modi loquendi* remains the work of Elizabeth Salter, *Piers Plowman: An Introduction* (Cambridge, MA: Harvard University Press; Oxford: Blackwell, 1962), together with her introduction to *Piers Plowman by William Langland: An Edition of the C-Text* (London: Arnold, 1967), ed. Elizabeth Salter and Derek Pearsall, 3–58, reprinted as chap. 5 of her collected essays, *English and International: Studies in the Literature, Art, and Patronage of Medieval England*, ed. Derek Pearsall and Nicolette Zeeman (Cambridge: Cambridge University Press, 1988).

10. Alasdair MacIntyre, *After Virtue: A Study in Moral Theory*, 2nd ed. (London: Duckworth, 1985), 222.

11. See Alasdair MacIntyre, *God, Philosophy, Universities: A Selective History of the Catholic Philosophical Tradition* (Lanham, MD: Rowman and Littlefield, 2009), 169. This book involves a far more affirmative account of Scotus and Ockham than MacIntyre's work habitually provides; compare *Three Rival Versions of Moral Enquiry: Encyclopaedia, Genealogy, and Tradition* (London: Duckworth, 1990), chap. 7.

12. Here I revisit and rehearse an argument made in "English Reformations" by myself and Nigel Smith in a special issue of the *Journal of Medieval and Early Modern Studies* 40 (2010): 425–38; here see 425–26, which comes from the part of the essay for which I was responsible. For the most relevant major work deploying this language, see James Simpson, *The Oxford English Literary History, Vol. 2, 1350–1547: Reform and Cultural Revolution* (Oxford: Oxford University Press, 2002).

13. Taylor, *A Secular Age*, 61–88, 773–76. For exemplification of this thesis, see Brian Tierney, *Religion, Law, and the Growth of Constitutional Thought, 1150–1650* (Cambridge: Cambridge University Press, 1982), 38, 49, 85–86, 103–8. With this, consult Gerhart B. Ladner, *The Idea of Reform: Its Imprint on Christian Thought and Action in the Age of the Fathers* (New York: Harper and Row, 1959).

14. *ST* II–II.11.3, resp.

15. See Gordon Leff, "The Apostolic Ideal in Later Medieval Ecclesiology," *Journal of Theological Studies* 18 (1967): 58–82; see, too, Anne Hudson, *The Premature Reformation: Wycliffite Texts and Lollard History* (Oxford: Clarendon Press, 1988), chap. 7.

16. Duffy, *Stripping of the Altars*: for my own somewhat critical comments on aspects of Duffy's work, see "Altars of Power: Reflections on Eamon Duffy's *The Stripping of the Altars*," *Literature and History* 3 (1994): 90–105; see Duffy's robust response in the second edition of *Stripping of the Altars*, Preface, xx–xxviii.

17. Simpson, *Reform and Cultural Revolution*, 328–65, 370–74. For a recent attempt to assess Langland's relations with the Reformation, see Robert Adams, "Langland as a Proto-Protestant: Was Thomas Fuller Right?," in *Yee? Baw for Bokes: Essays on Medieval Manuscripts and Poetics in Honor of Hoyt N. Duggan*, ed. Michael Calabrese and Stephen H. A. Shepherd (Los Angeles: Marymount Institute Press, 2013), 245–66; see, too, Robert Adams, "Langland and the *Devotio Moderna*: A Spiritual Kinship," in *Medieval Alliterative Poetry: Essays in Honour of Thorlac Turville-Petre*, ed. John A. Burrow and Hoyt N. Duggan (Dublin: Four Courts, 2010), 23–40. Adams asserts Langland's commitment to something called "democratic perfectionism" ("Langland as a Proto-Protestant," 258), which allegedly links him to "the Radicals" of the Reformation in what seems a version of the pelagianism with which Adams has associated Langland elsewhere. On these issues, see David Aers, *Salvation and Sin: Augustine, Langland, and Fourteenth-Century Theology* (Notre Dame: University of Notre Dame Press, 2009), chap. 4.

18. Duffy, *Stripping of the Altars*, Preface, xx–xxii; see, too, the treatment of Wycliffites in Richard Rex, *The Lollards* (Basingstoke: Palgrave Macmillan, 2002).

19. Throughout I cite *Piers Plowman* by passus and line numbers from Pearsall, ed., *Piers Plowman: A New Annotated Edition of the C-text*, unless otherwise stated.

20. On the widely discussed tradition of Constantinian donation and the angelic voice proclaiming that it has poisoned the church, see the following: Beryl Smalley, *English Friars and Antiquity in the Early Fourteenth Century* (Oxford: Blackwell, 1965), 154–57; Pamela Gradon, "Langland and the Ideology of Dissent," *Proceedings of the British Academy* 66 (1980): 179–205, here 185–86; Hudson, *Premature Reformation*, 330, 334–46; Wendy Scase, *Piers Plowman and the New Anti-Clericalism* (Cambridge: Cambridge University Press, 1989), 88–91. For John Howard Yoder's reflections on Constantinian Christianity and its different historical forms, see the following: *The Priestly Kingdom: Social Ethics as Gospel* (Notre Dame: University of Notre Dame Press, 1984), chap. 7; *The Royal Priesthood* (Grand Rapids: Eerdmans, 1994), 195–203; *Christian Attitudes to War, Peace, and Revolution* (Grand Rapids: Brazos, 2009), chap. 4. See, too, Stanley Hauerwas, *Approaching the End: Eschatological Reflections on Church, Politics, and Life* (Grand Rapids: Eerdmans, 2013), 22–36; D. H. Williams, *Retrieving the Tradition and Renewing Evangelicalism* (Grand Rapids: Eerdmans, 1999), chap. 5. An excellent account of the political history in the fourth century is offered by Timothy Barnes, *Athanasius and Constantine: Theology and Politics in the Constantinian Empire* (Cambridge, MA: Harvard University Press, 1993); and Rowan Williams, *Arius: Heresy and Tradition*, rev. ed. (Grand Rapids: Eerdmans, 2002), especially 82–91, 95–116, 266–67.

BEYOND REFORMATION?

1. All quotations of *Piers Plowman* unless otherwise stated are from *Piers Plowman: A New Annotated Edition of the C-text*, ed. Pearsall, citing passus and line numbers. I have also used Russell and Kane, *Piers Plowman: The C Version*. For the B version, I refer to *Piers Plowman: The B Version*, rev. ed., ed. Kane and Donaldson. I still use the astonishingly learned commentary by Skeat in the second volume of *The Vision of William concerning Piers the Plowman*.

2. For a discussion of the theology here and its relations to ideas of universal salvation, see Aers, *Salvation and Sin*, 114–19; for the notes to secondary material relevant to this, see 216–17. See too the introduction to Pearsall's *Piers Plowman*, 37–38.

3. And apocryphal material: here see *The Middle English Harrowing of Hell and Gospel of Nicodemus*, ed. W. W. Hulme, EETS, e.s., 100 (London: K. Paul, Trench, Trübner, and Co., 1907). My reference to "so many theologians" points to the fascination with God's *potentia absoluta* among the later medieval "moderni." For a careful and lucid definition of what this is (and is not), see William of Ockham, *Opus Nonaginta Deorum*, chap. 95, trans. John Kilcullen and John Scott as *Work of Ninety Days*, 2 vols. (Lewiston, NY: Mellen Press, 2001), vol. 2; and Ock-

ham's *Quodlibetal Questions*, trans. Alfred J. Freddoso and Francis E. Kelley, 2 vols. (New Haven: Yale University Press, 1991), VI.1.1 and VI.2. For an introduction to this topic with citation of relevant commentaries, see Aers, *Salvation and Sin*, 38–45.

4. For these conventional examples of speculation concerning what God could do *de potentia absoluta*, see Ockham, *Breviloquium* V.2, translated as *A Short Discourse of Tyrannical Government*, trans. John Kilcullen, ed. Arthur McGrade (Cambridge: Cambridge University Press, 1992), 132; Ockham, *Quodlibetal Questions*, VII.55; Robert Holcot, quoted in Gordon Leff, *Medieval Thought: St. Augustine to Ockham* (Harmondsworth: Penguin, 1968), 292. Leonard A. Kennedy, *The Philosophy of Robert Holcot: Fourteenth-Century Skeptic* (Lewiston, NY: Mellen, 1993), contains many arresting examples of such speculation. For an analysis of Holcot's deployment of such material that contrasts with Kennedy's, see Hester G. Gelber, *It Could Have Been Otherwise: Contingency and Necessity in Dominican Theology at Oxford, 1300–1350* (Leiden: Brill, 2004), chaps. 3–5.

5. This is not the place where I intend to exemplify this claim: suffice it to say that anyone who spends any time reading the treatment of the Trinity in the commentaries on the first book of Peter Lombard's *Sentences*, distinctions 1–34, will find this to be so, as they will also find scripture marginalized. For an enthusiastic introduction to this theological tradition, see Russell L. Friedman, *Medieval Trinitarian Thought from Aquinas to Ockham* (Cambridge: Cambridge University Press, 2010); and his essay "Medieval Trinitarian Theology from the Late Thirteenth to the Fifteenth Centuries," in *The Oxford Handbook of the Trinity*, ed. Gilles Emery and Matthew Levering (Oxford: Oxford University Press, 2011), 197–209.

6. For an example of the affirmation of scriptural foundations of doctrine, see Aquinas, *ST* I.1.1–2 and I.1.8–10.

7. See, e.g., Friedman, *Medieval Trinitarian Thought* and "Medieval Trinitarian Theology; William J. Courtenay, *Schools and Scholars in Fourteenth-Century England* (Princeton: Princeton University Press, 1987); and Hester Gelber's extraordinary doctoral dissertation, "Logic and the Trinity: A Clash of Values in Scholastic Thought, 1300–1335" (University of Wisconsin, 1974). For a useful overall introduction, see *The History of the University of Oxford*, vol. 2, *Late Medieval Oxford*, ed. J. L. Catto and Ralph Evans (Oxford: Clarendon Press, 1992).

8. See Gelber's "Logic and the Trinity" and *It Could Have Been Otherwise*.

9. I quote scripture from the Douay Rheims translation, *The Holy Bible*, rev. Richard Challoner (Rockford, IL: Tan Books, 1989); for the Latin text of the Vulgate, I use *Biblia Sacra iuxta Vulgatem Clementinam: Nova Editio*, 4th ed., ed. Alberto Colunga and Laurentio Turrado (Matriti: Biblioteca de Autores Cristianos, 1965).

10. Earlier in the poem, Conscience, who disputes with Mede, had included the Trinity in his discourse as well as an apocalyptic discourse which I discuss later: III.344–406, 437–82a.

11. Matthew 5:44–45; Luke 6:27, 35. See too Pearsall's note to XXI.114.

12. On "alle manere men," see 1 Timothy 2:4. From Augustine through the Reformation this text elicited some of the most bizarre exegesis in Christian traditions as theologians tried to make it talk Augustinian or Thomistic or Calvinist predestinarian theology. For a typical example of this distressing chain, see Augustine, *Enchiridion* 24.97–25.1, translated by Bruce Harbert as *The Augustine Catechism*, ed. John E. Rotelle (Hyde Park, NY: New City Press, 1999); Augustine, *The Predestination of the Saints* 8.14 and *Rebuke and Grace* 14.44, trans. Roland J. Teske, in *Answer to the Pelagians IV*, The Works of Saint Augustine: A Translation for the 21st Century (hereafter WSA), ed. John E. Rotelle, pt. 1, vol. 26 (Hyde Park, NY: New City Press, 1999). For Calvin, see *Institutes* III.24.16; I use the translation by John T. McNeill and Ford L. Battles, *Institutes of the Christian Religion*, 2 vols. (Louisville, KY: Westminster John Knox Press, 1960). For Aquinas's place in this tradition, see *ST* I.19.6 and I.23.4, ad 3.

13. For a very sympathetic account of indulgences, see R. N. Swanson, *Indulgences in Late Medieval England* (Cambridge: Cambridge University Press, 2007). This work is a hymn to positivist methodologies of history.

14. On purgatory and pilgrimage, see Duffy, *Stripping of the Altars*, 338–76, 205. This and subsequent references are to the second edition.

15. Ockham's work after he withdrew obedience from the Avignon papacy will have a role in this essay. Marsilius of Padua's critique of papal claims to plenitude of power in *The Defender of the Peace*, ed. and trans. Annabel Brett (Cambridge: Cambridge University Press, 2005), has some common ground with Ockham, but his solutions are strikingly different. See Cary Nederman, *Community and Consent: The Secular Political Theory of Marsilius of Padua's "Defensor Pacis"* (Lanham, MD: Rowman and Littlefield, 1995).

16. St. Augustine, *The Retractions*, trans. Mary I. Bogan (Washington, DC: Catholic University of America Press, 1968), I.20. See with this his exposition on Psalm 60:3 and Sermon 295.1–4, in *Expositions of the Psalms*, trans. Maria Boulding, ed. John E. Rotelle, 6 vols., WSA, pt. 3, vols. 15–20 (Hyde Park, NY: New City Press, 2001–4), here WSA, pt. 3, vol. 17; and *Sermons*, trans. Edmund Hill, 10 vols., WSA, pt. 3, vols. 1–10 (Brooklyn: New City Press, 1990–95), here WSA, pt. 3, vol. 8.

17. Augustine, Sermon 76.1, in *Sermons*, trans. Hill, WSA, pt. 3, vol. 3.

18. See *Catena Aurea*, ed. and trans. John Henry Newman, 4 vols. (London: Saint Austin Press, 1999), 1:584–85.

19. For a brief introduction to some of this history, see Walter Ullman, *A History of Political Thought: The Middle Ages*, rev. ed. (Harmondsworth: Penguin, 1976), 22–28; still indispensable in following the ideology of papal monarchism and debates around it is Michael Wilks, *The Problem of Sovereignty in the Middle*

Ages (Cambridge: Cambridge University Press, 1963). For Ockham here, see *Breviloquium* II.14, in *A Short Discourse on Tyrannical Government*.

20. *Breviloquium*, II.14, in *A Short Discourse on Tyrannical Government*.

21. As do even the best commentators on the poem: Skeat, *Vision of William concerning Piers the Plowman*, 2:130; Pearsall, IX.327a, note.

22. For a fascinating account of the kind of papal bulls Langland has in mind, see the "extraordinary" but "common rubric" in collections of prayers quoted by Duffy, *Stripping of the Altars*, 287–98, at 290–91.

23. For commentary on this much interpreted scene of pardon which turns out to be "no pardon" in any sense that participants in Passus IX can grasp, see Pearsall, *Piers Plowman*, 31–32, "The Pardon sent from Truth," with his note to IX.290. For my own reading, see David Aers, *Sanctifying Signs: Making Christian Tradition in Late Medieval England* (Notre Dame: University of Notre Dame Press, 2004), 107–14.

24. For a particularly good introduction to the issues of penance in both the B and C versions of *Piers Plowman*, see Gradon, "Langland and the Ideology of Dissent," 191–93; also Hudson, *Premature Reformation*, 294–310. In general, consult Thomas Tentler, *Sin and Confession on the Eve of the Reformation* (Princeton: Princeton University Press, 1977).

25. On Langland's use of the liturgy from Passus XVIII–XXI (B XVI–XIX), see M. F. Vaughan, "The Liturgical Perspectives of *Piers Plowman* B, XVI–XIX," *Studies in Medieval and Renaissance History* 3 (1980): 87–155; Raymond St.-Jacques, "Langland's Bells of the Resurrection and the Easter liturgy," *English Studies in Canada* 3 (1977): 129–35; Raymond St.-Jacques, "Langland's Christ-Knight and the Liturgy," *Revue de l'Université d'Ottawa* 37 (1967): 144–58; Raymond St.-Jacques, "The Liturgical Associations of Langland's Samaritan," *Traditio* 25 (1969): 217–30.

26. See Yves Congar, *I Believe in the Holy Spirit*, 3 vols. (New York: Crossroad, 1983), 1:104–11.

27. Augustine, Sermon 192.1, in *Sermons*, trans. Hill, WSA, pt. 3, vol. 6. On Langland's exquisite lyric, see especially Ben Smith, *Traditional Imagery of Charity in Piers Plowman* (The Hague: Mouton, 1966), 21–34. See too the eloquent discussion in Cristina M. Cervone, *Poetics of the Incarnation: Middle English Writing and the Leap of Love* (Philadelphia: University of Pennsylvania Press, 2012), 115–17. On becoming "a god . . . lyk oure lord" scholars often relate Langland's text to "The doctrine of 'deification,' as developed in the writings of St. Bernard": Pearsall, I.86, note, citing Edward Vasta, *The Spiritual Basis of Piers Plowman* (The Hague: Mouton, 1965), 66, and see 65–67. Langland's own combination of lyrical celebration, affirmation, and caution is shared and illustrated by the quotation from Augustine. As Augustine wrote in *De Trinitate*, IV.2.4, God took away

"the dissimilarity of our iniquity, and becoming a partaker of our mortality he made us partners of his divinity"; see *The Trinity*, trans. Edmund Hill, WSA, pt. 1, vol. 5 (Hyde Park, NY: New City Press, 1991). I draw on the illuminating discussion of "deification" in Gerald Bonner, *Freedom and Necessity: St. Augustine's Teaching on Divine Power and Human Freedom* (Washington, DC: Catholic University of America Press, 2007), 62–69.

28. For the Statute of Laborers and Langland's relations to its conflicts, see David Aers, *Community, Gender and Individual Identity* (London: Routledge, 1988), chap. 1; see too Anne Middleton, "Acts of Vagrancy," in *Written Work: Langland, Labor and Authorship*, ed. Stephen Justice and Kathryn Kerby-Fulton (Philadelphia: University of Pennsylvania Press, 1997), 208–317.

29. For this scene and its historical contexts, see the works cited in note 28. Already in the B version Langland was representing the struggle of relevant political forces in postplague England. To the materials cited in Aers and Middleton (note 29) should be added the perceptive essay by the historian John Hatcher, "England in the Aftermath of the Black Death," *Past & Present* 144 (1994): 3–35.

30. On the Folvilles, see E. L. G. Stones, "The Folvilles of Ashby Folville, Leicestershire, and Their Associates in Crime, 1326–1341," *Transactions of the Royal Historical Society* 7 (1957): 117–39; R. H. Bowers, "Foleyvyles Lawes," *Notes and Queries* 206 (1961): 327–28. For a recent attempt to trace the family of "Stacy de Rokayle, pater Willielmi de Langland" (from the famous entry in the Dublin C version of the poem, Trinity College, MS 212, fol. 89v), see Robert Adams, *Langland and the Rokele Family: The Gentry Background* (Dublin: Four Courts Press, 2013); and see 59–66 for the "reckless reputation" of some of this family, whom Adams sees as Folville-like. Adams imagines young William Langland growing up with stories of such "laudable" gentry violence (66).

31. For an illuminating explication of the political theology of this text, including its co-text in Acts 5:29 ("We ought to obey God rather than man"), see Aquinas on Romans 13:1–7 in his *In Omnes S. Pauli Apostoli Epistolas Commentaria*, 2 vols. (Turin: Marietti, 1912), chap. 13, lec. 1 in vol. 1, 180–85. The French translation offers superb annotations by Jean-Éric Stroobant and Jean Borella, *Commentaire de l'Épître aux Romains* (Paris: Cerf, 1999); here see 445–54. This commentary offers a salutary contrast with the magisterial reformation's thoroughly Constantinian reading of Romans 13:1–7. A good starting point for pursuing this undistinguished tradition is William Tyndale's 1535 *Obedience of a Christian Man*, ed. David Daniell (London: Penguin, 2000).

32. The best guides known to me in this field are the following: Pamela Nightingale, "Capitalists, Crafts, and Constitutional Change in Late Fourteenth Century London," *Past & Present* 124 (1989): 3–35; Caroline Barron, *London in the Later Middle Ages* (Oxford: Oxford University Press, 2004); Pamela Nightingale, *A Medieval Mercantile Community: The Grocers' Company and the Politics of*

Trade in London, 1000–1485 (New Haven: Yale University Press, 1995); Heather Swanson, *Medieval Artisans: An Urban Class in Late Medieval England* (Oxford: Blackwell, 1989). On Langland and artisan culture, the following has certainly been influential: James Simpson, "'After Craftes Conseil clotheth yow and fede': Langland and London City Politics," in *England in the Fourteenth Century: Proceedings of the 1991 Harlaxton Symposium*, ed. N. Rogers (Stamford: P. Watkins, 1993), 109–27.

33. The ways in which the Eucharist and rituals around it could sacralize social hierarchy have been richly displayed by the following: Miri Rubin, *Corpus Christi: The Eucharist in Late Medieval Culture* (Cambridge: Cambridge University, 1991); Miri Rubin, "The Eucharist and the Construction of Medieval Identities," in *Culture and History, 1350–1600: Essays on English Communities, Identities, and Writing*, ed. David Aers (Hemel Hempstead: Harvester Wheatsheaf, 1992), 43–63; Sarah Beckwith, *Christ's Body: Identity, Culture, and Society in Late Medieval Writing* (London: Routledge, 1993); Duffy, *Stripping of the Altars*, 126–27.

34. For an introduction to the relevant material, see David Aers, "The Sacrament of the Altar," in *Sanctifying Signs*, chap. 1; on Langland and the Eucharist, chap. 2; on Wyclif and the Eucharist, chap. 3.

35. Aquinas on the Pater Noster, section 1066, in his *Opuscula Theologica*, 2 vols., ed. R. A. Verardo, R. M. Spiazzi, and M. Calcaterra (Rome: Marietti, 1954), 2:228.

36. For an example of this pre-Wycliffite norm, see Robert of Basevorn's *Form of Preaching* (ca. 1322), ed. and trans. in James J. Murphy, *The Medieval Rhetorical Arts* (Berkeley: University of California Press, 1971), 144–215, here 124–25 (chap. 4).

37. See S. Bihel, "S. Franciscus Fuitne Angelus Sexti Sigilli (Apoc 7.2)?," *Antonianum* 2 (1927): 59–90; Marjorie Reeves, *The Influence of Prophecy in the Later Middle Ages: A Study in Joachimism*, 2nd ed. (Notre Dame: University of Notre Dame Press, 1993), esp. pt. 2.

38. I quote Chaucer from *The Riverside Chaucer*, ed. Larry D. Benson, 3rd ed. (Boston: Houghton Mifflin, 1987); with *The Canterbury Tales*, rev. ed., trans. Nevill Coghill (London: Penguin, 1977). Further references are to fragment and line numbers in the original, followed by page numbers in the translation. On Chaucer and the friars, see Penn Szittya, *The Antifraternal Tradition in Medieval Literature* (Princeton: Princeton University Press, 1986), chap. 6.

39. On Langland's treatment of the friars, especially of Franciscan ideology, see Aers, *Sanctifying Signs*, chap. 5; Szittya, *Antifraternal Tradition*, chap. 7.

40. Consult Pearsall's introduction to *Piers Plowman*, 24–25, together with Ralph Hanna, "'Meddling with Makings' and Will's Work," in *Late-Medieval Religious Texts and Their Transmission*, ed. A. J. Minnis (Cambridge: D. S. Brewer, 1994), 85–94.

41. On *status* in Christian lives, see Aquinas, *ST* II-II.183–89; on poverty and perfection, II-II.184.

42. On Aquinas in this paragraph, see the following seriatim: *In Omnes S. Pauli Apostoli Epistolas*, vol. 1, on 1 Cor. 12, Lectio 3, 355–60; *ST* II-II.39.1, resp.; *ST* II-II.183.2.

43. See *Documents of the Christian Church*, 2nd ed., ed. Henry Bettenson (London: Oxford University Press, 1965), 159–61.

44. These are abundantly and sympathetically illustrated in Friedman, *Medieval Trinitarian Thought*; and Gelber, *It Could Have Been Otherwise*.

45. On the traditions Langland deploys here, see D.W. Robertson and Bernard F. Huppé, *Piers Plowman and Scriptural Tradition* (Princeton: Princeton University Press, 1951), 17–20; S. A. Barney, "The Plowshare of the Tongue: The Progress of a Symbol from the Bible to *Piers Plowman*," *Medieval Studies* 35 (1973): 261–93.

46. See Aers, *Community, Gender, and Individual Identity*, 20–55; on London and the Statute, see Barron, *London*, 273–77, esp. 276 on the 1359 Proclamation that all able-bodied beggars are to leave London or be put in the stocks on Cornhill, a spectacle to Wille and Kytte, *Piers Plowman*, V.1–2.

47. Here I draw especially on Bertha Putnam, *The Enforcement of the Statutes of Labourers during the First Decade after the Black Death, 1349–1359* (New York: Columbia University, 1908), chaps. 1–3; and on Richard Smith, "'Modernization' and the Corporate Medieval Village Community in England: Some Skeptical Reflections," in *Explorations in Historical Geography*, ed. Alan R. H. Baker and Derek Gregory (Cambridge: Cambridge University Press, 1984), 140–79. On constables, see Helen Cam, "Shire Officials: Coroners, Constables, and Bailiffs," in *The English Government at Work, 1327–1336*, ed. J. F. Willard et al., 3 vols. (Cambridge, MA: Harvard University Press, 1950), 3:143–83, esp. 165–71.

48. *The Vision of Pierce Plowman, Nowe the Seconde Time Imprinted by Roberte Crowley* (1550): the copy I use is Cambridge University Library, Syn 7.55.25; the quotation is from an annotation to Passus VI (Crowley edits a copy of the B version). Unlike some modern critics, Crowley did see that the "wasters" are also *workers*.

49. See the texts in *The Peasant's Revolt of 1381*, ed. R. B. Dobson (London: Macmillan, 1970), 65 and 74 (1376 Petition).

50. Elizabeth Salter [Zeeman], "Piers Plowman and the Pilgrimage to Truth," *Essays and Studies* 11 (1958): 1–16, reprinted in Robert J. Blanch, ed., *Style and Symbolism in "Piers Plowman"* (Knoxville: University of Tennessee Press, 1969), 117–31. See too Vasta, *Spiritual Basis of "Piers Plowman*," 107–20.

51. See especially Henri de Lubac, *Exégèse médiévale: Les quatre sens de l'écriture*, 4 vols. (Paris: Aubier, 1959–64); on later medieval hermeneutics, consult

Christopher Ocker, *Biblical Poetics before Humanism and Reformation* (Cambridge: Cambridge University Press, 2002).

52. An excellent display of papalist ideology is provided by Giles of Rome, *On Ecclesiastical Power*, see the Latin and English texts edited by R.W. Dyson (New York: Columbia University Press, 2004), with a very useful introduction on the relevant historical contexts. With Giles of Rome, still extremely informative on papal monarchist ideology and the debates around it, see Wilks, *Problem of Sovereignty in the Later Middle Ages*. An illuminating example of this papalist ideology is offered by the Carmelite John Baconthorpe; see Beryl Smalley, "John Baconthorpe's Postill on St. Matthew," *Medieval and Renaissance Studies* 4 (1958): 91–115.

53. See Gradon, "Langland and the Ideology of Dissent"; Hudson, *Premature Reformation*, 398–408.

54. This is from *Opus Nonaginta Dierum*, chap. 93, trans. Kilcullen and Scott as *Work of Ninety Days*; also in Ockham, *Letter to the Friars Minor and Other Writings*, ed. McGrade and Kilcullen, 105–6.

55. Throughout I use the translation of the *Breviloquium* by McGrade and Kilcullen, *A Short Discourse on Tyrannical Government*, here, seriatim, II.1, II.2, II.3; further references are given in the text. I have been guided by the still indispensable study by Arthur S. McGrade, *The Political Thought of William of Ockham* (Cambridge: Cambridge University Press, 1974); and also by Takashi Shogimen, *Ockham and Political Discourse in the Late Middle Ages* (Cambridge: Cambridge University Press, 2007).

56. McGrade, *Political Thought*, 147.

57. Ibid., 147–48.

58. William of Ockham, *On the Power of Emperors and Popes*, ed. and trans. Annabel S. Brett (Bristol: Thoemmes Press, 1998), chap. 9.

59. McGrade shows how Ockham insists that "the gospel's law is a law of freedom" (140–49), and here I quote from 141. On the role of Ockham's teaching on Christian liberty, see too Shogimen, *Ockham and Political Discourse*, chap. 6; and on the Christian's right in relation to suspicions of heresy, see chap. 2.

60. On this scope and duty of Christians, see Shogimen, *Ockham and Political Discourse*, 83–104, 150–55, chaps. 2–3 passim, with special attention due to the section on "fraternal correction" and conscience, 118–35. Also see on this, McGrade, *Political Thought*, 219–24. Ockham's understanding of the universal church accords with his understanding of universals developed earlier in his life when he was doing work as a conventional academic theologian. So the universal church consists not of some metaphysical corporation but rather of all the individuals who throughout history believe the true faith: see Brian Tierney on Ockham in *On the Origins of Papal Infallibility, 1150–1350* (Leiden: Brill, 1972),

chap. 6; Janet Coleman, *History of Political Thought: From the Middle Ages to the Renaissance* (Oxford: Blackwell, 2000), 176, 179–80; Shogimen, *Ockham and Political Discourse*, 238–42, 256–61; McGrade, *Political Thought*, 224.

61. See Shogimen, *Ockham and Political Discourse*, 135–37; on women and a general council, see McGrade, *Political Thought*, 222 n. 9.

62. On Wyclif's "dualism" in contrast to Langland's ecclesiology, see Gradon, "Langland and the Ideology of Dissent," 197–201, esp. 199–200; also very helpful here is Gordon Leff's analysis of Wycliff's ecclesiology in his *Heresy in the Later Middle Ages*, 2 vols. (Manchester: Manchester University Press, 1967), 2:514–46. This account is not superseded in more recent work: Stephen Lahey, *John Wyclif* (Oxford: Oxford University Press, 2009); G. R. Evans, *John Wyclif* (Oxford: Lion, 2005); Takashi Shogimen, "Wyclif's Ecclesiology and Political Thought," in *A Companion to John Wyclif: Late Medieval Theologian*, ed. Ian C. Levy (Leiden: Brill, 2006), 199–240. For a recent attempt to emphasize the overlappings between what the author calls "mainstream Christian tradition" and Lollardy, see Fiona Somerset, *Feeling Like Saints: Lollard Writings after Wyclif* (Ithaca: Cornell University Press, 2014), 130.

63. Tierney, *Infallibility*, 210.

64. On the second, allegorical scene of plowing, see David Aers, *Piers Plowman and Christian Allegory* (London: Arnold, 1975), 128–31; see too Robertson and Huppé, *Piers Plowman and Scriptural Tradition*, 217–22.

65. See Thomas Gilby on this in his edition of Thomas's text in the Dominican *Summa Theologiae*, 61 vols. (London: Blackfriars, 1964–81), 1:133: "In the first question of the *Summa* the terms holy teaching and holy scripture are synonymous."

66. For an introduction to the relevant contemporary conflicts, see especially Leff, *Heresy*, 2:511–16; Ian C. Levy, *John Wyclif: Scriptural Logic, Real Presence, and the Parameters of Orthodoxy* (Milwaukee, WI: Marquette University Press, 2003).

67. On the virtues here, rightfully identified as *infused*, see Morton W. Bloomfield, *Piers Plowman as a Fourteenth-Century Apocalypse* (New Brunswick: Rutgers University Press, 1961), 134; John Burrow associates them with the seven gifts of the Holy Spirit in *Langland's Fictions* (Oxford: Clarendon Press, 1993), 68–69.

68. The central "duplex" structures I summarize here, natural and supernatural, pervade the *Summa Theologiae*: see, e.g., I.1.1, resp.; I-II.61.1, resp.; I.23.1, resp. Relevant here is Reinhard Hütter's treatment of the conflicts of interpretation in *Dust Bound for Heaven: Explorations in the Theology of Thomas Aquinas* (Grand Rapids, MI: Eerdmans, 2012), chap. 5. For a nuanced account of relations between Aquinas and Langland on the virtues, see Sheryl Overmyer, "The Wayfarer's Way and Two Guides for the Journey: The *Summa Theologiae* and *Piers Plowman*" (PhD diss., Duke University, 2010).

69. John Burrow asserts that Langland's figuration of the seeds being eaten is "at some cost to the coherence of his fiction" (*Langland's Fictions*, 70). This

might be true if Langland were writing a nineteenth-century novel or a manual on estates' management.

70. Skeat, *Piers the Plowman*, 2:271 n. 314.

71. Calvin, *Institutes* IV.6.5–7.

72. Augustine, *Retractions*, trans. Bogan, I.20.1; see too *Sermons*, trans. Hill, 295.1–2 and 5, in WSA, pt. 3, vol. 8.

73. Wilks, *The Problem of Sovereignty*, 360, 367. The work I have found most helpful in displaying such arguments in detail is Giles of Rome, *On Ecclesiastical Power*, trans. Dyson.

74. On Psalm 132, see Augustine, *Expositions of the Psalms*, trans. Boulding, WSA, pt. 3, vol. 20; for the Latin text of the homily on Psalm 132 from which I also quote, see *Enarrationes in Psalmos*, 2nd ed., 3 vols., ed. Eligius Dekkers et al., Corpus Christianorum Series Latina, vols. 38–40 (Turnholt: Brepols, 1956–90), 3:1927.

75. Pearsall's note to the earlier appearance of the *hayward* at XIII.45, *Piers Plowman* 229; see too Skeat, *Piers the Plowman*, 2:62 n. 16 and 174 n. 45.

76. On Langland's exploration of Franciscan ideologies and practices, see Aers, *Sanctifying Signs*, chap. 5; Szittya, *Antifraternal Tradition*, chap. 7.

77. *De Officio Regis* is a major text in one's understanding of the exorbitant role envisaged for the Crown in the disendowment of the church: see David Aers, *Faith, Ethics, and Church: Writing in England, 1360–1409* (Cambridge: D. S. Brewer, 2000), chap. 5.

78. The B version here and elsewhere is quoted from the revised edition by Kane and Donaldson, *Piers Plowman: The B Version*.

79. See *ST*: I-II.61.5, resp.; I-II.61.1–2, 4–5; I-II.58.1. I should note that while Pearsall ascribes the passage I have just quoted from the Prologue to "the dreamer," the one I designate the figure of the poet, George Russell and George Kane in their edition of the C version give the lines to Conscience. See Pearsall, *Piers Plowman*, Prol. 128 (note).

80. Augustine, *City of God* XI.2: for the Latin text I use *De civitate Dei*, ed. B. Dombart and A. Kalb, 5th ed., 2 vols. (Stuttgart: Teubner, 1993), 1:463; English trans. by R. W. Dyson, *The City of God against the Pagans* (Cambridge: Cambridge University Press, 1998), 451.

81. There is an excellent commentary on the terms, the ironic play, and the historical contexts in J. A. W. Bennett, *Piers Plowman: The Prologue and Passus I–VII of the B Text as Found in Bodleian MS Laud Misc. 581* (Oxford: Clarendon Press, 1972), 96.

82. See Bennett, *Piers Plowman*, 96.

83. Ibid.

84. Ibid.; and see J. A. W. Bennett, "The Date of the B-text of *Piers Plowman*," *Medium Aevum* 12 (1943): 55–64.

85. See John Finnis, *Aquinas on Moral, Political, and Legal Theory* (Oxford: Oxford University Press, 1998), 200–210.

86. Or, depending on how one is reading the poem's complex temporalities, the passage is a memory of the past Pentecostal community.

87. From a substantial literature on this topic, I have drawn especially on the following: John T. Noonan, *The Scholastic Analysis of Usury* (Cambridge, MA: Harvard University Press, 1957); John W. Baldwin, *The Medieval Theories of the Just Price* (Philadelphia: American Philosophical Society, 1959); Odd Langholm, *Economics in the Medieval Schools: Wealth, Exchange, Value, Money, and Usury according to the Paris Theological Tradition, 1200–1350* (Leiden: Brill, 1992); Joel Kaye, *Economy and Nature in the Fourteenth Century: Money, Market Exchange, and the Emergence of Scientific Thought* (Cambridge: Cambridge University Press, 1998); Lester K. Little, *Religious Poverty and the Profit Economy in Medieval Europe* (London: P. Elek, 1978); Norman Jones, *God and the Moneylenders: Usury and Law in Early Modern England* (Oxford: Blackwell, 1989). I have found R. H. Tawney's introduction to Thomas Wilson's Elizabethan work on usury extremely helpful, as in Wilson's *A Discourse upon Usury by Way of Dialogue and Orations*, ed. R. H. Tawney (London: Bell, 1925). Finally I should mention a great and apparently forgotten work: W. J. Ashley, *An Introduction to English Economic History and Theory, Part 2: The End of the Middle Ages*, 4th ed. (London: Longman, 1906); the study of the medieval *and* reformation history of usury is in chap. 6, "The Canonist Doctrine."

88. For an example of the former, Alexander of Hales, discussed in Little, *Religious Poverty*, 181; for Aquinas, *ST* II-II.78.2, ad 1.

89. Little, *Religious Poverty*, 180–83; and Kaye, *Economy and Nature*, esp. chaps. 4 and 7.

90. Giles of Lessines, *De Usuris*, printed as opusculum 66 in Thomas Aquinas, *Opera Omnia*, vol. 17 (Parma, 1864). Little dates this text as "about 1280" and discusses it in *Religious Poverty*, 181–82. It was his discussion that made me aware of this fascinating work. Here I refer to *De Usuris*, Proemium, 413–14; further references are given in the text to this edition.

91. Little, *Religious Poverty*, 182; see *De Usuris*, chaps. 6–8 and 13, esp. 419–22.

92. Little, *Religious Poverty*, 182–83.

93. Ibid., 183: see too Kaye, *Economy and Nature*, chap. 4.

94. Still indispensable here is Jill Mann's *Chaucer and Medieval Estates Satire* (Cambridge: Cambridge University Press, 1973); and T. A. Yunck, *The Lineage of Lady Meed: The Development of Mediaeval Venality Satire* (Notre Dame: University of Notre Dame Press, 1963).

95. I quote from John Paul II, *The Splendor of Truth: Veritatis Splendor* (Boston: Pauline Books, 1993). In the rest of the essay I give references to the work's paragraph numbering in my text.

96. I allude to Duffy's *Stripping of the Altars.*

97. Here I allude to Gregory's *The Unintended Reformation.*

98. Conscience is of course touched on by most commentators on *Piers Plowman*, but the following works have a substantive focus on this figure: M. W. Bloomfield, *Piers Plowman*; Sarah Wood, *Conscience and the Composition of "Piers Plowman"* (Oxford: Oxford University Press, 2012).

99. Pearsall's notes that XXI.335 echoes VIII.112 and observes that "the meaning is that he [Piers] leaves the vicinity of Unity to till truth elsewhere, as Jesus recommended to the Apostles (Matt. 16:15)" (XXI.335 note).

100. See Rowan Williams, *Why Study the Past? The Quest for the Historical Church* (Grand Rapids, MI: Eerdmans, 2005), chap. "Resident Aliens: The Identity of the Early Church."

101. See esp. *City of God*, I–VI; there is much illuminating commentary in Robert Dodaro, *Christ and the Just Society in the Thought of Augustine* (Cambridge: Cambridge University Press, 2004), esp. chaps. 1–3.

102. On the Donation of Constantine there is an understandable inclination to foreground Wycliffite attacks on this in discussions of *Piers Plowman*, but we need to remember the resonance of the angelic criticism in pre-Wycliffite and orthodox writers: see Gradon, "The Ideology of Dissent," 185–86; Anne Hudson, *Premature Reformation*, 335 (with 334–46); Beryl Smalley, *English Friars and Antiquity in the Early Fourteenth Century* (Oxford: Blackwell, 1960), 195–96.

103. On Wyclif's advocacy of coercive disendowment of the church by lay elites and their charity, see Hudson, *Premature Reformation*, 337–45; Scase, *"Piers Plowman" and the New Anti-Clericalism*, chap. 4.

104. On Wyclif's "strongly regalian" politics and his followers, see Hudson, *Premature Reformation*, 362–67; Michael Wilks, *Wyclif: Political Ideas and Practice* (Oxford: Oxbow, 2000), chap. 7, "Royal Patronage and Anti-Papalism from Ockham to Wyclif"; Leff, *Heresy*, 2:543–45.

105. See Hudson, *Premature Reformation*, 60; and, especially, Margaret Aston "John Wycliffe's Reformation Reputation," *Past & Present* 30 (1965): 23–51, reprinted in Aston, *Lollards and Reformers: Images and Literacy in Late Medieval Religion* (London: Hambledon Press, 1984), 243–72.

106. See G. W. Bernard, *The King's Reformation: Henry VIII and the Remaking of the English Church* (New Haven: Yale University Press, 2007): on connections with the medieval history, 43, 172, 173; but for substantial exploration of the relevant antecedents, see Gerald Harriss, *Shaping the Nation: England, 1360–1461* (Oxford: Clarendon Press, 2005), chaps. 3, 15; Jeremy Catto, "Religious Change under Henry V," in *Henry V: The Practice of Kingship*, ed. G. L. Harriss (Oxford: Oxford University Press, 1985), 97–116, at 97, 115. Catto argues that Henry V "had begun to act as supreme governor of the Church of England" (115).

107. William Langland, *Piers Plowman: A Parallel-Text Edition of the A, B, C, and Z Versions*, 2 vols., ed. A. V. C. Schmidt (Kalamazoo, MI: Medieval Institute Publications, 2008), 2:707 n. 215.

108. On the historical process of splitting off will from reason and its consequences, see Pfau, *Minding the Modern*, passim but especially chaps. 2–6, 8, 16. There is a relevant comment on the translation of *Liber arbitrium* in Brian Davies's introduction to Thomas Aquinas, *On Evil*, trans. Richard Regan (Oxford: Oxford University Press, 2003), 35–36.

109. My own understanding of Liberum Arbitrium is led by my reading of Langland's composition of the figure, but I have been helped to understand his choices and emphasis by the *quaestio* in Aquinas's *Summa Theologiae*, "De Libero Arbitrio," I-II.83, along with I-II.82.1–2. For an attempt to link Liberum Arbitrium with St. Bernard's writing, see Vasta, *Spiritual Basis of "Piers Plowman*," 81–83; and before him, E. Talbot Donaldson, *Piers Plowman: The C-Text and Its Poet* (New Haven: Yale University Press, 1949), 188–93. On Conscience, see note 98 above. According to Tierney, *On the Origins of Papal Infallibility*, 208 n. 1, all medieval theologians were "eclectic" in their philosophical theology, and to this Langland is no exception.

110. Norman Doe, *Fundamental Authority in Late Medieval English Law* (Cambridge: Cambridge University Press, 1990), chap. 6, "Conscience and the Human Law"; quotation at 132.

111. On the natural disposition to know first principles, known as *synderesis*, see *ST* I.79.12; conscience is then treated in I.79.13. T. C. Potts's book on conscience remains very helpful: *Conscience in Medieval Philosophy* (Cambridge: Cambridge University Press, 1980).

112. For my comments on the "duplex" (here and in note 68), see Laurence Feingold, *The Natural Desire to See God according to St. Thomas Aquinas and His Interpreters*, 2nd ed. (Naples, FL: Sapientia Press, 2010).

113. On the processes through which post-Nicene orthodoxy was made, see Lewis Ayres, *Nicaea and Its Legacy: An Approach to Fourth-Century Trinitarian Theology* (Oxford: Oxford University Press, 2004). It is striking that Faith's analogy did not have Augustine's admiration: compare XVIII.214–22 with *De Trinitate* XII.5 (Pearsall's note here in his edition mistakenly cites *De Trinitate* II.5).

114. Has Wille forgotten the discussion with Liberum Arbitrium about "Sarresynes," "the Iewes," and their conversion to trinitarian faith (XVII.315–20a)?

115. On Isaiah 1:18, I slightly adjust the Douay Rheims (Challoner) text. The text links to 1 Peter 3:15.

116. This is true however many contemporaries one can produce for whom it would have seemed mistaken and even dangerous. For a discussion of just such a contemporary, Nicholas Love, see Aers, *Sanctifying Signs*, 12–24, 165–73.

117. For Christ the Samaritan, Luke 10, and the exegetical tradition Langland deploys, see Pearsall, XIX.49 note and its references.

118. On "inwit" and its meanings, see R. Quirk, "Langland's Use of *Kind Wit* and *Inwit*," *JEGP* 52 (1953): 182–89; Nicolette Zeeman, *"Piers Plowman" and the Medieval Discourse of Desire* (Cambridge: Cambridge University Press, 2006), 100–108, 121–25.

119. Aquinas rejects the views of Bonaventure and Franciscan masters on this: consult Potts, *Conscience in Medieval Philosophy*, chaps. 3–4.

120. *Sermons*, 75.5, in WSA, pt. 3, vol. 3.

121. For a different approach, see Jill Mann, "Allegorical Buildings in Medieval Literature," *Medium Aevum* 63 (1994): 191–210.

122. I use Susan Powell's fine edition: *John Mirk's Festial*, 2 vols., EETS, o.s., 334 and 335 (Oxford: Oxford University Press, 2009–11), vol. 1, sermon 10, quotation at 42. Powell offers a helpful commentary on Mirk's sources (2:290–91). For a remarkable modern analogy, see the premonitory and posthumous testimony of the Trappist martyr murdered in Algeria by Islamic people in 1996, Christian de Charge: Stanley Hauerwas, *Cross-Shattered Christ: Meditations on the Seven Last Words* (Grand Rapids, MI: Brazos Press, 2004), 31–33.

123. I quote Duffy, *Stripping of the Altars*, 412.

124. From the copious literature on the sacrament of the altar I am especially indebted to the following: John Bossy, "The Mass as a Social Institution, 1200–1700," *Past & Present* 100 (1983): 29–61; James F. McCue, "The Doctrine of Transubstantiation from Berengar through Trent," *Harvard Theological Review* 61 (1968): 385–430; Henri de Lubac, *Corpus mysticum: L'Euchariste et l'église au moyen âge* (Paris: Aubier, 1949); Gary Macy, *The Banquet's Wisdom: A Short History of the Theologies of the Lord's Supper* (New York: Paulist, 1992); Rubin, *Corpus Christi*; Gary Macy, "Theologies of the Eucharist in the High Middle Ages," in *A Companion to the Eucharist in the Middle Ages*, ed. Ian Levy, Gary Macy, and Kristen Van Ausdall (Leiden: Brill, 2012), 365–98.

125. Aers, *Sanctifying Signs*, chap. 1.

126. Aquinas, *ST* III.76.1, resp. and ad 2; here I use the text and translation of the Blackfriars edition.

127. Duffy, *Stripping of the Altars*, 91: see chap. 3, "The Mass." References below to Duffy's work are given in the text.

128. Things had not always been thus. Gary Macy has recovered forgotten and denied histories: "The 'Invention' of Clergy and Laity in the Twelfth Century," in *A Sacramental Life: A Festschrift Honoring Bernard Cooke*, ed. Michael H. Barnes and W. P. Roberts (Milwaukee, WI: Marquette University Press, 2003), 117–35; Gary Macy, *The Hidden History of Women's Ordination* (Oxford: Oxford University Press, 2008), especially in the eucharistic context I address around Langland, 63–66, 82–85.

129. Duffy, *Stripping of the Altars*, 131.

130. Walter Brut's testament can be found in *Registrum Johannis Trefnant*, ed. W. W. Capes (London: Canterbury and York Society, 1916), 278–394. References in my text are to this edition. There is a discussion of this fascinating lay theologian in Aers, *Sanctifying Signs*, 67–82.

131. On Brut's lack of sustained attention to this issue, see Aers, *Sanctifying Signs*, 82.

132. John Wyclif, *De Eucharistia (Tractatus Maior)*, ed. Johann Loserth (London: Trübner and Co. for the Wyclif Society, 1892): "Nullus (inquam) fidelis dubitat quin Deus posset dare layco potentiam conficendi, sicut laycus cum possit esse sacerdos (ut dicit loyci [*sic*]) possit conficere" (98). The influence of Wyclif is very plain in the Lollard conclusions of 1395 so dramatically forced on Parliament's attention. Any faithful man or woman ("potest quilibet fidelis homo et mulier") can consecrate the sacrament (which is understood without the fictitious miracle of transubstantiation): *Fasciculi Zizaniorum Magistri Johannis Wyclif cum Tritico*, ascribed to Thomas Netter, ed. Walter W. Shirley (London: Longman, 1858), item 4, 361–62.

133. Hawisia Mone, in Norman Tanner, ed., *Heresy Trials in the Diocese of Norwich, 1428–31*, (London: Royal Historical Society, 1977), 142. These reflections on Conscience's ministry of the Eucharist, Walter Brut, the 1395 Lollard articles (item 4), and Hawisia Mone could include attention to a striking deletion in Langland's C version of *Piers Plowman*. In the B version Ymagenatyf teaches Wille that among the reasons Christians need *clergie* is the role of *clergie* in the sacrament of the altar: he affirms that God's body could not be of bread without "clergie" (B XII.85). In *The Premature Reformation*, Anne Hudson examines the relations of Langland's work to Wycliffite writing (398–408). There she considers the deletion of this line (B XII.85) from the final version of the poem. She decides that it is "probably . . . not the result of a change of heart by the author concerning transubstantiation, but rather of an increasing scepticism of the role of the clergy as honourable intermediaries between God and man" (403). I agree with Hudson's statement about the treatment of the clergy in the C version, and she may be right about Langland's deletion not being the result of reconsidering the doctrine of transubstantiation against the emphasis in B XII.85. However, this remains an open question for me since the statement about the sacrament in Conscience's offer of Passus XXI does *not* mandate that it be read according to the dogma of transubstantiation: we are given "bred yblessed" *and* "godes body thereunder" (XXI.385: as is B. XIX.385). This is perfectly compatible with the consubstantiational account of the sacrament. Condemned by the Roman Church, it was considered by Ockham to be the least incoherent of the models explaining the mystery as the church understood the conversion of the elements and rejected because, in those days before excommunication, he simply accepted the authority of

the church. For Ockham's summary of what he takes to be orthodox doctrine, see *De Corpore Christi*, chap. 2, esp. 91, in *Guillelmi de Ockham: Tractatus de Quantitate et Tractatus de Corpore Christi*, ed. Carlo A. Grassi, vol. 10 of William of Ockham, *Opera Philosophica et Theologica* (St. Bonaventure, NY: St. Bonaventure University, Franciscan Institute, 1986), 89–234.

134. See, e.g., Duffy, *Stripping of the Altars*, 93; it is, however, congruent with Aquinas's thought, *ST* III.80.10; and see Brian Davies, *The Thought of Thomas Aquinas* (Oxford: Clarendon Press, 1993), 363.

135. On Communion as the making of the community of Christ's body, see Duffy, *Stripping of the Altars*, 123–30; Bossy, "The Mass as Social Institution." For a theological statement of this theme, see Aquinas, *ST* III.73.3, resp., with III.80.4, resp.

136. On these producers two essays by Rodney Hilton are very informative: "Lords, Burgesses, and Hucksters" and "Women Traders in Medieval England," chaps. 15 and 16 in *Class Conflict and the Crisis of Feudalism: Essays in Social History* (London: Hambledon, 1985). Also relevant is Judith Bennett, *Ale, Beer, and Brewsters in England: Women's Work in a Changing World, 1300–1600* (New York: Oxford University Press, 1996).

137. See *Confessions* VIII.5.10; also VIII.7.18, VIII.11.26, VI.12.21–22, VII.17.23: *Confessions*, 3 vols., ed. James J. O'Donnell (Oxford: Clarendon Press, 1992); with *Confessions*, trans. Henry Chadwick (Oxford: Oxford University Press, 1991). Especially illuminating here is John G. Prendiville, "The Development of the Idea of Habit in the Thought of Saint Augustine," *Traditio* 28 (1972): 22–99. It is fascinating that in 1433 a statute was passed prohibiting people living in Southwark from being jurors: "This was because they were people 'without conscience and of evil governance.'" Here we encounter the idea that repeated action creates habits which can change our nature to create a lack of *conscience*, as Langland shows. I quote from Doe, *Fundamental Authority*, 146 (see note 110 above).

138. Pearsall, note to XXI.409; Robertson and Huppé, *Piers Plowman and Scriptural Tradition*, 225–27, quotation at 225.

139. For an example of such commentary, see Schmidt, *Piers Plowman*, 2:712–13, with its totally uncritical rehearsal of Rosanne Gasse, "Langland's 'Lewd Vicory' Reconsidered," *JEGP* 95 (1996): 322–35. For a recent Schmidtian reading of the "lewed vicory," see Emily Steiner, *Reading "Piers Plowman"* (Cambridge: Cambridge University Press, 2013), 215–16. For an admirably lucid and accurate account of the "lewed vicory," see James Simpson, *Piers Plowman: An Introduction*, 2nd ed. (Exeter: University of Exeter Press, 2007), 230; and Pearsall's notes at XXI.409, 413, 422, 426, and 427. Stephen A. Barney has a long note on this figure in *The Penn Commentary on "Piers Plowman,"* 5 vols. (Philadelphia: University of Pennsylvania Press, 2006), 5:166–79.

140. See Pearsall's notes to Prol. 132 and 134.

141. See XXI.424–28 and 434–39 with Pearsall's note on the two plows at XXI.426.

142. The most concise and relevant work of Ockham here is *On the Power of Emperors and Popes*, ed. and trans. Brett.

143. On the historical contexts, see Pearsall's notes at XVII.234 and XXI.428–29; and Scase, *Piers Plowman and the New Anti-Clericalism*, 102–19.

144. Commentators from Skeat on have drawn attention to the poem's allusions to the Great Schism: Skeat, *Piers the Plowman*, 2:198, 233, 273–74; Bennett, *Piers Plowman*, 96–97; Pearsall, Prol. 134 and XXI.428–29 with further references to commentary on the poem. On the Schism, I have found the following most helpful: Renate Blumenfeld-Kosinski, *Poets, Saints, and Visionaries of the Great Schism, 1375–1417* (University Park: Pennsylvania State University Press, 2006); Joëlle Rollo-Koster and Thomas Izbicki, *A Companion to the Great Western Schism, 1378–1417* (Leiden: Brill, 2009); Édouard Perroy, *L'Angleterre et le Grand Schisme d'Occident* (Paris: Monnier, 1933), esp. 175–205 on the Despenser crusade; Wendy L. Anderson, *The Discernment of Spirits: Assessing Visions and Visionaries in the Late Middle Ages* (Tübingen: Siebeck, 2011), esp. chaps. 4–5; Hudson, *Premature Reformation*, 330–34, 409–10.

145. Scholars disagree about the date of this passus (C XXI, B XIX). Compare, for example, Anne Hudson, "*Piers Plowman* and the Peasant's Revolt," *Yearbook of Langland Studies* 8 (1994): 85–106, esp. 100, with Barney, *Penn Commentary on "Piers Plowman,"* 5:174–76. My own commentary does not depend on the outcome of such an argument, although my opinion coincides with Hudson's. One has to acknowledge the relevance of Lawrence Warner's claim about the relations between the B version and C versions, although I expect these claims will also divide opinion among Langland scholars. See Warner, *The Lost History of "Piers Plowman"* (Philadelphia: University of Pennsylvania Press, 2011).

146. The sources on which I draw, giving references in my text, are the following: Norman Housley, "The Bishop of Norwich's Crusade, May 1383," *History Today* 33 (1983): 15–20; Margaret Aston, "The Impeachment of Bishop Despenser," *Bulletin of the Institute of Historical Research* 38 (1965): 127–48; Perroy, *L'Angleterre et le Grand Schisme*, 175–205. For an extremely rich and much-needed account of the diversity of crusading discourses and the implied politics, see Lee Manion, *Narrating the Crusades: Loss and Recovery in Medieval and Early Modern English Literature* (Cambridge: Cambridge University Press, 2014): on Despenser's crusade, see 19–20, 108, 117; and Christopher Tyerman, *England and the Crusades, 1095–1588* (Chicago: University of Chicago Press, 1988), 333–38.

147. On "his military tastes," see Aston, "The Impeachment," 133; and Housley, "The Bishop," 16.

148. Aston, "The Impeachment," 133.

149. Ibid., 134.

150. Housley, "The Bishop," 18.

151. On Courtenay's public support for Despenser's crusade, see Housley, "The Bishop," 18.

152. References are to Henry Knighton, *Knighton's Chronicle, 1337–1396*, ed. and trans. G. H. Martin (Oxford: Clarendon Press, 1995), citing the parallel English and Latin texts.

153. Housley, "The Bishop," 18.

154. For the ideology and practice of this treasury, see Swanson, *Indulgences*, 309–12; and Robert W. Shaffern, *The Penitents' Treasury: Indulgences in Latin Christendom, 1175–1375* (Scranton, PA: University of Scranton Press, 2007).

155. *Knighton's Chronicle*, 324/325. I have revised Martin's translation to reflect Knighton's second use of the important phrase "a pena et a culpa," and I have modernized the spelling.

156. There is a substantial and discordant literature on this pardon in C IX and in its earlier form, B VII. In the latter, Piers tears the pardon in response to the priest's challenge. For an introduction to the interpretations and arguments, see Pearsall, *Piers Plowman*, "The Pardon Sent from Truth," 31–32. Cf. Aers, *Sanctifying Signs*, 107–16.

157. Marc Bloch, *Feudal Society*, 2 vols. (London: Routledge, 1982), 2:430, 431.

158. Philip Corrigan and Derek Sayer, *The Great Arch: English State Formation as Cultural Revolution* (Oxford: Blackwell, 1985), 16.

159. Housley, "The Bishop," 17.

160. Aston, "The Impeachment," 134, 135, 136.

161. Duffy, *Stripping of the Altars*. In "Altars of Power" I have drawn attention to the striking rhetorical and grammatical differences between the part of Duffy's book devoted to the Middle Ages and that on the sixteenth century. In the second edition of *Stripping of the Altars*, Duffy responded persuasively to some of my criticisms but not to the one addressing the different analytic and narrative modes deployed in his treatments of the Middle Ages and Reformation, a difference with serious and unexamined consequences. See *Stripping of the Altars*, xxi–xxii.

162. Aston, "The Impeachment," 133.

163. Ibid., 137–41.

164. William of Ockham, *On the Power of Emperors and Popes*, trans. Brett, chap. 7, 94.

165. James Simpson, *Piers Plowman*, 202, citing Mary Carruthers, *The Search for St. Truth: A Study of Meaning in "Piers Plowman"* (Evanston, IL: Northwestern University Press, 1973), 157–73.

166. Passus VIII had already represented an example of the latter in "the statuyt" of laborers and the laborers' anger (VIII.337–40). See section III of this essay.

167. Skeat, *Piers the Plowman*, 2:274–75; Pearsall, *Piers Plowman*, note to XXI.459–64.

168. J. L. Bolton, *The Medieval English Economy, 1150–1500* (London: Dent, 1980), 92.

169. Augustine, *De doctrina christiana*, ed. and trans. R. P. H. Green (Oxford: Clarendon Press, 1995), III.20–21 (140–41).

170. That Christ is the key to scripture, the one whose incarnation discloses the allegorical meaning of the Old Testament, was an exegetical commonplace. The best introduction to the theology of medieval interpretation of scripture remains de Lubac, *Exégèse mèdièvale*.

171. For the comment that "hermaphrodite or ambidexter" would be good names for the fusion of temporal and spiritual powers in the church, see item 6 in the 1395 Lollard "libellus" in *Fasciculus Zizaniorum*, 361. There is an English translation in Bettenson, ed., *Documents of the Christian Church*, 245–51.

172. See *ST* II-II.58.1, resp. with obj. 1 and ad 1.

173. The king's assumption that his will and the law are synonymous was to become one of the marks of tyranny used to justify the deposition of Richard II in 1399. For a useful collection of documents concerning the deposition and its ideology, see *Chronicles of the Revolution, 1397–1400: The Reign of Richard II*, ed. and trans. Chris Given-Wilson (Manchester: Manchester University Press, 1993), 213–23.

174. Skeat, *Piers the Plowman*, 2:275.

175. An example of this convention is provided by Thomas of Wimbledon in his famous Paul's Cross Sermon of 1388, edited by N. H. Owen, *Medieval Studies* 28 (1966): 176–97, here 179. The sermon is also edited by Ione Kemp Knight in *Wimbledon's Sermon* (Pittsburgh: Duquesne University Press, 1967).

176. See XVII.227–32. See references given in note 103 above to Wyclif's "strongly regalian" politics.

177. Consult the materials cited in notes 105 and 106 above, with Duffy, *Stripping of the Altars*, pt. 2.

178. See Aquinas, *ST* I.79.12–13 with I-II.19.5–6.

179. John Paul II, *The Splendor of Truth*, par. 106, original emphasis; subsequent references in the text are to paragraph numbers.

180. I draw on Quentin Skinner, "Thomas Hobbes: Rhetoric and the Construction of Morality," *Proceedings of the British Academy* 76 (1990): 1–61, here at 7–8. Subsequent citations are given in the text. For the place of this analysis in Skinner's wider reading of Hobbes, see his *Reason and Rhetoric in the Philosophy of Hobbes* (Cambridge: Cambridge University Press, 1996), 138–80. In an essay on preaching the virtues, Richard Newhauser, without identifying paradiastolic speech and its traditions, as Skinner does, mentions the way medieval "moral theologians" seek "to strip off the disguises used by vices to masquerade as virtues." See his

"Preaching the 'Contrary Virtues,'" *Mediaeval Studies* 70 (2008): 135–62. The Wycliffite William Taylor provides a nice example of paradiastolic speech in the sermon edited by Anne Hudson in *Two Wycliffite Texts: The Sermon of William Taylor (1406); The Testimony of William Thorpe (1407)*, EETS, o.s., 301 (Oxford: Oxford University Press, 1993), 14, lines 415–27. Taylor notes how the devil baptizes sins under the names of virtue. Another nice example of paradiastolic speech is ascribed to the wicked ("implii") in the Book of Wisdom. In chapter 2, they determine to "let our strength be the law of justice" (*Sit autem fortitudo nostra lex iustitiae*). This is, of course, closely related to the speech of the lord toward the end of *Piers Plowman*: there the infused cardinal virtues of prudence and fortitude become identified with tyranny (XXI.459–65). Robert Holcot's ruminations on the Book of Wisdom are always very engaging, and he addresses this text (Sapientia 2.1) in Lectio 23 of his *In Librum Sapientiae Regis Salomonis Praelectiones CCXIII* (Basel, 1586).

181. For a more searching and critical exploration of Hobbes in a grand narrative of extraordinary erudition and attention to detail, so rare in such narratives, see Pfau, *Minding the Modern*, chap. 8.

182. For recent work on Hobbes most germane to my own concerns, alongside Pfau's *Minding the Modern*, see A. P. Martinich, *The Two Gods of "Leviathan": Thomas Hobbes on Religion and Politics* (Cambridge: Cambridge University Press, 1992); and the essays in parts 3 and 4 of *The Companion to Hobbes's "Leviathan,"* ed. Patricia Springborg (Cambridge: Cambridge University Press, 2007), esp. chaps. 12, 15, 16–17.

183. For some reflections on such possible connections, see Noel R. Malcolm, "Thomas Hobbes and Voluntarist Theology" (PhD diss., Cambridge University, 1983). For some fascinating reflections in the seventeenth century on Hobbes's relations with late medieval theology of the "moderni," see Ralph Cudworth, *A Treatise concerning Eternal and Immutable Morality: With a Treatise on Freewill* (Cambridge: Cambridge University Press, 1996), I.4–5. Such relations seem still very much understudied.

184. For a skillful description of conflicting interpretations followed by a wide-ranging investigation of a "need ethos" in *Piers Plowman*, see Jill Mann, "The Nature of Need Revisited," *Yearbook of Langland Studies* 18 (2006): 3–29.

185. See Aers, *Sanctifying Signs*, chap. 5, on Nede, 150–56. Probably the most sustained commentary on "temperance" in the poem remains Bloomfield, *Piers Plowman*, 135–43.

186. R. M. Adams, "The Nature of Need in *Piers Plowman XX*," *Traditio* 34 (1978): 273–301, quotation at 278.

187. For a different reading of this scene, see Anne Middleton, "Acts of Vagrancy: The C Version 'Autobiography' and the Statute of 1388," in *Written Work: Langland, Labor, and Authorship*, ed. Stephen Justice and Kathryn Kerby-Fulton

(Philadelphia: University of Pennsylvania Press, 1997), 208–317. She links the questioning of Wille in Passus V with Nede's in Passus XXII and seeks to bind the former to the enforcement of the Statute of Laborers and its 1388 version.

188. I offer some reflections on the significance of this in Langland's theology and ecclesiology in *Sanctifying Signs*, 149–50.

189. See, e.g., *ST* II-II.66.7, sed contra and resp.

190. I quote from Szittya, *Antifraternal Tradition*, 272. On Nede's relations to Kynde, see Zeeman, *"Piers Plowman" and the Medieval Discourse of Desire*, 263–83.

191. See *ST* II-II.66.7, resp.

192. See *ST* II-II.141.2–6; II-II.152–54.

193. Nede's assumption that Temperance should primarily govern the destitute is shared by another fascinating figure in the poem, Patience, as is his confidence that destitution must generate Christlike humility (XXII.35–37; see Pearsall's note to XXII.37 linking with Patience at XVI.57–99). For mistakes in Nede's and Patience's assumptions, see Aers, *Sanctifying Signs*, 127–32. Ironically, both figures propagate a materialist determination which occludes the need for divine grace in the making of Christocentric virtues, grace mediated by sacraments, according to Jesus the Samaritan (XIX.83–95).

194. See too Bloomfield, *Piers Plowman*, 137, 104. Bloomfield claims that Langland disagrees with Aquinas and agrees with Nede in the hierarchy of the virtues. This stance ignores both Grace's account of the virtues, which I have been following, and Conscience's insistence that Justice is the chief seed that Piers has sown (XXI.406).

195. On Nede's attempt to appropriate Christ's Incarnation for Franciscan ideology, see Aers, *Sanctifying Signs*, 151–52.

196. On *mundus*, see Zeeman, *"Piers Plowman" and the Medieval Discourse of Desire*, 211 n. 20.

197. There is a substantial literature on Antichrist and Langland's version of this figure. A good introduction is Pearsall, *Piers Plowman*, 36–37; and I have found the following helpful: Richard K. Emmerson, *Antichrist in the Middle Ages* (Seattle: University of Washington Press, 1981); Reeves, *Influence of Prophecy*; Henri de Lubac, *La postérité spirituelle de Joachim de Flore*, 2 vols. (Paris: Lethielleux, 1979); R. E. Lerner, "Antichrists and Antichrist in Joachim of Fiore," *Speculum* 60 (1985): 553–70. Two scholars of Langland have presented him as a Joachite writer: Bloomfield, *Piers Plowman*; and Kathryn Kerby-Fulton, *Reformist Apocalypticism and "Piers Plowman"* (Cambridge: Cambridge University Press, 1990). For my own critical distance from such presentations, see David Aers, "Visionary Eschatology in *Piers Plowman*," *Modern Theology* 15 (2000): 3–17. I continue aspects of this discussion below.

198. Perhaps one might expect something like Huon de Mery's tournament of Antichrist; see Emmerson, *Antichrist*, 188–93.

199. Kerby-Fulton is confident that Piers is metamorphosing from St. Peter into the evangelist St. John in accord with Joachim's schemes of sacred history and the third *status* of the Holy Spirit manifested in contemplatives; she is also confident that "Piers will return to reform the Church" (*Reformist Apocalypticism*, 170). As my discussion of the poem's closing lines will make clear, I see no grounds for such confidence. It is salutary to read a work by John of Rupescissa closely alongside the long version of *Piers Plowman*: even when there is some thematic overlapping (as on disendowment, or ecclesial apostasy) the difference of literary and theological modes should be very striking and the modes of speaking, as Aquinas taught, yield decisive doctrinal differences. A very manageable work of John of Rupescissa to read alongside Langland's poem is *Vade Mecum in Tribulatione*. This was published by Edward Brown in the second volume of his *Fasciculus Rerum Expetendarum & Fugiendarum* (London: Chiswell, 1690), 496–508.

200. John Hatcher describes mortality in the plague of 1348–49 as "at least a third of the population of the known world," in "England in the Aftermath of the Black Death," 3.

201. The processes I designate as de-Christianization are considerably broader and deeper than Scase's "anti-clericalism." In fact what she terms "the new anti-clericalism" in her *"Piers Plowman" and the New Anti-Clericalism* seems to be a name for an aspect of Wycliffite ideology and generates a Wycliffite obsession with sacerdotal failings from which the church will be rescued by the king and lay elites, a new Constantinianism.

202. Dante locates simoniac leaders of the church in the *Inferno*, canto 19.

203. Langland wrote the final version of the poem after the Earthquake Council; Hudson, *Premature Reformation*, 402; see Joseph H. Dahmus, *The Prosecution of John Wyclif* (New Haven: Yale University Press, 1952), chap. 5.

204. E.g., Prol. 56–94, 95–127; II.59–80, 158–59; III.26–67, 185–95; V.173–77.

205. See Scase, *Piers Plowman*, 112–19.

206. See Margaret Aston, "William White's Lollard Followers," *Catholic Historical Review* 68 (1982): 469–97.

207. The history of Henry VIII's revolution illustrates the range of theology and contradictory dogmatics compatible with enforcing this revolution. On the theology, J. J. Scarisbrick's work is especially helpful: *Henry VIII* (London: Eyre and Spottiswoode, 1968; repr. London: Methuen, 1983), chap. 12. For what seems to me a far more superficial account of Henry's theology as a coherent "middle way," see Bernard, *The King's Reformation*, chap. 6; for examples of Bernard's claims about this "middle way," see 475, 478–80, 488, 490–91, 494, 507, 521, 543, 546, 558.

208. Gradon, "Langland and the Ideology of Dissent"; and Hudson, *Premature Reformation*, 398–408.

209. Since Gradon, "Langland and the Ideology of Dissent," and Hudson, *Premature Reformation*, the most distinguished contributions to this topic have been by Scase, *Piers Plowman*; and Andrew Cole, *Literature and Heresy in the Age of Chaucer* (Cambridge: Cambridge University Press, 2008), chaps. 2–3.

210. Gradon, "Langland and the Ideology of Disent," 187–88.

211. Margaret Aston, "'Caim's Castles': Poverty, Politics, and Disendowment," in *The Church, Politics, and Patronage in the Fifteenth Century*, ed. R. B. Dobson (Gloucester: Sutton, 1984), 45–81, here 50. This superb essay is reprinted in Margaret Aston, *Faith and Fire* (London: Hambledon, 1997), chap. 4. References in my text are to the original printing in 1984.

212. On the theological virtues in this context, see Aquinas, *ST* I-II.62.1–3; on charity, II-II.23.1–2 and 24.1–2 (charity as a *habit* of the *will* leading to friendship with God).

213. Scase, *Piers Plowman*, chap. 4.

214. On this extraordinary episode and its centrality in *Piers Plowman*, see Aers, *Salvation and Sin*, chap. 4.

215. For lucid commentary and reference to secondary literature, see Pearsall, *Piers Plowman*, XX.11 note.

216. For an example of my understanding of how Langland's dialectic works on a specific topic of inquiry (Franciscan ideologies of poverty), see Aers, *Sanctifying Signs*, chap. 5.

217. See Elizabeth Salter's fine *"Piers Plowman*: An Introduction," in *Piers Plowman: Selections from the C-Text*, ed. Elizabeth Salter and Derek Pearsall (London: Arnold, 1967), 3–58; reprinted in the collection of essays by Salter, *English and International: Studies in the Literature, Art, and Patronage of Medieval England*, ed. Derek Pearsall and Nicolette Zeeman (Cambridge: Cambridge University Press, 1988), 111–57; together with her *Piers Plowman: An Introduction*. Note, in the latter, her description of the poem's "episodic quality" (20, 22), perceptions elaborated by Anne Middleton, "Narration and the Invention of Experience: Episodic Form in *Piers Plowman*," in *The Wisdom of Poetry: Essays in Early English Literature in Honor of Morton W. Bloomfield*, ed. Larry D. Benson and Sigfried Wenzel (Kalamazoo, MI: Medieval Institute Publications, 1982), 91–122.

218. I am drawing especially on Wyclif's *Tractatus De Officio Regis*, ed. A. W. Pollard and C. Sayle (London: Trübner, 1887), esp. chap. 1 (pp. 14 and 13) and chap. 3. On this topic, consult Hudson, *Premature Reformation*, 362–67; Leff, *Heresy in the Later Middle Ages*, 2:542–45; Michael Wilks, "Royal Patronage and Anti-Papalism from Ockham to Wyclif," *Studies in Church History Subsidia* 5 (1987): 135–63; reprinted in his *Wyclif: Political Ideas and Practice*, ed. Anne Hudson (Oxford: Oxbow, 2000), 135–63; Shogimen, "Wyclif's Ecclesiology and Political Thought."

219. See Hudson, *Premature Reformation*, 60 ("stella matutina," Bale's term for Wyclif); Aston, "John Wycliffe's Reformation Reputation."

220. See Scarisbrick, *Henry VIII*, chaps. 9–12; Bernard, *The King's Reformation*, chaps. 3, 5, 6; Duffy, *Stripping of the Altars*, chaps. 11–12.

221. I refer to the printing of the B version by Robert Crowley, *The Vision of Pierce Plowman, now the second time imprinted by Roberte Crowley* (1550), using the copy in the Cambridge University Library, Syn 7.55.25. The B version's passage on disendowment is at XV.553–69. I draw here from Crowley's "Printer to the Reader" and "A briefe summe of the principall poynts" and from his marginalia. Crowley is an evangelist who admires the way Langland "doth most christianlie instructe the weake, and sharplye rebuke the obstynate blynde" ("Printer to the Reader"). There is discussion of Crowley's *Piers Plowman* in Sarah A. Kelen, *Langland's Early Modern Identities* (New York: Palgrave, 2007); Jamie K. Taylor, *Fictions of Evidence: Witnessing, Literature, and Community in the Late Middle Ages* (Columbus: Ohio State University Press, 2013), 146–48; Brewer, *Editing "Piers Plowman,"* chap. 1.

222. So despite disagreements over wider issues concerning Langland's theology, I agree with James Simpson's emphasis on the differences between Langland's work and Wycliffite Christianity in *Reform and Cultural Revolution*, 371–74.

223. Leff, *Heresy in the Later Middle Ages*, 2:543.

224. See the brilliant essay on the *Knight's Tale* by Elizabeth Salter, *Chaucer: The Knight's Tale and the Clerk's Tale* (London: Arnold, 1962); see too her essay "Chaucer and Boccaccio: *The Knight's Tale*," in *Fourteenth-Century English Poetry: Contexts and Readings* (Oxford: Clarendon Press, 1983), 141–81.

225. Skeat, *Piers the Plowman*, 2:279.

226. Repentaunce is both an act of the soul and, according to Pearsall, a "priest-confessor" (note to VI.1).

227. Sources for the "horn" of Hope and the quotations here are discussed by Pearsall in his notes to VI.151–54; some amplification is offered by Schmidt, *Piers Plowman*, 2:544.

228. See Skeat, *Piers the Plowman*, 2:63–65, as so often in Skeat, a thoroughly engaging commentary.

229. Pearsall, *Piers Plowman*, VI.115, note.

230. See VIII.23–55, 149–66, 329–38 (with notes 47–48 above).

231. For characteristic examples of this basic distinction, *ST* I.1.1, resp.; I.23.1, resp.; I-II.5.3–5; I-II.62.1. For relevant literature on the debates around this "duplex," see note 68 above.

232. The most sustained study of "kynde" in *Piers Plowman* is by Nicolette Zeeman in her *"Piers Plowman" and the Medieval Discourse of Desire*, chaps. 5–7. I acknowledge this to be an outstanding work which I greatly admire. But her understanding of "kynde," in my view, turns Langland into a natural theologian with

little interest in Christology. It is significant in this respect that her capacious index does not even have an entry for "Christ."

233. See, e.g., Kenneth Surin's informative study, *Theology and the Problem of Evil* (Oxford: Blackwell, 1986).

234. Excellent notes by Pearsall link the relevant passages in VIII and XXII at his *Piers Plowman* XXII.80 and VIII.168. Schmidt seeks to gloss away the obvious meaning of Conscience's final prayer for vengeance (*Piers Plowman*, 2:726). Here it is appropriate to recall the *Prick of Conscience*, that immensely popular medieval poem so helpfully reedited by Ralph Hanna and Sara Wood in *Richard Morris's "Prick of Conscience": A Corrected and Amplified Reading Text*, EETS, o.s., 242 (Oxford: Oxford University Press, 2013). The preface of the poem articulates the view that people can be terrified into virtue (lines 320–47). Much in the work's treatment of purgatory and hell enacts this view.

235. On this episode and its relevant secondary literature, see Aers, *Salvation and Sin*, chap. 4.

236. Ockham, *A Short Discourse on Tyrannical Government*, ed. and trans. Kilcullen, 59 (chap. 19).

237. For Walter Brut, see my admiring discussion in *Sanctifying Signs*, 67–82. For relevant views by East Anglian Wycliffites, persecuted by the church, see *Heresy Trials in the Diocese of Norwich*, ed. Tanner, e.g., 71 (John Pyrye of Martham), 96 (Robert Cavell of Bungay), 42 (Margery Baxter of Martham), 86 (Richard Fleccher of Beccles), 142 (Hawisia Mone of Loddon), 148 (John Skylan of Bergh Apton), 153 (William Hardy of Mundeham). Similar views are expressed in the 1395 Lollard "libellus," in Netter, *Fasciculi Zizaniorum*, item 10 (366–67). On Christian discipleship and nonviolence among Wycliffites, see Hudson, *Premature Reformation*, 367–70.

238. T. S. Eliot, *Little Gidding*, pt. 2, in *The Four Quartets* (New York: Harcourt, Brace and Co., 1971).

239. I have just quoted from Pearsall's note on XXII.183.

240. Calvin, *Institutes*, II.8.44.

241. I refer to passages of disputation in Passus XVI–XIX, XXI.

242. See *ST* III.46.6–8 and III.47.3; also III.15.5–10. My understanding of what Aquinas is doing here and of his motivations has been immeasurably helped by Paul Gondreau, *The Passions of Christ's Soul in the Theology of St. Thomas Aquinas* (Münster: Aschendorff, 2002; repr. Scranton: University of Scranton Press, 2009).

243. These were, of course, traditional affirmations in orthodox Christianity, commonplaces of late medieval preaching. Our resurrection is enabled by and prefigured by Christ's (1 Cor. 15). A classic example of the tradition is in Augustine, *City of God*, XXII.4–30; see also *ST* III prologue and III.56.1–2; and Aquinas, *Summa contra Gentiles*, trans. Anton C. Pegis, 5 vols. (Notre Dame: University of Notre Dame Press, 1975), IV.79–88 (vol. 5).

244. I refer to *City of God* XX.7; further references are given in the text. I use *De civitate Dei*, ed. Dombart and Kalb; and the English translation by Henry Bettenson, *The City of God against the Pagans* (London: Penguin, 1984), together with that by Dyson, *The City of God against the Pagans*.

245. For an example of such calculation in 397, see R. A. Markus, *Saeculum: History and Society in the Theology of St. Augustine* (Cambridge: Cambridge University Press, 1970; repr. 1988), 20.

246. I have found the following accounts of Joachite ideology and exegesis especially helpful: Reeves, *Influence of Prophecy*; Bernard McGinn, *The Calabrian Abbot: Joachim of Fiore* (London: Macmillan, 1985); Jeanne Bignami-Odier, *Études sur Jean de Roquetaillade (Johannes de Rupescissa)* (Paris: Vrin, 1952); Blumenfeld-Kosinski, *Poets, Saints, and Visionaries*.

247. See Lerner, "Antichrist and Antichrists in Joachim of Fiore," 563, 567.

248. On Jean, see Bignami-Odier, *Études*; E. Jacob, "John of Roquetaillade," *Bulletin of the John Rylands Library* 39 (1956–57): 75–96.

249. Reeves, *Influence of Prophecy*, 226–27.

250. See Reeves, *Influence of Prophecy*, 227 and chap. 3; further references are given in the text. She draws on Bignami-Odier, *Études*, using her detailed and lucid summaries of Jean's works. I have also drawn here on Blumenfeld-Kosinski, *Poetry, Saints, and Visionaries*, 181–82. Kerby-Fulton addresses Jean de Roquetaillade in her *Reformist Apocalypticism and "Piers Plowman*,*"* 188–91. Her commitment to offering "a Joachite perspective on *Piers Plowman*" (191–200 passim) tends to encourage the confusion of what a text reminds her of with the establishment of influence.

251. The summary of Jean's prophetic work is drawn from Bignami-Odier, *Études*, 53–172; Reeves, *Influence of Prophecy*, 320–24; Blumenfeld-Kosinski, *Poetry, Saints, and Visionaries*, 181–82. On the making of God into an Englishman, see Michael Wilks, "Royal-Patronage and Anti-Papalism from Ockham to Wyclif," *Studies in Church History Subsidia* 5 (1987): 135–63, reprinted in his *Wyclif: Political Ideas and Practice* (Oxford: Oxbow, 2000), 135–63, where he uses J. W. McKenna, "How God became an Englishman," in *Tudor Rule and Revolution: Essays for G. R. Elton from His American Friends*, ed. D. G. Guth and J. W. McKenna (Cambridge: Cambridge University Press, 1982), 25–43. For examples of the life of Joachite traditions in the Reformation, see Diarmaid MacCulloch, *Reformation: Europe's House Divided, 1490–1700* (London: Penguin, 2004), 189, 205–7.

252. On Mede, see Yunck, *Lineage of Lady Meed*.

253. Pearsall observes: "The story . . . is not intrinsically a very good one for the illustration of meed" (III.409–42, note).

254. See *ST* II-II.4.2 with III.47.2.

255. See *ST* II-II.4.2 with III.47.2; and Milton, *Paradise Lost*, I.1–5, in *The Complete Poetry and Essential Prose of John Milton*, ed. William Kerrigan, John Rumrich, and Stephen Fallon (New York: Modern Library, 2007).

256. See *1 Henry IV*, 3.1.11–66, and *King Lear*, 1.2.102–33, in *The Riverside Shakespeare*, ed. G. Blakemore Evans (Boston: Houghton Mifflin, 1974).

257. See Szittya, *Antifraternal Tradition*, chap. 4 (Wyclif) and chap. 2 (William of St. Amour).

258. See Aers, "Visionary Eschatology," 7, and citations in n. 17 of this essay to Jean of Roquetaillade.

259. Isaiah 2:2–5 was "read at matins in the first week of Advent" (Bennett, *Piers Plowman*, 141).

260. Henri de Lubac discusses the compromising of Christ Jesus's full significance in the economy of salvation in *Exégèse médiévale*, II/1:538; see the whole of chap. 6 on Joachite exegesis and ideology.

261. Here I rehearse distinctions basic to Aquinas, as in *ST* I-II.109.1–2 or I-II.62.1; see note 68 above.

262. See Aers, *Sanctifying Signs*, 88–92, 97–107.

263. Holcot, *In Librum Sapientiae*.

264. In Lectio 58: "Nam circa eius adventum calculatores & pseudoastronomi seducti sunt," *In Librum Sapientiae*, 206–7. For a study that goes against the grain of current inclinations to reject the Leffian and Gilsonian accounts of "skepticism" in fourteenth-century theology, see Kennedy, *Philosophy of Robert Holcot*.

265. For John Wyclif's similar rejection of Joachite projects to discover the times and moments, see the statement quoted in Leff, *Heresy in the Later Middle Ages*, 2:543 n. 2, from *Johannis Wyclif Opera Minora*, ed. Johann Loserth (London: Trübner, 1913), 375.

266. Tierney, *Origins of Papal Infallibility*, chap. 6, here at 210.

267. See Ockham, *A Letter to the Friars Minor and Other Writings*, 13.

268. Ibid., 206.

269. Ibid., 218.

270. Tierney, *Origins of Papal Infallibility*, 232; cf. Shogimen, *Ockham and Political Discourse*, 238. Tierney strongly disapproves of Ockham's teaching on authority and hermeneutics (e.g., 228, 235–36). In my view, his conviction that Ockham's teaching is anarchic and subjective simply evades the problems that Ockham identified in his church. Contrast Shogimen, 256–61.

271. John Milton, *The Ready and Easy Way to Establish a Free Commonwealth*, in Kerrigan, Rumrich, and Fallon, eds., *Complete Poetry and Essential Prose*, 1136. Abdiel's arguments and acts are recounted in *Paradise Lost*, V.803–VI.198; the Abdiel-like just men are encountered through books XI and XII. For Milton's articulation of his ecclesiology after the Revolution, see his *De doctrina christiana*, I.29 and 31; as in Ockham, his ecclesiology is inseparable from his teaching on Christian liberty (I.27). For *De doctrina christiana*, see the parallel-text edition by John K. Hale and J. D. Cullington, in vol. 8 of *The Complete Works of John Milton*, 2 vols. (Oxford: Oxford University Press, 2012). On Ockham's innovative account

of Christian liberty, see McGrade, *Political Thought of William of Ockham*, 141–49, 160–66; with Shogimen, *Ockham and Political Discourse*, chap. 6.

272. On this topic, the fusion of ecclesiology and predestinarian dogmatics, Pamela Gradon offers a lucid and decisive account of the differences between Langland and Wyclif, in "Langland and the Ideology of Dissent," 199–202; as does Leff, *Heresy in the Later Middle Ages*, 2:516–46; and Hudson, *Premature Reformation*, chap. 7; also more recently Shogimen, "Wyclif's Ecclesiology and Political Thought," 220–21.

273. *Breviloquium*, V.4, in *A Short Discourse on Tyrannical Government*, 136.

274. Ibid., 137.

275. Ibid., 138.

276. I quote from the fine translation by Maria Boulding, *Expositions of the Psalms*, exposition on Psalm 73:1. For the Latin text, see Augustine, *Enarrationes In Psalmos*, 1004–23. Milton's version of the remnant pervades both editions of *The Readie and Easie Way to Establish a Free Commonwealth*; see *The Complete Works of John Milton*, vol. 6, *Vernacular Regicide and Republican Writings*, ed. N. K. Keeble and Nicholas McDowell (Oxford: Oxford University Press, 2013), 461–523, esp. 520–23. Keeble's comments on Milton's version of the remnant rightly bring out its "elitism and exclusivity" (106). Unlike Milton, Langland has absolutely no idea that his "fools" should wield the sword and civil power in a republican politics of "elitism and exclusivity" with rabid contempt for the people. Milton, we recall, had long before judged the people to be "an inconstant, irrational and Image-doting rabble" (*Eikonoklastes*, 424, in the same volume). After the Restoration, in political defeat, Milton offers a version of the remnant separate from the lust for dominion: see, e.g., *Paradise Lost* XII.479–551.

277. For the commonplaces here, see Tentler, *Sin and Confession on the Eve of the Reformation*, 104–33; on penance in *Piers Plowman* in relation to Wycliffite views, see Gradon, "Langland and the Ideology of Dissent," 191–93; and Hudson, *Premature Reformation*, 294–301.

278. Netter, *Fasciculus Zizaniorum*, 278: "Item quod si homo fuerit debite contritus, omnis confessio exterior est sibi superflua, vel inutilis."

279. William Thorpe, *Testimony of William Thorpe*, in Hudson, ed., *Two Wycliffite Texts*, 80–84. Such views were common among Hawisia Mone and her friends in Norfolk and Suffolk; see Tanner, ed., *Heresy Trials in the Diocese of Norwich*, 140–41 (Hawisia Mone), 135 (John Eldon), 48–49 (Margery Baxter, a more elaborate story), and many more similarly, one of the most widespread beliefs in opposition to church dogmatics.

280. I am not persuaded by Scase's description of the final passus as "anticlerical apocalypticism," in *"Piers Plowman" and the New Anti-Clericalism*, 113. This classification occludes Langland's critique of lay elites alongside clergy. Perhaps Scase's terminology is shaped by her preoccupation with Wyclif.

281. Conscience's dismissal of Clergie is proximate to Rechelessnesse's wrathful dismissal of "clergie" which Ymagenatyf later corrects: XI.272–303; XIII.129–30; XIV.99–130. On *clergie*, see Zeeman, *"Piers Plowman"and the Medieval Discourse of Desire*, 23–24 and chaps. 4, 6, 7.

282. Aers, *Sanctifying Signs*, chap. 5, provides references to primary and secondary sources.

283. For William of St. Amour, see Szittya, *Antifraternal Tradition*, chap. 1; on Jean de Meun, 184–90.

284. Like the reader, he may remember III.38–76 and XII.11–36.

285. On Chaucer's friars in his *Summoner's Tale*, see Szittya, *Antifraternal Tradition*, chap. 6. Jill Mann's discussion of the friar of the *General Prologue* and the traditions of satire to which he belongs remains indispensable: *Chaucer and Medieval Estates Satire*, 37–54.

286. For an exploration of what constitutes a state of perfection, see Aquinas, *ST* II-II.186.1–2.

287. Wyclif, *Tractatus De Blasphemia*, ed. Michael Henry Dziewicki (London: Trübner and Co. for the Wyclif Society, 1893), 46; see also 218. On Wyclif's teaching on the friars, see Hudson, *Premature Reformation*, 347–51, 168–73.

288. On the friars here, see Pearsall's note to XXII.276, with Szittya, *Antifraternal Tradition*, 282.

289. On the Fourth Lateran Council's canon 21, "Omnis utriusque sexus" (1215), see *Decrees of the Ecumenical Councils*, ed. Norman Tanner, Latin and English, 2 vols. (London: Sheed and Ward, 1990), 1:245, par. 21.

290. I refer to Scase, *"Piers Plowman" and the New Anti-Clericalism*, 119; contrast Sarah Wood, *Conscience and the Composition of "Piers Plowman,"* 88: "as earlier a king's knight and now castellan of Unity," Conscience in Passus XXII becomes "a lordly conscience easily misled by friars." Yet on the consequences of this, Wood and I seem far apart.

291. There is an engaging passage in Wyclif's *De Blasphemia* where he discusses how friars are generally the confessors and counselors of lay lords (192–93) and where he attacks clerical elites for taking on the most secular work for the Crown (199, 200). Indeed: but had he forgotten his own earlier missions for Crown and elites? For an extremely informative study of the ecclesial contexts, see Robert C. Palmer, *Selling the Church: The English Parish in Law, Commerce, and Religion, 1350–1550* (Chapel Hill: University of North Carolina Press, 2002), which presents a striking comparison with Duffy's materials in his *Stripping of the Altars*.

292. Szittya gives a fine exposition of *penetrantes domos* in *Antifraternal Tradition*, 58–61, 185–86, 284–85.

293. *Jacob's Well: An English Treatise on the Cleansing of Man's Conscience*, ed. A. Brandeis (pt. 1), EETS, o.s., 115 (London: K. Paul, Trench, Trübner, and Co., 1900).

294. Similarly Szittya, *Antifraternal Tradition*, 276, 286.

295. On *dwale* I follow Skeat, *Piers the Plowman*, 2:284–85: "an opiate, a sleeping draught," citing Chaucer's usage in his *Reeve's Tale*, *CT* I.4161; the *Riverside Chaucer* glosses *dwale* as "sleeping potion."

296. See *ST* III.62, III.64.1, III.64.7, III.84.7, III.85.3.

297. Below I will address the relations between Holy Church in Passus I–II and Holy Church in Passus XXII.

298. It is important to recognize the history congealed and reified in the encyclical's language of "Magisterium." For a helpful introduction by a Roman Catholic theologian, see Yves M.-J. Congar, "Pour une histoire sémantique du terme 'magisterium'" and "Bref historique des formes du 'magistère' et de ses relations avec les docteurs," *Revue des Sciences Philosophiques et Théologiques* 60 (1976): 85–98, 99–112.

299. Recent examples can be found in Schmidt's annotations in *Piers Plowman*, vol. 2: rejecting readings of the poem's ending which have some affinities with the one offered in this book, he asserts that they simply must be wrong because they "would be out of keeping with his [Conscience's? Langland's?] upright and loyal nature." So how are we to read Conscience leaving the church in the final lines? "The possibility therefore [*sic!*] cannot be excluded that the ending was to receive further revision, perhaps on the scale of the text up to Passus XX" (726). Luckily for Langland, assumed to share Schmidt's version of Christian orthodoxy and authority, the modern editor's gloss now in effect provides the "further revision" Langland failed to provide in *either* long version of his work. Schmidt thus now makes it into a fitting conclusion for an "upright and loyal" Christian in his own rather un-Langlandian image of orthodoxy.

300. 1377, Parliament: the quotation is from Michael Wilks's discussion of the text on "Royal Patronage and Anti-Papalism," in his *Wyclif*, 131–32.

301. See Siegfried Wenzel, *Latin Sermon Collections from Later Medieval England: Orthodox Preaching in the Age of Wyclif* (Cambridge: Cambridge University Press, 2005), 371–72, 375.

302. See Harriss, *Shaping the Nation*, 590; also consult the important essay by Jeremy Catto, "Religious Change under Henry V."

303. *De Blasphemia*, 197; see too 200.

304. So I reject the arguments of Aers in *Chaucer, Langland, and the Creative Imagination* (London: Routledge, 1980), 59–60, but develop some strands found on 61.

305. On this aspect of the later Ockham, see the fine commentary in McGrade, *Political Thought of William of Ockham*, 68–71, 72–74; with Annabel Brett's introduction to her translation of Ockham's *On the Power of Emperors and Popes*, 28. Shogimen's account of Ockham's "ecclesiastical republicanism" is intriguing but seems to me an imposition of alien political structures and institutions on Ockham's theology of evangelical liberty.

306. McGrade, *Political Thought of William of Ockham*, 141; and see 140–49. See also Shogimen, *Ockham and Political Discourse*, chap. 6.

307. On some of the ironies here, Lester Little is particularly illuminating in *Religious Poverty and the Profit Economy*.

308. Aquinas, *In Orationem Dominicam Videlicet "Pater Noster" Expositio*, par. 1066, in *Opuscula Theologica*, ed. Verardo, Spiazzi, and Calcaterra, 2:228.

309. Milton, "On the New Forcers of Conscience under the Long Parliament," in *Complete Poetry and Essential Prose*, line 20—a characteristic piece of Miltonic wordplay rather congruent with one of Langland's pleasures. On *formalism* and *antiformalism* in the revolution, see J. C. Davis, "Against Formality: One Aspect of the English Revolution," *Transactions of the Royal Historical Society* 3 (1993): 265–88. Still helpful is William Lamont's account of shifts in the understanding of liberty, "Pamphleteering, the Protestant Consensus, and the English Revolution," in *Freedom and the English Revolution*, ed. R. C. Richardson and G. M. Ridden (Manchester: Manchester University Press, 1986), 72–92.

310. Dymmok's *Liber* was edited by H. S. Cronin for the Wyclif Society (London: K. Paul, Trench, Trübner, and Co., 1922); page references to this edition are cited in the text.

311. For a good account of medieval appeals to the early church, see Leff, "Apostolic Ideal in Later Medieval Ecclesiology."

312. The Supremacy Act of 1559 is reprinted in G. R. Elton, ed., *Tudor Constitution: Documents and Commentary* (Cambridge: Cambridge University Press, 1982), document 184; and in Bettenson, ed., *Documents of the Christian Church*, 329–30. For Milton's comments on the Donation of Constantine, see, e.g., *Of Reformation* (1641), in *Complete Prose Works of John Milton*, ed. Don M. Wolfe et al., 8 vols. (New Haven: Yale University Press, 1953–82), 1:615; on the Constantinianism of the Reformation, 1:535, 554–55. The central place of Constantinianism in Foxe's *Acts and Monuments* is illustrated throughout William Haller, *Foxe's Book of Martyrs and the Elect Nation* (London: Cape, 1963), also published as *The Elect Nation: The Meaning and Relevance of Foxe's Book of Martyrs* (New York: Harper and Row, 1963). William Lamont has some sharply relevant observations on how "the saints" of the 1640s and 1650s "had to destroy Foxe and his idols—the martyr-bishops, the Godly Prince, Constantine, Elizabeth"—in "Puritanism as History and Historiography," *Past & Present* 44 (1969): 133–46, here 139.

313. Still indispensable is Margaret Aston's "Lollardy and Sedition, 1381–1431," *Past & Present* 17 (1960): 1–44, reprinted in her *Lollards and Reformers*, 1–47; also H. G. Richardson, "Heresy and the Lay Power under Richard II," *English Historical Review* 51 (1936): 1–28.

314. Catto, "Religious Change under Henry V," esp. 115; on this nexus, see A. H. McHardy, "Liturgy and Propaganda in the Diocese of Lincoln during the

Hundred Years War," *Studies in Church History* 20 (1983): 171–78; Harriss, *Shaping the Nation*, chaps. 3, 15.

315. From different motives, grand narratologists tend to stress *discontinuities* and ignore *continuities*. One can readily witness this in works referred to in the preface to this book, such as Duffy, *Stripping of the Altars*; Simpson, *Reform and Cultural Revolution*; Gregory, *Unintended Reformation*; Gillespie, *Theological Origins of Modernity*.

316. A good example of Constantinian modes is displayed in the statute of 1401 legitimizing the burning to death of English Wycliffites, in Bettenson, ed., *Documents of the Christian Church*, 251–55; here *heresy* is explicitly identified with "sedition and insurrection" (252). Aston, "Lollardy and Sedition," is extremely informative on this period, as is Peter McNiven's *Heresy and Politics in the Reign of Henry IV* (Woodbridge: Boydell, 1987). On the magisterial reform of the sixteenth century and Langland, I concur with James Simpson, *Reform and Cultural Revolution*, 343–45, albeit for different reasons.

317. I refer to Ockham, *On the Power of Emperors and Popes*, chap. 27 (p. 168).

318. Aers, *Sanctifying Signs*, 99–156.

319. See Hudson, *Premature Reformation*, 334, quoting Netter, *Fasciculi Zizaniorum*, 279 (item IX): "Item quod post Urbanum sextum non est aliquis recipiendus in papam, sed vivendum est, more Graecorum sub legibus propriis." Hudson notes that this view "appeared several times around 1395 in English writing concerning the Schism" (334). This should surely be seen as among the many *continuities* between the later fourteenth/early fifteenth century and the theological resources of the sixteenth-century Reformation, as should the line taken at the Council of Constance to subordinate the papacy to general council. On Wyclif and Antichrist, see Leff, *Heresy in the Later Middle Ages*, 2:536–41.

320. Consult Salter, *Piers Plowman: An Introduction*, 89.

321. I discuss the theology, compassion, and rhetorical brilliance of this speech in *Salvation and Sin*, 115–19.

322. Skeat, *Piers the Plowman*, 2:285.

323. *De heretico comburendo*, in Bettenson, ed., *Documents of the Christian Church*, 252–53.

324. See the still unsurpassed essay on this passus by Elizabeth Salter, "Piers Plowman and the Pilgrimage to Truth," together with her *Piers Plowman: An Introduction*, 84–90, 100–102.

325. Elizabeth Salter, "Introduction," in Salter and Pearsall, *Piers Plowman*, 31, 32; original emphasis. Her quotation from Hilton comes from *The Scale of Perfection*, II.29, ed. Evelyn Underhill (London: J. M. Watkins, 1923; repr. 1948), 355; in the reprint of the essay as chap. 5 in her *English and International*, this quotation is at 134.

326. Augustine, *Homilies on the Gospel of John, Homilies on the First Epistle of John, Soliloquies*, ed. Philip Schaff (Grand Rapids, MI: Eerdmans, 1986), 68.3.

327. Salter, "Piers Plowman and the Pilgrimage to Truth," 126–27 (original emphasis), reprinted in Blanch, ed., *Style and Symbolism*, chap. 6; Middleton, "Langland's Lives: Reflections on Late-Medieval Religious and Literary Vocabulary," in *The Idea of Medieval Literature*, ed. James M. Dean and Christian K. Zacher (Newark: University of Delaware Press, 1992), 227–42, here at 233.

328. Wilks, *Problem of Sovereignty in the Later Middle Ages*; W. Ullmann, *Medieval Papalism: The Political Theories of the Medieval Canonists* (London: Methuen, 1949). Of course, I am aware that here, as in much of my reading of *Piers Plowman*, I would encounter responses such as that offered to Crowley by the seventeenth-century Roman Catholic Andrew Bostock, as he opposed the editor's marginalia: Langland, insists Bostock, "must not be understood to scorn the Authority of the Chief Pastor, as the Heretical margin, wold suggest" (from Bostock's own marginalia on Crowley's marginalia, printed by Charlotte Brewer in *Editing Piers Plowman*, 18–19). Brewer herself is sure that Bostock's reading of Langland's work is correct and Crowley's wrong since Langland's reformation is "always in terms that implicitly or explicitly reinforce traditional social and religious structures" (7–8). This represents the dominant view in scholarship on *Piers Plowman* and was nicely expressed by my own teacher assessing Crowley's editorial comments: "it comes about, ironically, that a work so fundamentally Catholic and orthodox was used as a support for the Reformation" (Salter, *Piers Plowman: An Introduction*, 12). It is worth juxtaposing Langland's treatment of the relations between the absent Piers and the very present pope in the lines just quoted from Passus XXII with Dante's *Paradiso* 27.19–66. There Dante hears St. Peter describe the modern popes as usurpers of his own place in the church. They have turned this into a foul place of blood in the service of Satan, turning the church into an institution whose teleology is the acquisition of earthly gold instead of beatitude. They have betrayed the papal office by turning its keys into signs under which the papacy promotes wars between Christians. Everywhere he looks, complains St. Peter, he sees rapacious wolves dressed as sheep ("In vesta di pastor lupi rapaci"). I have used the text of the *Divine Comedy* with translation by Geoffrey L. Bickersteth (Oxford: Blackwell for the Shakespeare Head Press, 1965). Given the quotation from Milton's *Ready and Easy Way* in section XIII above, I also wish to recall Milton's own brilliant attack on the papacy and his own reformed church in *Lycidas*, lines 109–31: the links with Dante are made in the edition by Barbara K. Lewalski and Estelle Haan, *The Complete Works of John Milton*, vol. 3, *The Shorter Poems* (Oxford: Oxford University Press, 2014), 54–55, 388; on *Paradiso* 29.103–8 in *Lycidas* 126, see p. 389.

329. Brewer, *Editing Piers Plowman*, chap. 1 (on Crowley); and see note 222 in this essay.

330. John Paul II, *The Splendor of Truth (Veritatis Splendor)*, 88 and 106 (pp. 110 and 128); original emphasis.

331. I refer to Augustine, *City of God*, XIX.15 and XIX.17.

332. William of Ockham, *A Letter to the Friars Minor and Other Writings*, 13; he alludes to 3 Kings 19:10 and 18. Most famously, of course, the Virgin Mary alone remained true during the crucifixion of Christ; Shogimen, *Ockham and Political Discourse*, 238.

333. See Karl Barth, *The Doctrine of Reconciliation*, in *Church Dogmatics*, 4 pts. in 12 vols., trans. Geoffrey W. Bromiley (Edinburgh: T. and T. Clark, 1962), vol. 4, pt. 3.2; and Augustine's second exposition on Psalm 29:6 in *Expositions of the Psalms*, trans. Boulding, WSA, pt. 3, vol. 15, 305.

334. I depend on the illuminating and detailed study by Beryl Smalley, "John Baconthorpe's Postill on St. Matthew," in her *Studies in Medieval Thought and Learning: From Abelard to Wyclif* (London: Hambledon, 1981), 289–343; I quote from 321 and draw on 319–33. However, the most thorough expression of papalist absolutism, a papalist version of Constantinian Christianity, known to me is Giles of Rome, *On Ecclesiastical Polity*, ed. and trans. Dyson. This edition contains a helpful introduction on the historical contexts of Giles and this work.

335. *De heretico comburendo* quoted here from Bettenson, ed., *Documents of the Christian Church*, 251–55.

336. Prologue to Ockham, *On the Power of Emperors and Popes*, 71–72.

337. Milton, *Areopagitica*, in *Complete Prose Works*, II.529. For a pertinent discussion of "sect" and Lollards, see Hudson, *Premature Reformation*, 168–73, 347–51; and there is a characteristically eloquent and ruminative essay by Patrick Collinson on such issues: "Night Schools, Conventicles, and Churches: Continuities and Discontinuities in Early Protestant Ecclesiology," in *The Beginnings of English Protestantism*, ed. Peter Marshall and Alec Ryrie (Cambridge: Cambridge University Press, 2002), 209–35.

338. For the 1593 act, see Bettenson, ed., *Documents of the Christian Church*, 340–42.

339. Tanner, *Heresy Trials in the Diocese of Norwich*, 138–44; further references are given in the text. See Hudson, *Premature Reformation*, 33–34, 38–41, 162–63, 168–73, 180–200.

340. For the punishments with which these East Anglian Christians were afflicted, see Tanner's summary in *Heresy Trials in the Diocese of Norwich*, 22–25, 29–30.

341. On women in Lollardy, compare Margaret Aston, "Lollard Women Priests?," *Journal of Ecclesiastical History* 31 (1980): 441–61, reprinted in her *Images and Literacy in Late Medieval Religion* (London: Hambledon Press, 1984), 49–70; Clare Cross, "'Great Reasoners in Scripture': The Activities of Women Lollards, 1380–1530," *Studies in Church History Subsidia* 1 (1978): 359–80;

Shannon McSheffrey, *Gender and Heresy: Women and Men in Lollard Communities,
1420–1530* (Philadelphia: University of Pennsylvania Press, 1995).

342. See Hudson, *Premature Reformation*, chap. 3 and also 450–51, 456–72;
see too Wyclif, *De Eucharistia*, ed. Loserth, 119, on Christians breaking bread in
their homes.

343. Wyclif, *De Blasphemia*, 62.

344. Ibid., 72.

345. Here I think of René Girard, *Things Hidden since the Foundation of the
World* (London: Athlone, 1977).

346. For this language and its unfolding, see Henry Jacob, *A Collection of
Sundry Matters* (1616) with *A Confession and Protestation of the Faith of Certaine
Christians* (1616), bound together in Cambridge University Library, Rare Books
Room, shelfmark Bb*.12.47.

347. For introduction to these, see Rollo-Koster and Izbicki, *Companion to
the Great Western Schism*; and I have found especially helpful Anderson, *Discernment of Spirits*; with Blumenfeld-Kosinski, *Poets, Saints, and Visionaries*.

348. I am aware of J. Patrick Hornbeck's denial that any Wycliffite held to
"the principles of congregationalism in church governance, at least not as those
concepts were later articulated by the reformers of the sixteenth century"; see
What Is a Lollard? Dissent and Belief in Late Medieval England (Oxford: Oxford
University Press, 2010), 172. I have no problems with a denial couched in such
terms. No Wycliffite in Earsham or Loddon in the 1420s would formulate the
same ecclesiastic polity as ones being worked out by Brownists and later sepa-
ratists in Elizabethan and Jacobean England or in the very different contexts of
the 1650s. My quotation from Henry Jacob does not indicate that I equate Jacob
or Thomas Helwys or John Goodwin with Langland or Hawisia Mone. But nor
do I think of "congregationalism" as having determinate "principles" articulated in
sixteenth-century Europe. Rather "congregationalism" gestures toward complex,
fascinating processes of reformation as groups of Protestants came to resist the ecclesiology and theology of the magisterial Reformation to which the Church of
England belonged. Still extremely useful here is Murray Tolmie, *The Triumph of
the Saints: The Separate Churches of London, 1616–1649* (Cambridge: Cambridge
University Press, 1977). Here I should acknowledge the complexity and important nuances of the terminology used to think about different aspects of reformation, restitution, renewal, and regeneration within the traditions of Reformation
in the sixteenth and seventeenth centuries. This is nicely exemplified in Peter
Wilcox's essay on an aspect of Calvin's writing, "'The Restoration of the Church'
in Calvin's 'Commentaries in Isaiah the Prophet,'" *Archiv für Reformationsgeschichte*
85 (1994): 68–95. Hornbeck's approach to change and continuity within Christian traditions does not seem a productive one, since it is unlikely that many con-

cepts are articulated in precisely the same way across the centuries even within a strand that seeks continuity with what its adherents recognize as their predecessors. In this area we address implications and potentialities, not univocal concepts and practices. In fact, Hornbeck himself ascribes what he says "might seem to imply almost a congregationalist understanding of authority" to the Lollard sermon *Of Mynystris in the Chirche* (185). The grammar Hornbeck uses here seems to me thoroughly appropriate to such texts and their places in histories of reformation. I concur with him on this particular reading. In the present contexts I want to remember the shrewd reflections by St. Thomas More related to a term I use very tentatively: *congregationalism*. In his often brilliant *Dialogue concerning Heresies*, More discusses Tyndale's translation of the New Testament and explains why it deserves to be burned. He says it should not be called the New Testament but "Tyndals testament or Luthers testament." This is because the "holsom doctryne of Cryste" is displaced in Tyndale's translation which time and again substitutes "deuylysh heresyes" (285). Among the symptomatic choices illustrated by More is the substitution of "chyrch" by "congregacyon" (286). More himself had earlier used "chyrche" and "congregacyon of Cryste" as synonymous (e.g., 190, 192–93). Indeed, in principle, he saw no problem in naming a gathering of Christians as a "chyrche or congregacyon of Cryste" (190). He had earlier said that Christ intended to "gather a flocke and congregacyon of people that should serue god and be hus specyall people" (173). The problem arose when a Lutheranizing author refused any use of "chyrche" and always translates "*ecclesia*" as "congregacyon." This Tyndale did: "he calleth the chyrche alwway the congregacyon." But More points out that although "the chyrche" is indeed "a congregacyon," not every "congregacyon" is "the chyrche." Only "a congregacyon of crysten people" is "the chyrche." And in common English "a congregacyon of crysten people hath ben in Englande always called and knowen by the name of chyrche." So to exclude "chyrche" completely from his translation and only use the term *congregacyon* represents an ideological decision, a Lutheran polemic embodied in remaking the New Testament. References and text from *A Dialogue concerning Heresies* are to the edition by Thomas M. C. Lawler, Germain Marc'Hadour, and Richard C. Marius in vol. 6 of *The Complete Works of St. Thomas More*, ed. Louis Martz et al. (New Haven: Yale University Press, 1981). There is a fine essay on More's work by Eamon Duffy, "'The comen knowen multytude of crysten men': *A Dialogue concerning Heresies* and the Defence of Christendom," in *The Cambridge Companion to Thomas More*, ed. George M. Logan (Cambridge: Cambridge University Press, 2011), 191–215; on Tyndale's translation and More's criticisms, see 206–7. I should also note here that my visit to the church in Corinth in conjunction with a discussion of Langland's "fools" would hardly surprise many medieval exegetes of scripture. Take the commentary on the Bible by the distinguished theologian Peter Auriol:

thinking about Paul's first letter to the Corinthians, he observes that the word of the cross ("verbum crucis") is the word of folly among the worldly wise and prudent. But, he says, God did not choose to save people through such wisdom but through the foolishness of preaching accepted in faith, faith perceived as folly ("stulta & fatua") by the world's common sense. See *Petri Aureoli Franciscani . . . Compendiosa in vniversam sacram scripturam commentaria* (Paris, 1585), 141. There is one further question that should be addressed: how do the "fools" of Passus XXII relate to those beggars who are called "lunatyk lollares and lepares about" in Passus IX.105–40? Following Derek Pearsall, I discussed the latter at some length in *Sanctifying Signs* (110–15) in a chapter on Langland's exploration of forms and ideologies of poverty. As I showed there, Langland makes very clear that these male and female mendicants "wanteth wyt" (i.e., lack wit, or the capacity to reason): they are driven by "the mone [moon's phases]," "meuynge aftur the mone." Lacking the power of intellect, "they preche nat." Nevertheless, in their vulnerable and "moneyeles" witlessness they present a challenge to the community's charity and openness: as such, they are as God's "postles" and his "priue," or secret, disciples (IX.105–20a). In all these features they are as significantly different from the "fools" of Passus XXII as they are from St. Paul preaching and teaching in Corinth. But they do *foreshadow* the fools of Passus XXII, and Langland stresses this by linking them to Paul's comment that if anyone in the church seems ("videtur") to be wise in the present world let him become a fool ("stultus," 1 Cor. 3:18; see Passus IX.127a). But foreshadowing is not identification. The "lunatyk" and witless beggars of Passus IX offer a typological anticipation of the fools of Passus XXII who will challenge the modern church as it follows "Antichrist" (XXII.56–75). For Pearsall's "'Lunatyk Lollares' in *Piers Plowman*," see *Religion in the Poetry and Drama of the Late Middle Ages in England*, ed. Piero Boitani and Anna Torti (Cambridge: D. S. Brewer, 1988), 163–78.

349. For Margery Kempe on *noli me tangere*, see Book I.81. I use *The Book of Margery Kempe*, ed. Barry Windeatt (London: Longman, 2000).

350. I quote from and allude to *The Book*, 352–57.

351. Augustine, *Homilies on the Gospel of John*, 121.3–5.

352. For relevant material and arguments, see David Aers and Lynn Staley, *The Powers of the Holy: Religion, Politics, and Gender in Late Medieval English Culture* (University Park: Pennsylvania State University Press, 1996), chaps. 1–3. Consult John P. Kenney, *The Mysticism of Saint Augustine: Rereading the Confessions* (New York: Routledge, 2005).

353. See Aers, *Sanctifying Signs*, chap. 1, "The Sacrament of the Altar in the Making of Orthodox Christianity."

354. Dymmok, *Liber*, 94–101.

355. See Wyclif, *De Eucharistia*, 11–13, 16–17; I outlined Wyclif's teaching on the Eucharist in *Sanctifying Signs*, chap. 3; see too Ian C. Levy, "*Christus Qui*

Mentiri Non Potest: John Wyclif's Rejection of Transubstantiation," *Recherches de Théologie et Philosophie Médiévales* 66 (1999): 316–34; Leff, *Heresy in the Later Middle Ages*, 2:249–57. But perhaps, as one considers Langland's Piers and the blocks the poet has placed against those seeking affinities between Piers and the church's papal institution, the Wycliffite text most pertinent is *De Potestate Pape*; see *Tractatus de Potestate Pape*, ed. Johann Loserth and F. D. Matthew (London: Trübner and Co. for the Wyclif Society, 1907).

356. *ST* III.76.1, resp. and ad 2.

357. Dymmok, *Liber*, 100–101: "Cum Christus ex hoc mundo transiturus esset ad Patrem, ne sponsam suam sanctam, scilicet ecclesiam, solacio sue corporalis presencie destitueret in cena hoc sacramentum instituit" (100).

358. Nicholas Love, *Mirror of the Blessed Life of Jesus Christ*, ed. Michael G. Sargent (New York: Garland, 1992), 152, 153; see Duffy, *Stripping of the Altars*, 91–102.

359. Aers and Staley, *Powers of the Holy*, chaps. 1–2.

360. For a contrasting account of iconoclasm and of Milton (who has been in the margins of the present essay), see James Simpson, *Under the Hammer: Iconoclasm in the Anglo-American Tradition* (Oxford: Oxford University Press, 2010).

361. See Pearsall's note to I.3; Galloway has many words on this subject in Barney and Galloway, *The Penn Commentary on "Piers Plowman,"* 1:147–53 with 147–218 passim.

362. Smith, *Traditional Imagery of Charity in "Piers Plowman,"* 21–34. See too the eloquent discussion in Cervone, *Poetics of the Incarnation*, 115–17.

363. I quote from Ayres, *Nicaea and Its Legacy*, 255.

364. Pearsall glosses *on my knees*: "a more humble act of obeisance than kneeling on one knee, as to a secular lord" (I.76 note).

365. For my attempt to explore this dialectic in Langland's treatment of the Eucharist, see *Sanctifying Signs*, chap. 2.

366. I quote from *The Complete Poetry and Essential Prose of John Milton*, ed. Kerrigan, Rumrich, and Fallon.

367. I have already drawn attention to the immense differences between Wyclif's ecclesiology and Langland's, observing the central role of predestinarian dogmatics in Wyclif's account; once again see Gradon, "Langland and the Ideology of Dissent," 197–201; and Leff, *Heresy in the Later Middle Ages*, 2:516–46. For Langland on predestination, see XII.41–74a.

368. Pearsall's notes to Prol. 1–4.

369. On Langland's relations to contemplative traditions concerning the love of God and the reformation of the image of God within people, Elizabeth Salter's work has not been superseded: "Piers Plowman and the Pilgrimage to Truth"; *Piers Plowman: An Introduction*, chap. 3; "*Piers Plowman*: An Introduction," in her *English and International*, 131–49. Edward Vasta attempted to develop

connections made by Salter in *The Spiritual Basis of "Piers Plowman."* Pearsall provides helpful annotations for the loci I have been discussing at I.86 note (*Piers Plowman*, 60) and VII, notes at 269 and 270 (153); as does Bennett, *Piers Plowman*, 108.

370. Barth, *Church Dogmatics*, vol. 4, pt. 3, 668.

371. "Dictamen conscientiae plus obligat quam obligat praeceptum praelati," in Robert Holcot, *In Librum Sapientiae Regis Salomonis Praelectiones*, 387. The Lectio from which this comes, Lectio 115 (*Sapientia* 8.16, misprinted as 8.26 on p. 385) includes a characteristically engaging account of the house of Conscience.

372. *The Showings of Julian of Norwich*, ed. Denise N. Baker (New York: W.W. Norton, 2005), chap. 86 (124).

BIBLIOGRAPHY

PRIMARY SOURCES

Aquinas, Thomas. *Catena Aurea: Commentary on the Four Gospels Collected out of the Works of the Fathers.* 4 vols. Translated and edited by John Henry Newman. London: Saint Austin Press, 1999.

———. *Commentaire de l'Épître aux Romains.* Edited by Jean-Éric Stroobant and Jean Borella. Paris: Cerf, 1999.

———. *De Malo.* Translated by Richard Regan in *On Evil*, edited by Brian Davies. Oxford: Oxford University Press, 2003.

———. *The Literal Exposition on Job.* Translated by Anthony Damico. Atlanta: Scholars Press, 1989.

———. *In Omnes S. Pauli Apostoli Epistolas Commentaria.* 2 vols. Turin: Marietti, 1912.

———. *Opuscula Theologica.* 2 vols. Edited by R. A. Verardo, R. M. Spiazzi, and M. Calcaterra. Rome: Marietti, 1954.

———. *Summa contra Gentiles.* 5 vols. Translated by Anton C. Pegis. Notre Dame: University of Notre Dame Press, 1975.

———. *Summa Theologiae.* 61 vols. London: Blackfriars, 1964–81.

———. *Summa Theologica.* 6 vols. Rome: Ex typographia Forzani, 1894.

Augustine. *The Augustine Catechism: The Enchiridion on Faith, Hope, and Love.* Translated by Bruce Harbert. Edited by John E. Rotelle. Hyde Park, NY: New City Press, 1999.

———. *The City of God against the Pagans.* Translated by Henry Bettenson. London: Penguin, 1984.

———. *The City of God against the Pagans.* Translated by R. W. Dyson. Cambridge: Cambridge University Press, 1998.

——. *Confessions.* Edited by James J. O'Donnell. 3 vols. Oxford: Clarendon Press, 1992.

——. *Confessions.* Translated by Henry Chadwick. Oxford: Oxford University Press, 1991.

——. *De civitate Dei.* Edited by B. Dombart and A. Kalb. 5th ed. 2 vols. Stuttgart: Teubner, 1993.

——. *De doctrina christiana.* Edited and translated by R. P. H. Green. Oxford: Clarendon Press, 1995.

——. *Enarrationes in Psalmos.* 2nd ed. 3 vols. Edited by Eligius Dekkers et al. Corpus Christianorum Series Latina, vols. 38–40. Turnhout: Brepols, 1956–90.

——. *Expositions of the Psalms.* Translated by Maria Boulding. Edited by John E. Rotelle. 6 vols. The Works of Saint Augustine: A Translation for the 21st Century (hereafter WSA), pt. 3, vols. 15–20. Hyde Park, NY: New City Press, 2001–4.

——. *Homilies on the Gospel of John, Homilies on the First Epistle of John, Soliloquies.* Edited by Philip Schaff. Grand Rapids, MI: Eerdmans, 1986.

——. *The Predestination of the Saints.* Translated by Roland J. Teske. In *Answer to the Pelagians IV.* WSA, pt. 1, vol. 26. Hyde Park, NY: New City Press, 1999.

——. *Rebuke and Grace.* Translated by Roland J. Teske. In *Answer to the Pelagians IV.* WSA, pt. 1, vol. 26. Hyde Park, NY: New City Press, 1999.

——. *The Retractions.* Translated by Mary I. Bogan. Washington, DC: Catholic University of America Press, 1999.

——. *Sermons.* Translated by Edmund Hill. 10 vols. WSA, pt. 3, vols. 1–10. Brooklyn: New City Press, 1990–95.

——. *The Trinity.* Translated by Edmund Hill. WSA, pt. 1, vol. 5. Hyde Park, NY: New City Press, 1991.

Auriol, Peter. *Petri Aureoli Franciscani . . . Compendiosa in vniversam sacram scripturam commentaria.* Paris, 1585.

Barth, Karl. *Church Dogmatics.* Translated by Geoffrey W. Bromiley. 4 pts. in 12 vols. Edinburgh: T. and T. Clark, 1956–75.

Bettenson, Henry, ed. *Documents of the Christian Church.* 2nd ed. London: Oxford University Press, 1965.

Bible. *Biblia Sacra iuxta Vulgatem Clementinam: Nova Editio.* 4th ed. Edited by Alberto Colunga and Laurentio Turrado. Matriti: Biblioteca de Autores Cristianos, 1965.

——. *The Holy Bible, Translated from the Latin Vulgate.* Revised by Richard Challoner. Rockford, IL: Tan Books, 1989.

Brut, Walter. "Proceedings in the Trial of Walter Brut for Heresy." In *Registrum Johannis Trefnant,* edited by W. W. Capes, 278–394. London: Canterbury and York Society, 1916.

Calvin, John. *Institutes of the Christian Religion*. Edited by John T. McNeill. Translated by Ford L. Battles. 2 vols. Louisville, KY: Westminster John Knox Press, 1960.

Chaucer, Geoffrey. *The Canterbury Tales*. Rev. ed. Translated by Nevill Coghill. London: Penguin, 1977.

———. *The Riverside Chaucer*. 3rd ed. Edited by Larry D. Benson. Boston: Houghton Mifflin, 1987.

Cudworth, Ralph. *A Treatise concerning Eternal and Immutable Morality: With a Treatise on Freewill*. Cambridge: Cambridge University Press, 1996.

Dante Alighieri. *Divine Comedy*. Edited and translated by Geoffrey L. Bickersteth. Oxford: Blackwell for the Shakespeare Head Press, 1965.

Dymmok, Roger. *Liber contra XII errores et hereses lollardorum*. Edited by H. S. Cronin. London: K. Paul, Trench, Trübner, and Co., 1922.

Eliot, T. S. *Four Quartets*. New York: Harcourt, Brace, and Co., 1971.

Giles of Lessines. *De Usuris*. Printed as opusculum 66 in Thomas Aquinas, *Opera Omnia*, vol. 17. New York: Musurgia Press, 1948–49.

Giles of Rome. *On Ecclesiastical Polity*. Edited and translated by R. W. Dyson. New York: Columbia University Press, 2004.

———. *On Ecclesiastical Power: A Medieval Theory of World Government; A Critical Edition and Translation*. Edited by R. W. Dyson. New York: Columbia University Press, 2004.

Hanna, Ralph, and Sara Wood, eds. *Richard Morris's "Prick of Conscience": A Corrected and Amplified Reading Text*. EETS, o.s., 242. Oxford: Oxford University Press, 2013.

Hilton, Walter. *The Scale of Perfection*. Edited by Evelyn Underhill. London: J. M. Watkins, 1923; repr. 1948.

Holcot, Robert. *In Librum Sapientiae Regis Salomonis Praelectiones CCXIII*. Basel, 1586.

Horner, Patrick J., ed. *A Macaronic Sermon Collection from Late Medieval England: Oxford, MS Bodley 649*. Toronto: Pontifical Institute of Mediaeval Studies, 2006.

Hulme, W. W., ed. *The Middle English Harrowing of Hell and Gospel of Nicodemus*. EETS, e.s., 100. London: K. Paul, Trench, Trübner, and Co., 1907.

Jacob, Henry. *A Collection of Sundry Matters* (1616) with *A Confession and Protestation of the Faith of Certaine Christians* (1616) bound together in Cambridge University Library, shelfmark Bb*.12.47.

Jacob's Well: An English Treatise on the Cleansing of Man's Conscience. Edited by A. Brandeis (pt. 1). EETS, o.s., 115. London: K. Paul, Trench, Trübner, and Co., 1900.

John of Rupescissa, *Vade Mecum in Tribulatione*. In Edward Brown, *Fasciculus Rerum Expetendarum & Fugiendarum*, vol. 2, 496–508. London: Chiswell, 1690.

Julian of Norwich. *A Book of Showings to the Anchoress Julian of Norwich*. 2 vols. Edited by Edmund Colledge, O. S. A., and James Walsh, S. J. Toronto: Pontifical Institute of Mediaeval Studies, 1978.

———. *The Showings of Julian of Norwich*. Edited by Denise N. Baker. New York: W. W. Norton, 2005.

Kempe, Margery. *The Book of Margery Kempe*. Edited by Barry Windeatt. London: Longman, 2000.

Knighton, Henry. *Knighton's Chronicle, 1337–1396*. Edited and translated by G. H. Martin. Oxford: Clarendon Press, 1995.

Langland, William. *Piers Plowman: A Parallel-Text Edition of the A, B, C, and Z Versions*. 2 vols. Edited by A. V. C. Schmidt. Kalamazoo: Medieval Institute Publications, 2008.

———. *Piers Plowman: A New Annotated Edition of the C-text*. 2nd ed. Edited by Derek Pearsall. Exeter: University of Exeter Press, 2008.

———. *Piers Plowman: The B Version*. Rev. ed. Edited by George Kane and E. Talbot Donaldson. London: Athlone, 1988.

———. *Piers Plowman: The C Version; Will's Vision of Piers Plowman, Do-Well, Do-Better, and Do-Best*. Edited by George Russell and George Kane. London: Athlone, 1997.

———. *The Vision of Pierce Plowman: now the second tyme imprinted by roberte crowley* (1550). Cambridge University Library, shelfmark Syn 7.55.25.

———. *The Vision of William concerning Piers the Plowman in Three Parallel Texts: Together with Richard the Redeless*. Edited by Walter W. Skeat. 2 vols. Oxford: Clarendon Press, 1886; repr. Oxford: Oxford University Press, 1968.

———. *William Langland's "Piers Plowman": The C Version*. Translated by George Economou. Philadelphia: University of Pennsylvania Press, 1996.

Love, Nicholas. *Mirror of the Blessed Life of Jesus Christ*. Edited by Michael G. Sargent. New York: Garland, 1992.

Marsilius of Padua. *The Defender of the Peace*. Edited and translated by Annabel Brett. Cambridge: Cambridge University Press, 2005.

Milton, John. *The Complete Poetry and Essential Prose of John Milton*. Edited by William Kerrigan, John Rumrich, and Stephen Fallon. New York: Modern Library, 2007.

———. *The Complete Works of John Milton*, vol. 3, *The Shorter Poems*. Edited by Barbara K. Lewalski and Estelle Haan. Oxford: Oxford University Press, 2014.

———. *The Complete Works of John Milton*, vol. 6, *Vernacular Regicide and Republican Writings*. Edited by N. H. Keeble and Nicholas McDowell. Oxford: Oxford University Press, 2013.

———. *De Doctrina Christiana*. In vol. 8 of *The Complete Works of John Milton*, edited by John K. Hale and J. D. Cullington. 2 vols. Oxford: Oxford University Press, 2012.

———. *Of Reformation* (1641). In vol. 1 of *Complete Prose Works of John Milton*, edited by Don M. Wolfe et al. 8 vols. New Haven: Yale University Press, 1953–82.

Mirk, John. *John Mirk's Festial*. Edited by Susan Powell. 2 vols. EETS, o.s., 334 and 335. Oxford University Press, 2009–11.

More, St. Thomas. *Dialogue concerning Heresies*. In *The Complete Works of St. Thomas More*, edited by Thomas M. C. Lawler, Germain Marc'Hadour, and Richard C. Marius, vol. 6. New Haven: Yale University Press, 1981.

Netter, Thomas. *Fasciculi Zizaniorum Magistri Johannis Wyclif cum Tritico*. Edited by Walter W. Shirley. London: Longman, 1858.

Robert of Basevorn. *Form of Preaching*. Edited and translated by James J. Murphy. In *Three Medieval Rhetorical Arts*, edited by James J. Murphey. Berkeley: University of California Press, 1971.

Shakespeare, William. *The Riverside Shakespeare*. Edited by G. Blakemore Evans. Boston: Houghton Mifflin, 1974.

Tanner, Norman P., ed. *Decrees of the Ecumenical Councils*. 2 vols. London: Sheed and Ward, 1990.

———. *Heresy Trials in the Diocese of Norwich, 1428–31*. London: Royal Historical Society, 1977.

Thomas of Wimbledon. "Paul's Cross Sermon of 1388." Edited by N. H. Owen. *Medieval Studies* 28 (1966): 176–97.

———. *Wimbledon's Sermon*. Edited by Ione Kemp Knight. Pittsburgh: Duquesne University Press, 1967.

Thorpe, William. *The Testimony of William Thorpe*. In *Two Wycliffite Texts: The Sermon of William Taylor (1406); The Testimony of William Thorpe (1407)*, edited by Anne Hudson. EETS, o.s., 301. Oxford: Oxford University Press, 1993.

Tyndale, William. *The Obedience of a Christian Man*. Edited by David Daniell. London: Penguin, 2000.

William of Ockham. *Breviloquium (A Short Discourse of Tyrannical Government)*. Edited by Arthur Stephen McGrade. Translated by John Kilcullen. Cambridge: Cambridge University Press, 1992.

———. *De Corpore Christi*. In *Guillelmi de Ockham: Tractatus de Quantitate et Tractatus de Corpore Christi*. Edited by Carlo A. Grassi, in vol. 10 of William of Ockham, *Opera Philosophica et Theologica*, 87–234. St. Bonaventure, NY: St. Bonaventure University, Franciscan Institute, 1986.

———. *A Letter to the Friars Minor and Other Writings*. Edited by Arthur S. McGrade and John Kilcullen. Cambridge: Cambridge University Press, 1995.

———. *On the Power of Emperors and Popes*. Edited and translated by Annabel S. Brett. Bristol: Thoemmes Press, 1998.

———. *Quodlibetal Questions*. Translated by Alfred J. Freddoso and Francis E. Kelley. 2 vols. New Haven: Yale University Press, 1991.

———. *Work of Ninety Days*. Translated by John Kilcullen and John Scott. 2 vols. Lewiston, NY: Edwin Mellen, 2001.

Wyclif, John. *De Eucharistia (Tractatus Maior)*. Edited by Johann Loserth. London: Trübner and Co. for the Wyclif Society, 1892.

———. *Johannis Wyclif Opera Minora*. Edited by Johann Loserth. London: Trübner, 1913.

———. *Tractatus De Blasphemia*. Edited by Michael Henry Dziewicki. London: Trübner and Co. for the Wyclif Society, 1893.

———. *Tractatus De Officio Regis*. Edited by A. W. Pollard and C. Sayle. London: Trübner and Co. for the Wyclif Society, 1887.

———. *Tractatus De Potestate Pape*. Edited by Johann Loserth and F. D. Matthew. London: Trübner and Co. for the Wyclif Society, 1907.

SECONDARY SOURCES

Adams, Robert. "Langland and the *Devotio Moderna*: A Spiritual Kinship." In *Medieval Alliterative Poetry: Essays in Honour of Thorlac Turville-Petre*, edited by John A. Burrow and Hoyt N. Duggan, 23–40. Dublin: Four Courts, 2010.

———. *Langland and the Rokele Family: The Gentry Background.* Dublin: Four Courts Press, 2013.

———. "Langland as a Proto-Protestant: Was Thomas Fuller Right?" In *Yee? Baw for Bokes: Essays on Medieval Manuscripts and Poetics in Honor of Hoty N. Duggan*, edited by Michael Calabrese and Stephen H. A. Shepherd, 245–66. Los Angeles: Marymount Institute Press, 2013.

———. "The Nature of Need in *Piers Plowman* XX." *Traditio* 34 (1978): 273–301.

Aers, David. "Altars of Power: Reflections on Eamon Duffy's *The Stripping of the Altars*." *Literature and History* 3 (1994): 90–105.

———. *Chaucer, Langland, and the Creative Imagination*. London: Routledge, 1980.

———. *Community, Gender, and Individual Identity*. London: Routledge, 1988.

———. *Faith, Ethics, and Church: Writing in England, 1360–1409*. Cambridge: D. S. Brewer, 2000.

———. *Piers Plowman and Christian Allegory*. London: Arnold, 1975.

———. *Salvation and Sin: Augustine, Langland, and Fourteenth-Century Theology*. Notre Dame: University of Notre Dame Press, 2009.

———. *Sanctifying Signs: Making Christian Tradition in Late Medieval England*. Notre Dame: University of Notre Dame Press, 2004.

———. "Visionary Eschatology in *Piers Plowman*." *Modern Theology* 15 (2000): 3–17.

Aers, David, and Lynn Staley. *The Powers of the Holy: Religion, Politics, and Gender in Late Medieval English Culture*. University Park: Pennsylvania State University Press, 1996.

Aers, David, and Nigel Smith. "English Reformations." *Journal of Medieval and Early Modern Studies* 40 (2010): 425–38.

Anderson, Wendy L. *The Discernment of Spirits: Assessing Visions and Visionaries in the Late Middle Ages*. Tübingen: Siebeck, 2011.

Ashley, W. J. *An Introduction to English Economic History and Theory, Part 2: The End of the Middle Ages*. 4th ed. London: Longman, 1906.

Aston, Margaret. "'Caim's Castles': Poverty, Politics, and Disendowment." In *The Church, Politics, and Patronage in the Fifteenth Century*, edited by R. B. Dobson, 45–81. Gloucester: Sutton, 1984.

———. *Faith and Fire*. London: Hambledon, 1997.

———. "The Impeachment of Bishop Despenser." *Bulletin of the Institute of Historical Research* 38 (1965): 127–48.

———. "John Wycliffe's Reformation Reputation." *Past & Present* 30 (1965): 23–51. Reprinted in Aston, *Lollards and Reformers: Images and Literacy in Late Medieval Religion*, 243–72. London: Hambledon Press, 1984.

———. "Lollard Women Priests?" *Journal of Ecclesiastical History* 31 (1980): 441–61. Reprinted in Aston, *Lollards and Reformers: Images and Literacy in Late Medieval Religion*, 49–70. London: Hambledon Press, 1984.

———. "Lollardy and Sedition, 1381–1431." *Past & Present* 17 (1960): 1–44. Reprinted in Aston, *Lollards and Reformers: Images and Literacy in Late Medieval Religion*, 1–47. London: Hambledon Press, 1984.

———. "William White's Lollard Followers." *Catholic Historical Review* 68 (1982): 469–97.

Ayres, Lewis. *Nicaea and Its Legacy: An Approach to Fourth-Century Trinitarian Theology*. Oxford: Oxford University Press, 2004.

Baldwin, John W. *The Medieval Theories of the Just Price*. Philadelphia: American Philosophical Society, 1959.

Barnes, Timothy. *Athanasius and Constantine: Theology and Politics in the Constantinian Empire*. Cambridge, MA: Harvard University Press, 1993.

Barney, Stephen A., and Andrew Galloway. *The Penn Commentary on "Piers Plowman."* 5 vols. Philadelphia: University of Pennsylvania Press, 2006.

Barrey, S. A. "The Plowshare of the Tongue: The Progress of a Symbol from the Bible to *Piers Plowman*." *Medieval Studies* 35 (1973): 261–93.

Barron, Caroline. *London in the Later Middle Ages*. Oxford: Oxford University Press, 2004.

Beckwith, Sarah. *Christ's Body: Identity, Culture, and Society in Late Medieval Writing*. London: Routledge, 1993.

Bennett, J. A. W. "The Date of the B-text of *Piers Plowman.*" *Medium Aevum* 12 (1943): 55–64.

———. *Piers Plowman: The Prologue and Passus I–VII of the B Text as Found in Bodleian MS Laud Misc. 581.* Oxford: Clarendon Press, 1972.

Bennett, Judith. *Ale, Beer, and Brewsters in England: Women's Work in a Changing World, 1300–1600.* New York: Oxford University Press, 1996.

Bernard, G. W. *The King's Reformation: Henry VIII and the Remaking of the English Church.* New Haven: Yale University Press, 2007.

Bignami-Odier, Jeanne. *Études sur Jean de Roquetaillade (Johannes de Rupescissa).* Paris: J. Vrin, 1952.

Bihel, S. "S. Franciscus Fuitne Angelus Sexti Sigilli (Apoc 7.2)?" *Antonianum* 2 (1927): 59–90.

Bloch, Marc. *Feudal Society.* 2 vols. London: Routledge, 1982.

Bloomfield, Morton W. *Piers Plowman as a Fourteenth-Century Apocalypse.* New Brunswick, NJ: Rutgers University Press, 1961.

Blumenfeld-Kosinski, Renate. *Poets, Saints, and Visionaries of the Great Schism, 1375–1417.* University Park: Pennsylvania State University Press, 2006.

Bolton, J. L. *The Medieval English Economy, 1150–1500.* London: Dent, 1980.

Bonner, Gerald. *Freedom and Necessity: St. Augustine's Teaching on Divine Power and Human Freedom.* Washington, DC: Catholic University of America Press, 2007.

Bossy, John. "The Mass as a Social Institution, 1200–1700." *Past & Present* 100 (1983): 29–61.

Bowers, R. H. "Foleuyles Lawes." *Notes and Queries* 206 (1961): 327–28.

Brewer, Charlotte. *Editing "Piers Plowman": The Evolution of the Text.* Cambridge: Cambridge University Press, 1996; repr. 2006.

Burrow, John. *Langland's Fictions.* Oxford: Clarendon, 1993.

Cam, Helen. "Shire Officials: Coroners, Constables, and Bailiffs." In *The English Government at Work, 1327–1336,* edited by J. F. Willard et al., 3:143–83. 3 vols. Cambridge, MA: Harvard University Press, 1950.

Carruthers, Mary. *The Search for St. Truth: A Study of Meaning in "Piers Plowman."* Evanston, IL: Northwestern University Press, 1973.

Catto, J. L. "Religious Change under Henry V." In *Henry V: The Practice of Kingship,* edited by G. L. Harriss, 92–115. Oxford: Oxford University Press, 1985.

Catto, J. L., and Ralph Evans, eds. *The History of the University of Oxford,* vol. 2, *Late Medieval Oxford.* Oxford: Clarendon Press, 1992.

Cervone, Cristina M. *Poetics of the Incarnation: Middle English Writing and the Leap of Love.* Philadelphia: University of Pennsylvania Press, 2012.

Cole, Andrew. *Literature and Heresy in the Age of Chaucer.* Cambridge: Cambridge University Press, 2008.

Coleman, Janet. *A History of Political Thought: From the Middle Ages to the Renaissance*. Oxford: Blackwell, 2000.

Collinson, Patrick. "Night Schools, Conventicles, and Churches: Continuities and Discontinuities in Early Protestant Ecclesiology." In *The Beginnings of English Protestantism*, edited by Peter Marshall and Alec Ryrie, 209–35. Cambridge: Cambridge University Press, 2002.

Congar, Yves M.-J. "Bref historique des formes du 'magistère' et de ses relations avec les docteurs." *Revue des Sciences Philosophiques et Théologiques* 60 (1976): 99–112.

———. *I Believe in the Holy Spirit*. 3 vols. New York: Crossroad, 1983.

———. "Pour une histoire sémantique du terme 'magisterium.'" *Revue des Sciences Philosophiques et Théologiques* 60 (1976): 85–98.

Corrigan, Philip, and Derek Sayer. *The Great Arch: English State Formation as Cultural Revolution*. Oxford: Blackwell, 1985.

Courtenay, William J. *Schools and Scholars in Fourteenth-Century England*. Princeton: Princeton University Press, 1987.

Cross, Clare. "'Great Reasoners in Scripture': The Activities of Women Lollards, 1380–1530." *Studies in Church History Subsidia* 1 (1978): 359–80.

Dahmus, Joseph H. *The Prosecution of John Wyclif*. New Haven: Yale University Press, 1952.

Davies, Brian. *The Thought of Thomas Aquinas*. Oxford: Clarendon Press, 1993.

Davis, J. C. "Against Formality: One Aspect of the English Revolution." *Transactions of the Royal Historical Society* 3 (1993): 265–88.

Dobson, R. B., ed. *The Peasant's Revolt of 1381*. London: Macmillan, 1970.

Dodaro, Robert. *Christ and the Just Society in the Thought of Augustine*. Cambridge: Cambridge University Press, 2004.

Doe, Norman. *Fundamental Authority in Late Medieval English Law*. Cambridge: Cambridge University Press, 1990.

Donaldson, E. Talbot. *Piers Plowman: The C-Text and Its Poet*. New Haven: Yale University Press, 1949.

Duffy, Eamon. "'The comen knowen multytude of crysten men': *A Dialogue concerning Heresies* and the Defence of Christendom." In *The Cambridge Companion to Thomas More*, edited by George M. Logan, 191–215. Cambridge: Cambridge University Press, 2011.

———. *The Stripping of the Altars: Traditional Religion in England, 1400–1580*. 2nd ed. New Haven: Yale University Press, 2005.

Elton, G. R., ed. *Tudor Constitution: Documents and Commentary*. Cambridge: Cambridge University Press, 1982.

Emmerson, Richard K. *Antichrist in the Middle Ages*. Seattle: University of Washington Press, 1981.

Evans, G. R. *John Wyclif*. Oxford: Lion, 2005.

Feingold, Laurence. *The Natural Desire to See God according to St. Thomas Aquinas and His Interpreters.* 2nd ed. Naples: Sapientia Press, 2010.

Finnis, John. *Aquinas on Moral, Political, and Legal Theory.* Oxford: Oxford University Press, 1998.

Friedman, Russell L. "Medieval Trinitarian Theology from the Late Thirteenth to the Fifteenth Centuries." In *The Oxford Handbook of the Trinity*, edited by Gilles Emery and Matthew Levering, 197–209. Oxford: Oxford University Press, 2011.

———. *Medieval Trinitarian Thought from Aquinas to Ockham.* Cambridge: Cambridge University Press, 2010.

Gasse, Rosanne. "Langland's 'Lewed Vicory' Reconsidered." *JEGP* 95 (1996): 322–35.

Gelber, Hester G. *It Could Have Been Otherwise: Contingency and Necessity in Dominican Theology at Oxford, 1300–1350.* Leiden: Brill, 2004.

———. "Logic and the Trinity: A Clash of Values in Scholastic Thought, 1300–1335." PhD diss., University of Wisconsin, 1974.

Gillespie, Michael. *The Theological Origins of Modernity.* Chicago: University of Chicago Press, 2007.

Girard, René. *Things Hidden since the Foundation of the World.* London: Athlone, 1977.

Given-Wilson, Chris, ed. *Chronicles of the Revolution, 1397–1400: The Reign of Richard II.* Manchester: Manchester University Press, 1993.

Gondreau, Paul. *The Passions of Christ's Soul in the Theology of St. Thomas Aquinas.* Münster: Aschendorff, 2002; repr. Scranton: University of Scranton Press, 2009.

Gradon, Pamela. "Langland and the Ideology of Dissent." *Proceedings of the British Academy* 66 (1980): 179–205.

Gregory, Brad S. *The Unintended Reformation: How a Religious Revolution Secularized Society.* Cambridge, MA: Harvard University Press, 2012.

Haller, William. *Foxe's Book of Martyrs and the Elect Nation.* London: Cape, 1963. Republished as *The Elect Nation: The Meaning and Relevance of Foxe's Book of Martyrs.* New York: Harper and Row, 1963.

Hanna, Ralph. *Introducing English Medieval Book History: Manuscripts, Their Production, and Their Reading.* Liverpool: Liverpool University Press, 2013.

———. "'Meddling with Makings' and Will's Work." In *Late-Medieval Religious Texts and Their Transmission: Essays in Honour of A.I. Doyle*, edited by A.J. Minnis, 85–94. Cambridge: D. S. Brewer, 1994.

———. *William Langland.* Aldershot: Variorum, 1993.

Harriss, Gerald. *Shaping the Nation: England, 1360–1461.* Oxford: Clarendon Press, 2005.

Hatcher, John. "England in the Aftermath of the Black Death." *Past & Present* 144 (1994): 3–35.

Hauerwas, Stanley. *Approaching the End: Eschatological Reflections on Church, Politics, and Life.* Grand Rapids: Eerdmans, 2013.

———. *Cross-Shattered Christ: Meditations on the Seven Last Words.* Grand Rapids, MI: Brazos Press, 2004.

Hilton, Rodney. *Class Conflict and the Crisis of Feudalism: Essays in Social History.* London: Hambledon, 1985.

Hornbeck, J. Patrick. *What Is a Lollard? Dissent and Belief in Late Medieval England.* Oxford: Oxford University Press, 2010.

Housley, Norman. "The Bishop of Norwich's Crusade, May 1383." *History Today* 33 (1983): 15–20.

Hudson, Anne. "*Piers Plowman* and the Peasant's Revolt." *Yearbook of Langland Studies* 8 (1994): 85–106.

———. *The Premature Reformation: Wycliffite Texts and Lollard History.* Oxford: Clarendon Press, 1988.

Hütter, Reinhard. *Dust Bound for Heaven: Explorations in the Theology of Thomas Aquinas.* Grand Rapids, MI: Eerdmans, 2012.

Jacob, E. "John of Roquetaillade." *Bulletin of the John Rylands Library* 39 (1956–57): 75–96.

John Paul II, Pope. *The Splendor of Truth: Veritatis Splendor.* Boston: Pauline Books, 1993.

Jones, Norman. *God and the Moneylenders: Usury and Law in Early Modern England.* Oxford: Blackwell, 1989.

Kane, George. *Piers Plowman: The Evidence for Authorship.* London: Athlone, 1965.

Kaye, Joel. *Economy and Nature in the Fourteenth Century: Money, Market Exchange, and the Emergence of Scientific Thought.* Cambridge: Cambridge University Press, 1998.

Kelen, Sarah A. *Langland's Early Modern Identities.* New York: Palgrave Macmillan, 2007.

Kennedy, Leonard A. *The Philosophy of Robert Holcot: Fourteenth-Century Skeptic.* Lewiston, NY: Edwin Mellen, 1993.

Kenney, John P. *The Mysticism of Saint Augustine: Rereading the "Confessions."* New York: Routledge, 2005.

Kerby-Fulton, Kathryn. *Reformist Apocalypticism and "Piers Plowman."* Cambridge: Cambridge University Press, 1990.

Ladner, Gerhart B. *The Idea of Reform: Its Impact on Christian Thought and Action in the Age of the Fathers.* New York: Harper and Row, 1959.

Lahey, Stephen. *John Wyclif.* Oxford: Oxford University Press, 2009.

Lamont, William. "Pamphleteering, the Protestant Consensus, and the English Revolution." In *Freedom and the English Revolution*, edited by R. C. Richardson and G. M. Ridden, 72–92. Manchester: Manchester University Press, 1986.

———. "Puritanism as History and Historiography." *Past & Present* 44 (1969): 133–46.

Langholm, Odd. *Economics in the Medieval Schools: Wealth, Exchange, Value, Money, and Usury according to the Paris Theological Tradition, 1200–1350.* Leiden: Brill, 1992.

Leff, Gordon. "The Apostolic Ideal in Later Medieval Ecclesiology." *Journal of Theological Studies* 18 (1967): 58–82.

———. *Heresy in the Later Middle Ages.* 2 vols. Manchester: Manchester University Press, 1967.

———. *Medieval Thought: St. Augustine to Ockham.* Harmondsworth: Penguin, 1958.

Lerner, R. E. "Antichrists and Antichrist in Joachim of Fiore." *Speculum* 60 (1985): 553–70.

Levy, Ian C. "*Christus Qui Mentiri Non Potest*: John Wyclif's Rejection of Transubstantiation." *Recherches de Théologie et Philosophie Médiévales* 66 (1999): 316–34.

———. *John Wyclif: Scriptural Logic, Real Presence, and the Parameters of Orthodoxy.* Milwaukee: Marquette University Press, 2003.

Little, Lester K. *Religious Poverty and the Profit Economy in Medieval Europe.* London: P. Elek, 1978.

Lubac, Henri de. *Corpus mysticum: L'Euchariste et l'église au moyen âge.* Paris: Aubier, 1949.

———. *Exégèse médiévale: Les quatre sens de l'écriture.* 4 vols. Paris: Aubier, 1959–64.

———. *La postérité spirituelle de Joachim de Flore.* 2 vols. Paris: Lethielleux, 1979.

MacCulloch, Diarmaid. *Reformation: Europe's House Divided, 1490–1700.* London: Penguin, 2004.

MacIntyre, Alasdair. *After Virtue: A Study in Moral Theory.* 2nd ed. London: Duckworth, 1985.

———. *God, Philosophy, Universities: A Selective History of the Catholic Philosophical Tradition.* Lanham, MD: Rowman and Littlefield, 2009.

———. *Three Rival Versions of Moral Enquiry: Encyclopaedia, Genealogy, and Tradition.* London: Duckworth, 1990.

Macy, Gary. *The Banquet's Wisdom: A Short History of the Theologies of the Lord's Supper.* New York: Paulist Press, 1992.

———. *The Hidden History of Women's Ordination: Female Clergy in the Medieval West.* Oxford: Oxford University Press, 2008.

———. "The 'Invention' of Clergy and Laity in the Twelfth Century." In *A Sacramental Life: A Festschrift Honoring Bernard Cooke*, edited by Michael H. Barnes and W. P. Roberts, 117–35. Milwaukee, WI: Marquette University Press, 2003.

———. "Theologies of the Eucharist in the High Middle Ages." In *A Companion to the Eucharist in the Middle Ages*, edited by Ian Levy, Gary Macy, and Kristen Van Ausdall, 365–98. Leiden: Brill, 2012.

Malcolm, Noel R. "Thomas Hobbes and Voluntarist Theology." PhD diss., Cambridge University, 1983.

Manion, Lee. *Narrating the Crusades: Loss and Recovery in Medieval and Early Modern English Literature.* Cambridge: Cambridge University Press, 2014.

Mann, Jill. "Allegorical Buildings in Medieval Literature." *Medium Aevum* 63 (1994): 191–210.

———. *Chaucer and Medieval Estates Satire.* Cambridge: Cambridge University Press, 1973.

———. "The Nature of Need Revisited." *Yearbook of Langland Studies* 18 (2006): 3–29.

Markus, R. A. *Saeculum: History and Society in the Theology of St. Augustine.* Cambridge: Cambridge University Press, 1970; repr. 1988.

Martinich, A. P. *The Two Gods of "Leviathan": Thomas Hobbes on Religion and Politics.* Cambridge: Cambridge University Press, 1992.

McCue, James F. "The Doctrine of Transubstantiation from Berengar through Trent." *Harvard Theological Review* 61 (1968): 385–430.

McGinn, Bernard. *The Calabrian Abbot: Joachim of Fiore.* London: Macmillan, 1985.

McGrade, Arthur Stephen. *The Political Thought of William of Ockham.* Cambridge: Cambridge University Press, 2002.

McHardy, A. H. "Liturgy and Propaganda in the Diocese of Lincoln during the Hundred Years War." *Studies in Church History* 20 (1983): 171–78.

McKenna, J. W. "How God Became an Englishman." In *Tudor Rule and Revolution: Essays for G. R. Elton from His American Friends*, edited by D. G. Guth and J. W. McKenna, 25–43. Cambridge: Cambridge University Press, 1982.

McNiven, Peter. *Heresy and Politics in the Reign of Henry IV.* Woodbridge: Boydell, 1987.

McSheffrey, Shannon. *Gender and Heresy: Women and Men in Lollard Communities, 1420–1530.* Philadelphia: University of Pennsylvania Press, 1995.

Middleton, Anne. "Acts of Vagrancy: The C Version 'Autobiography' and the Statute of 1388." In *Written Work: Langland, Labor, and Authorship*, edited by Stephen Justice and Kathryn Kerby-Fulton, 208–317. Philadelphia: University of Pennsylvania Press, 1997.

———. "Langland's Lives: Reflections on Late-Medieval Religious and Literary Vocabulary." In *The Idea of Medieval Literature*, edited by James M. Dean and Christian K. Zacher, 227–42. Newark: University of Delaware Press, 1992.

———. "Narration and the Invention of Experience: Episodic Form in *Piers Plowman*." In *The Wisdom of Poetry: Essays in Early English Literature in Honor of Morton W. Bloomfield*, edited by Larry D. Benson and Siegfried Wenzel, 91–122. Kalamazoo, MI: Medieval Institute Publications, 1982.

Nederman, Cary. *Community and Consent: The Secular Political Theory of Marsilius of Padua's "Defensor Pacis."* Lanham, MD: Rowman and Littlefield, 1995.

Newhauser, Richard. "Preaching the 'Contrary Virtues.'" *Mediaeval Studies* 70 (2008): 135–62.

Nightingale, Pamela. "Capitalists, Crafts, and Constitutional Change in Late Fourteenth Century London." *Past & Present* 124 (1989): 3–35.

———. *A Medieval Mercantile Community: The Grocers' Company and the Politics of Trade in London, 1000–1485.* New Haven: Yale University Press, 1995.

Noonan, John T. *The Scholastic Analysis of Usury.* Cambridge, MA: Harvard University Press, 1957.

Ocker, Christopher. *Biblical Poetics before Humanism and Reformation.* Cambridge: Cambridge University Press, 2002.

Overmyer, Sheryl. "The Wayfarer's Way and Two Guides for the Journey: The *Summa Theologiae* and *Piers Plowman*." PhD diss., Duke University, 2010.

Palmer, Robert C. *Selling the Church: The English Parish in Law, Commerce, and Religion, 1350–1550.* Chapel Hill: University of North Carolina Press, 2002.

Pearsall, Derek. "'Lunatyk Lollares' in *Piers Plowman*." In *Religion in the Poetry and Drama of the Late Middle Ages in England*, edited by Piero Boitani and Anna Torti, 163–78. Cambridge: D. S. Brewer, 1988.

Perroy, Édouard. *L'Angleterre et le Grand Schisme d'Occident.* Paris: Monnier, 1933.

Pfau, Thomas. *Minding the Modern: Human Agency, Intellectual Traditions, and Responsible Knowledge.* Notre Dame: University of Notre Dame Press, 2013.

Potts, T. C. *Conscience in Medieval Philosophy.* Cambridge: Cambridge University Press, 1980.

Prendiville, John G. "The Development of the Idea of Habit in the Thought of Saint Augustine." *Traditio* 28 (1972): 22–99.

Putnam, Bertha. *The Enforcement of the Statutes of Labourers during the First Decade after the Black Death, 1349–1359.* New York: Columbia University, 1908.

Quirk, R. "Langland's Use of *Kind Wit* and *Inwit*." *JEGP* 52 (1953): 182–89.

Reeves, Marjorie. *The Influence of Prophecy in the Later Middle Ages: A Study in Joachimism.* 2nd ed. Notre Dame: University of Notre Dame Press, 1993.

Rex, Richard. *The Lollards.* Basingstoke: Palgrave Macmillan, 2002.

Richardson, H. G. "Heresy and the Lay Power under Richard II." *English Historical Review* 51 (1936): 1–28.

Robertson, D.W., and Bernard. F. Huppé. *"Piers Plowman" and Scriptural Tradition*. Princeton: Princeton University Press, 1951.

Rollo-Koster, Joëlle, and Thomas Izbicki. *A Companion to the Great Western Schism, 1378–1417*. Leiden: Brill, 2009.

Rubin, Miri. *Corpus Christi: The Eucharist in Late Medieval Culture*. Cambridge: Cambridge University Press, 1991.

———. "The Eucharist and the Construction of Medieval Identities." In *Culture and History, 1350–1600: Essays on English Communities, Identities, and Writing*, edited by David Aers, 43–63. Hemel Hempstead: Harvester Wheatsheaf, 1992.

Salter, Elizabeth. "Chaucer and Boccaccio: *The Knight's Tale*." In *Fourteenth-Century English Poetry: Contexts and Readings*, 141–81. Oxford: Clarendon Press, 1983.

———. *Chaucer: The Knight's Tale and the Clerk's Tale*. London: Arnold, 1962.

———. *English and International: Studies in the Literature, Art, and Patronage of Medieval England*. Edited by Derek Pearsall and Nicolette Zeeman. Cambridge: Cambridge University Press, 1988.

———. *"Piers Plowman": An Introduction*. Oxford: Blackwell; Cambridge, MA: Harvard University Press, 1962.

———. "*Piers Plowman* and the Pilgrimage to Truth." *Essays and Studies* 11 (1958): 1–16. Reprinted in *Style and Symbolism in "Piers Plowman"*, edited by Robert J. Blanch, 117–31. Knoxville: University of Tennessee Press, 1969.

———. "*Piers Plowman*: An Introduction." In *Piers Plowman: Selections from the C-text*, edited by Elizabeth Salter and Derek Pearsall, 3–58. London: Arnold, 1967. Reprinted in Salter, *English and International: Studies in the Literature, Art, and Patronage of Medieval England*, edited by Derek Pearsall and Nicolette Zeeman, 111–57. Cambridge: Cambridge University Press, 1988.

Scarisbrick, J. J. *Henry VIII*. London: Eyre and Spottiswoode, 1968; repr. London: Methuen, 1968.

Scase, Wendy. *"Piers Plowman" and the New Anti-Clericalism*. Cambridge: Cambridge University Press, 1989.

Shaffern, Robert W. *The Penitents' Treasury: Indulgences in Latin Christendom, 1175–1375*. Scranton: University of Scranton Press, 2007.

Shogimen, Takashi. *Ockham and Political Discourse in the Late Middle Ages*. Cambridge: Cambridge University Press, 2007.

———. "Wyclif's Ecclesiology and Political Thought." In *A Companion to John Wyclif: Late Medieval Theologian*, edited by Ian C. Levy, 199–240. Leiden: Brill, 2006.

Skinner, Quentin. *Reason and Rhetoric in the Philosophy of Hobbes*. Cambridge: Cambridge University Press, 1996.

———. "Thomas Hobbes: Rhetoric and the Construction of Morality." *Proceedings of the British Academy* 76 (1990): 1–61.

Simpson, James. "'After Craftes Conseil clotheth yow and fede': Langland and London City Politics." In *England in the Fourteenth Century: Proceedings of the 1991 Harlaxton Symposium*, edited by N. Rogers, 109–27. Stamford: P. Watkins, 1993.

———. *The Oxford English Literary History*, vol. 2, *1350–1547: Reform and Cultural Revolution*. Oxford: Oxford University Press, 2002.

———. *"Piers Plowman": An Introduction*. 2nd ed. Exeter: University of Exeter Press, 2007.

———. *Under the Hammer: Iconoclasm in the Anglo-American Tradition*. Oxford: Oxford University Press, 2010.

Smalley, Beryl. *English Friars and Antiquity in the Early Fourteenth Century*. Oxford: Blackwell, 1965.

———. "John Baconthorpe's Postill on St. Matthew." *Medieval and Renaissance Studies* 4 (1958): 91–115. Reprinted in Beryl Smalley, *Studies in Medieval Thought and Learning: From Abelard to Wyclif*, 289–343. London: Hambledon, 1981.

Smith, Ben. *Traditional Imagery of Charity in "Piers Plowman."* The Hague: Mouton, 1966.

Smith, Richard. "'Modernization' and the Corporate Medieval Village Community in England: Some Skeptical Reflections." In *Explorations in Historical Geography*, edited by Alan R. H. Baker and Derek Gregory, 140–79. Cambridge: Cambridge University Press, 1984.

Somerset, Fiona. *Feeling Like Saints: Lollard Writings after Wyclif*. Ithaca: Cornell University Press, 2014.

Springborg, Patricia, ed. *The Companion to Hobbes's "Leviathan."* Cambridge: Cambridge University Press, 2007.

St.-Jacques, Raymond. "Langland's Bells of the Resurrection and the Easter Liturgy." *English Studies in Canada* 3 (1977): 129–35.

———. "Langland's Christ-Knight and the Liturgy." *Revue de l'Université d'Ottowa* 37 (1967): 144–58.

———. "The Liturgical Associations of Langland's Samaritan." *Traditio* 25 (1969): 217–30.

Steiner, Emily. *Reading "Piers Plowman."* Cambridge: Cambridge University Press, 2013.

Stones, E. L. G. "The Folvilles of Ashby Folville, Leicestershire, and Their Associates in Crime, 1326–1341." *Transactions of the Royal Historical Society* 7 (1957): 117–39.

Surin, Kenneth. *Theology and the Problem of Evil*. Oxford: Blackwell, 1986.

Swanson, Heather. *Medieval Artisans: An Urban Class in Late Medieval England*. Oxford: Blackwell, 1989.

Swanson, R. N. *Indulgences in Late Medieval England.* Cambridge: Cambridge University Press, 2007.

Szittya, Pen. *The Antifraternal Tradition in Medieval Literature.* Princeton: Princeton University Press, 1986.

Tawney, R. H. Introduction to Thomas Wilson, *A Discourse upon Usury by Way of Dialogue and Orations*, edited by Tawney. London: G. Bell, 1925.

Taylor, Charles. *A Secular Age.* Cambridge, MA: Harvard University Press, 2007.

Taylor, Jamie K. *Fictions of Evidence: Witnessing, Literature, and Community in the Late Middle Ages.* Columbus: Ohio State University Press, 2013.

Tentler, Thomas. *Sin and Confession on the Eve of the Reformation.* Princeton: Princeton University Press, 1977.

Tierney, Brian. *On the Origins of Papal Infallibility, 1150–1350.* Leiden: Brill, 1972.

———. *Religion, Law, and the Growth of Constitutional Thought, 1150–1650.* Cambridge: Cambridge University Press, 1982.

Tolmie, Murray. *The Triumph of the Saints: The Separate Churches of London, 1616–1649.* Cambridge: Cambridge University Press, 1977.

Tyerman, Christopher. *England and the Crusades, 1095–1588.* Chicago: University of Chicago Press, 1988.

Ullman, Walter. *A History of Political Thought: The Middle Ages.* Rev. ed. Harmondsworth: Penguin, 1976.

———. *Medieval Papalism: The Political Theories of the Medieval Canonists.* London: Methuen, 1949.

Warner, Lawrence. *The Lost History of "Piers Plowman."* Philadelphia: University of Pennsylvania Press, 2011.

Vasta, Edward. *The Spiritual Basis of "Piers Plowman."* The Hague: Mouton, 1965.

Vaughan, M. F. "The Liturgical Perspectives of *Piers Plowman* B XVI–XIX." *Studies in Medieval and Renaissance History* 3 (1980): 87–155.

Wenzel, Siegfried. *Latin Sermon Collections from Later Medieval England: Orthodox Preaching in the Age of Wyclif.* Cambridge: Cambridge University Press, 2005.

Wilcox, Peter. "'The Restoration of the Church' in Calvin's 'Commentaries in Isaiah the Prophet.'" *Archiv für Reformationsgeschichte* 85 (1994): 68–95.

Wilks, Michael. *The Problem of Sovereignty in the Middle Ages.* Cambridge: Cambridge University Press, 1963.

———. "Royal Patronage and Anti-Papalism from Ockham to Wyclif." *Studies in Church History Subsidia* 5 (1987): 135–63. Reprinted in Michael Wilks, *Wyclif: Political Ideas and Practice*, 117–46. Oxford: Oxbow, 2000.

———. *Wyclif: Political Ideas and Practice.* Edited by Anne Hudson. Oxford: Oxbow, 2000.

Williams, D. H. *Retrieving the Tradition and Renewing Evangelicalism.* Grand Rapids, MI: Eerdmans, 1999.

Williams, Rowan. *Arius: Heresy and Tradition*. Rev. ed. Grand Rapids, MI: Eerdmans, 2002.

———. *Why Study the Past? The Quest for the Historical Church*. Grand Rapids,
MI: Eerdmans, 2005.

Wood, Sarah. *Conscience and the Composition of "Piers Plowman."* Oxford: Oxford
University Press, 2012.

Yoder, John Howard. *Christian Attitudes to War, Peace, and Revolution*. Grand
Rapids: Brazos, 2009.

———. *The Priestly Kingdom: Social Ethics as Gospel*. Notre Dame: University of
Notre Dame Press, 1984.

———. *The Royal Priesthood*. Grand Rapids, MI: Eerdmans, 1994.

Yunck, T. A. *The Lineage of Lady Meed: The Development of Mediaeval Venality
Satire*. Notre Dame: University of Notre Dame Press, 1963.

Zeeman, Nicolette. *"Piers Plowman" and the Medieval Discourse of Desire*. Cambridge: Cambridge University Press, 2006.

INDEX

DAVID AERS

is James B. Duke Professor of English and Historical Theology with appointments in both the English Department and in the Divinity School at Duke University. His many publications include *Sanctifying Signs: Making Christian Tradition in Late Medieval England* (2004) and *Salvation and Sin: Augustine, Langland, and Fourteenth-Century Theology* (2009), both published by the University of Notre Dame Press.

Milton Keynes UK
Ingram Content Group UK Ltd.
UKHW021310130923
428604UK00022B/443